Sports and Education

• A Reference Handbook

CONTEMPORARY EDUCATION ISSUES

Sports and Education WITHDRAWN

•◦ A REFERENCE HANDBOOK

Anna Marie Frank

A B C CLIO

Santa Barbara, California • Denver, Colorado • Oxford, England

Library of Congress Cataloging-in-Publication Data
Frank, Anna Marie.
  Sports and education : a reference handbook / Anna Marie Frank.
    p. cm. — (Contemporary education issues)
  ISBN 1-85109-525-X (hardcover : alk. paper); ISBN 1-85109-530-6 (e-book)
  1. School sports—United States. 2. School sports—Social aspects—
United States. I. Title. II. Series.
GV346.F73 2003
796.071—dc22   2003017180

08 07 06 05 04 03   10 9 8 7 6 5 4 3 2 1

This book is also available on the World Wide Web as an e-book.
Visit www.abc-clio.com for details.

ABC-CLIO, Inc.
130 Cremona Drive, P.O. Box 1911
Santa Barbara, California 93116-1911

This book is printed on acid-free paper ⊗.
Manufactured in the United States of America

*Writing this book has been an
unexpectedly enjoyable yet challenging endeavor.
It is dedicated to those family members, friends,
and colleagues who have supported me through the process.
Special thanks to "Grumpy," "Happy," "Sleepy," and "Doc."*

❧ Contents

Series Editor's Preface

The Contemporary Education Issues series is dedicated to providing readers with an up-to-date exploration of the central issues in education today. Books in the series will examine such controversial topics as home schooling, charter schools, privatization of public schools, Native American education, African American education, literacy, curriculum development, and many others. The series is national in scope and is intended to encourage research by anyone interested in the field.

Because education is undergoing radical if not revolutionary change, the series is particularly concerned with how contemporary controversies in education affect both the organization of schools and the content and delivery of curriculum. Authors will endeavor to provide a balanced understanding of the issues and their effects on teachers, students, parents, administrators, and policymakers. The aim of the Contemporary Education Issues series is to publish excellent research on today's educational concerns by some of the finest scholar/practitioners in the field while pointing to new directions. The series promises to offer important analyses of some of the most controversial issues facing society today.

Danny Weil
Series Editor

● Preface

This book seeks to examine the role of sport in the educational process. All aspects of sport involvement—whether as a participant, a spectator, a fan, a coach, or a parent—allow individuals to learn or change from the experience. Therefore, education is considered as a broad concept, one not limited to the explicit lessons that athletes learn from their involvement in the sport experience; however, I examine these lessons as well. Sport is indeed a significant phenomenon in U.S. society, and it is the effect of this phenomenon in many contexts and at a variety of levels that we should review to gain an understanding of the complex issues and challenges related to sports in educational settings.

Sport skill acquisition and athletic development were among the most significant forces in the establishment of structured education. In chapter 2, I present the evolution of sport and athletic development within the history of education, as well as the history of physical education as a profession and the initial endeavors in organized sport competition. Along with the history of sport and education, I discuss several individuals who have made a significant impact on sport and who have taught us important lessons.

Chapter 3 considers the challenges and benefits of including sport within the educational context and considers its impact on society as a whole, organized around the following themes: Does sport participation benefit children? What are the primary coaching and administrative issues? Does the collegiate athletic system need to change? Have we crossed the line by engaging in unethical behavior? Should sport be eliminated from school settings?

I examine many significant issues in this text, but it should not be seen as a complete discussion. Many of the topics included here are complex, making a comprehensive presentation impossible. Race and gender issues are briefly discussed in chapter 4 along with profiles of significant African American and female athletes and educators who have had an impact on the world of sport. Chapters 5 and 6 provide readers with resources and organizations to seek additional information on specific issues of most interest to them.

Anna Marie Frank

Sports and Education

•⬦ A REFERENCE HANDBOOK

Chapter One

✦ Introduction

EDUCATION IN AMERICA

Most Americans believe that through education we can produce literate, responsible, productive citizens, resulting in a society in which freedom and equality can be guaranteed, regardless of one's sociocultural or racial background. Education thus has become a legal right, and free pubic schooling the means to achieve these goals. Over the years, many structural variations within the educational system have developed in an attempt to provide the best possible setting for American children to learn and grow into productive citizens. Getting it right has become the major focus of federal, state, and local governments, as well as of individual educational institutions from Head Start Centers to schools of education within universities across the country. One roadblock to accomplishing our educational goals, however, is that the broad concept of education has been replaced by the concept of schooling. Having our nation's children go to school is intended to provide an effective means of socioeconomic mobility, as well as the vehicle to resolve various social and moral problems. Learning in schools may assist in providing children with the opportunity to become literate and responsible and to understand how to be a productive member of society, but the education required to achieve these goals is much broader than schooling. This is why the term "education" cannot become synonymous with the act of attending school.

Think about how much one learns that does not take place in the formal school setting. Family, television, newspapers, magazines, books, billboards, music, movies, conversations, conflicts, daily observations, and sport all teach certain lessons. Therefore, when talking about education, the formal system of schooling may become a focus, but additional venues for learning cannot be neglected because of the profound influence they have on the education of a society.

Becoming literate implicitly means reading and writing in a common language. Developing responsibility assumes that there has been an established and accepted set of morals and values for which one is responsible. Additionally, attempting to become a productive member of a society implies that all members of that society are working for a common goal. Some have referred to this process as "Americanization," but if the previous statements have sparked questions, it is probably because over the years the term "American" has been so narrowly defined that groups of people are excluded from becoming "full-fledged" citizens of the United States because of their race or socioeconomic situations. As a result, the act of schooling as a means of Americanization has become inconsistent with what many children learn in the varied experiences of their lives. It is understandable that all societies attempt to transmit their cultures to the next generation through both formal and informal educational systems, but in the United States this has become a complicated and problematic process as school districts provide services to at least six racial groups. Various entities are constantly reviewing, researching, and restructuring our nation's schools as society fails to meet the goal of providing the opportunity for socioeconomic mobility through the formal educational system—and rightfully so, for no aspect of this system should be spared critique. One of the most visible aspects of the educational system are the established sport programs of elementary schools, secondary schools, and university. Therefore, it is appropriate to present sport as an aspect of education and to attempt to determine what it teaches our children.

SPORT AS A REFLECTION OF SOCIETY

In December of 2002, the sports network ESPN aired a series of commercials that were extremely timely, thought provoking, and clever. The writers probably did not intend them to be as profound as I found them to be, and they probably never thought they would be referred to in an academic book. These commercials provide the viewer with a series of clips of people doing things, followed by the words, "Without sports ..." I will attempt to recapture the commercials for you here.

> ➤ One of the commercials shows a cab driver listening to a football game on the radio, followed by a group of young men watching the game on television in a bar, a man watching it in a hotel room, a family of four watching it in the bedroom, and finally an elderly man sitting beside what looks to be his grandson as they watched the game together. As we listen to all these people passionately critique the game and provide their ideas for what the players should do, we are presented with the words, "Without sports, there'd be no one to coach."

➥ Another commercial captures three young men at their place of employment playing a makeshift game in which points are scored by bouncing a Nerf ball into an emptied shelf. As the players argue about the number of points that should be awarded in relation to the number of bounces, we are presented with the words, "Without sports, a shelf would be nothing but a shelf."

➥ Another commercial presents the television audience with a man passionately recapping the Chicago Cubs' recently completed baseball season. As he rattles off excuses and "what ifs" for the team's inability to make postseason play, we are presented with the words, "Without sports, there would be no next year."

➥ Yet another commercial shows groups of teenagers singing, dancing, and socializing, all dressed in shorts, T-shirts, and hats with sport team logos and names. The words appear, "Without sports there would be nothing to wear."

➥ My personal favorite presents clips of an interview with a few of Jackie Robinson's former teammates. Those interviewed recount the hardships he endured for being the first African American to play professional baseball. One shares a specific memory of how the fans yelled racist insults from the stands at Jackie during a game in Cincinnati. He then explains how Pee Wee Reese, a white teammate, went over to Jackie who was at second base and put his arm around him. The EPSN commercial declares, "Without sports there would be no teammates!"

I found these ESPN commercials to document what sport sociologists study and what this book is about: sport is more than mere activity affecting only the participants and observers. Sport is much more. Sport is powerful. Sport is everywhere. Sport has seeped into the crevices of U.S. culture in places where we did not anticipate it would and to a level we could never have imagined. I am writing these words on the eve of Super Bowl XXXVII, yet as I write them they feel inadequate in describing this phenomenon we call sport.

Sport is a cultural phenomenon that is explicitly connected to the social and political developments of a given society. Embedded in every society are the conceptualization, value, and formation of an educational system. It would therefore follow that sport, as it has been influenced by the educational systems in the society, is also capable of influencing education and the society in general. In fact, historically educational systems of various societies have developed in response to and along with the need for physical development and the interest in sports. This text provides readers with a better understanding of the relationship between sport and the formal and informal educational systems. I present this relationship from a historical perspective up to the present and attempt to encourage readers to question whether this relationship has been beneficial for both parties.

As I noted earlier, education in our society takes many forms. From infancy to adulthood, we are continuously learning, both implicitly and explicitly and in many settings. We learn to crawl, walk, eat, and talk in the unique and informal educational environment of the home. Caregivers are increasingly realizing the benefits of early childhood education in day-care or preschool settings. Whether we agree or not that "everything I ever needed to learn I learned in kindergarten," the sentiment points to the significance of our early development. The "formative years" in this country are spent in a formal public or private school setting consisting of elementary, middle school or junior high, high school, and various forms of schooling after receipt of a high school diploma. Learning in these settings is based on many factors. Within schools, however, "curriculum" is a term for what experts have agreed should be taught. Additionally, different kinds of curricula are recognized. Specifically, a *written curriculum* includes what should be taught, an *actual curriculum* includes only what is actually taught, and a *hidden curriculum* includes what is taught implicitly and often without intent. We can discuss, for example, whether sex education is the responsibility of an educational institution; however, the reality is that sex education *is* part of the written curriculum in schools from junior high through college. Nonetheless, what students actually learn about sex in school depends on (1) what is actually taught, (2) who teaches it, (3) what students hear other students say in discussions beyond the classroom, (4) what happens in the school hallways, and (5) what the students brings to the educational setting. As a result, we hope students learn facts that will help them make appropriate life decisions, but we know they learn much more. Often, they learn the current societal standards regarding sexual behaviors. It is with this same understanding of education and of these different curriculums that we also approach the issue of education and sport.

Sport is included in our educational settings because it has been widely accepted that sport teaches the participants valuable life lessons. The list of physical, mental, psychological, and social benefits is long and impressive (Lumpkin 1998, 11). Agreeing on what sports *can* teach is similar to our written curriculum of what it *should* teach; what sport actually teaches, however, is a problem that has received the attention of parents, teachers, coaches, administrators, scholars, and athletes alike. Many studies document the successes of student athletes and the abuses that take place in programs at all levels. What is known is that sport in every setting is a complex phenomenon. The list of problems associated with sport is significant with opposing viewpoints on each side of every issue.

SPORT AS A SOCIAL PHENOMENON

Sports are a part of people's lives that cannot be ignored because they are such a pervasive part of life in contemporary society (Coakley 1994). They are connected to the major social institutions of family, education, politics, the economy, and religion. A summary of sport sociologists, Jay Coakley's statements about sport within these institutions are included in the following paragraphs.

Family

In this country, millions of children are involved in organized sports, and it is primarily their parents who organize, coach, and attend the competitive events. As a result, the family schedule is affected by the demands of one or several family members' involvement in sport. The dinner hour must be adjusted or even eliminated because of participant demands. Even watching sport on television alters family rituals. These experiences can result in a deterioration of the family unit, or they can act as a bonding agent.

Education

Most middle and high schools in the United Stated provide interscholastic sports teams. In many of these schools, it is not uncommon for the athletic events to attract more attention than the academic programs. At the university level, many schools use the achievements of their athletic teams to promote the quality of their academic programs, whereas other schools face public relations problems because of abuses within their sports programs.

Politics

Despite the controversy, it is widely accepted to display national flags or play the national anthem at sporting events. It has become a tradition for U.S. presidents to congratulate sport teams upon winning championships. International sports are steeped in political controversies because most countries use sports to enhance their reputation in international political relationships.

Economy

Billions of sport dollars are spent annually for event tickets, equipment, participation fees, athletic club memberships, wagering, and apparel. These financial interests have an effect at the national, state, local, and individual levels. Television networks pay unprecedented amounts to attract the advertising dollars connected to popular televised sports.

Religion

Across the United States, religious congregations are often the sponsors of athletic teams and leagues, with these and other televised sporting events altering normal worship schedules. The objective of some religious organizations is to convert athletes to their religion; others recruit athletes as spokespersons in the hope of converting people who identify with sports.

Self-concept

Aside from the link to major social structures, sport is also a major factor in the way many people construct meaning. Sport experiences may inform factors such as attractiveness, pleasure and pain, excellence, sexuality, masculinity and femininity, and self-worth (Coakley 1994). An individual's self-concept is constructed as a result of the way people respond to him or her by way of recognition, rejection, or various other forms of feedback. Sport, particularly in the social setting of the school, provides participants with this valuable feedback. Quite often it is positive, occasionally it is negative, but never is it avoidable. The coach, the parent, the fans, the friends, and, most significantly, the athlete evaluate the experience and attach value. This may be what draws people to participate in sports, and it may also explain why certain sport experiences receive widespread criticism.

DOES EVERYONE SUPPORT SPORT IN SCHOOLS?

After experiencing sport in any capacity at the high school level in many Midwestern states, one would hesitate even to contemplate this question. In rural areas across the nation, towns literally close down each week as the majority of the population attends the local high school football game each Friday night. Bissinger's (1990) best-selling book, *Friday Night Lights: A Town, A Team, and A Dream,* is written about this phenomenon, presenting both the glory and the destruction of a high school football legacy. Even in large urban settings, the support for high school athletics can become unprecedented. In Chicago in 1937, it was estimated that more than 120,000 people attended a high school football game to determine the city championship. This game, called the Prep Bowl, is still held annually between the winner of the public league and the winner of the Catholic league. In 1937, Austin High School beat St. Leo, 26–0. Amid this support, the reality is that not all people support the inclusion of sport in the formal educational setting. Because it has become an expected aspect of the educational system in the United States, however, opposition was insignificant or thought to be irrelevant until recently. Because of the tremendous amount of explicit public support that sport receives in educational settings, its value often remains unquestioned. In support of this notion, John Gerdy, editor of *Sports in Schools: The Future of an Institution,* writes, "the late University of Alabama coach Bear Bryant was correct in pointing out that 50,000 people don't pay to watch English class; the mere fact that sport is wildly popular does not dismiss the need to critically evaluate its wide-ranging effects on our nation's educational goals and well-being" (Gerdy 2000, 5). Controversy regarding sport is not new, however; it's simply receiving more attention because the problems become more apparent as its popularity increases in all settings.

It should be recognized that interscholastic sports programs, those within high schools, are one of if not the most important elements in the development of a school's culture. Schools with highly recognized and supported athletic programs have cultures very different from schools that do not. Those who participate as athletes and cheerleaders are often awarded an elevated social status within the school. Making the team or squad provides much more than the opportunities to attend practices and compete or perform. Of course, this is not part of any written policy or even spoken of explicitly, but it is indisputably part of the hidden curriculum that was described at the beginning of this chapter. This hidden curriculum is not merely confined to the student population. Peers, teachers, administrators, parents, and other members of the local community recognize athletes for their accomplishments. One might suggest that recognition for a participant's hard work, dedication, and commitment should be recognized; however, many students participate in school functions such as theater, band, various journalistic activities, student government, and other clubs. Many large, affluent high schools can boast of their ability to offer more than one hundred school-sponsored activities in which their students may participate. Yet it is the successful athlete on the high-profile sport team that usually maintains the highest social status in the school community. From a sociological perspective it should be asked what impact this has on the overall school culture. What implicit messages are drawn from this phenomenon regarding the way students evaluate themselves and one another? What impact does this have on how students construct meaning about social structures, race, gender, relationships, and power? This is one broad and complex issue regarding sport and educational settings, but it is a good example of the controversies surrounding what has become accepted educational practice within the United States.

What is so fascinating about the issues regarding education and sport, both individually and collectively, is how dichotomous the positions become. Just as athletes may not wish to trade a moment of their athletic experience for another activity, another student may perceive that the athletic program has ruined the school culture, and this perception may develop into a lifelong deep-seated resentment of sports and those who participate in them. Ramifications of the elitist status of athletes at that high school might have been a contributing component that triggered the massacre at Columbine High School in Colorado, given that many of the targeted victims were athletes and cheerleaders.

From junior high to professional athletics, the use of performance-enhancing substances has become a problem that must be addressed. One athlete might believe that whatever form of performance enhancement is necessary to win a National Collegiate Athletic Association (NCAA) championship or an Olympic gold medal is warranted, while another student dies suddenly after taking an over-the-counter stimulant to get through practice. Injuries are "part of the game," but should the death of a high school football player from heat exhaustion during practice be considered an unfortunate circumstance, or should it be pursued as negligence?

Many professors with doctorates at universities across the country make less than one-sixth the minimum salary mandated for a rookie in the National Football League (NFL). How does this fact affect the career plans of high school students as they negotiate successes and failures in school? What implicit value does is attach to the professional academic and professional athlete?

Fans at National Hockey League games seem to cheer louder when the board checking is the hardest and rise to their feet when a fight breaks out. Could this accepted hockey culture that supports violence have anything to do with the fatal beating of a father of a high school–age hockey player by a teammate's father, which took place at a practice when a confrontation developed between the two men?

The "winning at all cost" attitude and coaching ethic are routinely addressed in every aspect of sport. Good sportsmanship and respect for authority are two lessons young athletes should learn from their sport experience, but what coaches and parents demonstrate on and off the field often contradicts these lessons. There are several organizations in place to provide training and support for coaches in youth sport programs, but is it unrealistic to allow only certified coaches to work with young children? Will the number of qualified coaches meet the demand?

We know that the role of a teacher in a high school should be valued more than the role of the coach. The physical education teacher provides lessons for every student in the school. The coach provides practice and guided competition for a small group of elite athletes. The demands placed on professionals who must assume both roles often dictates that they spend more time, energy, and effort preparing for their athletic responsibilities. Students in their classes are savvy enough to realize this and eventually come to accept the situation. What implicit messages are these students receiving regarding the role of the coach compared with the role of a teacher at their school?

What does the average American really know about Duke University, besides that is has one of the most successful basketball programs in the country? The athletic vision of the university administration is often a key reason for the financial stability of the academic institution. As an example, because the University of Notre Dame's football games have been recognized for their enormous television popularity, all of its games are now televised. As a result, this university can maintain its independent status and collect significant revenues from television broadcasts that will not be shared with other institutions. Most universities are members of an athletic conference that provides revenue sharing between its member institutions.

These are just a sampling of the issues that are presented in subsequent chapters of this text—issues that should be discussed by the most passionate supporters of sports and by those who are the most opposed. It is through this understanding of opposing viewpoints that the middle ground might become most appealing to all. As we think about the future of the institution of sport in this country, we affirm the need to question its value. Should athletics be eliminated from the formal school program? Why not confine sport activities to after-school community and private establishment programs? Can an athletic program be the only reason a poor urban male finishes high school and eventually receives a college scholarship? What other aspects of our educational system teach students discipline, dedication, teamwork, perseverance, and respect? Much has been written about these questions, and much more will be written in the future. We may not uncover their answers but only reach an understanding of the issues.

DEFINITIONS AND TERMS

When thinking about sport, many thoughts come to mind. This is related to past experiences, culture, socioeconomic class, gender, race, and even the part of the country in which a person grew up. Whatever thoughts surface, there are several that are common to people across the United States—Little League baseball, the American Youth Soccer Organization, Olympic gymnastics, figure skating, swimming, World Cup soccer, marathons, various professional league games, and even dodge ball played in physical education. Involvement in the sport experience is another concept that should be considered. One can be a participant, a spectator, or a coach, or one can participate in sporting organizations through governance or a variety of other capacities. What follows is that the school sport experience takes place in many settings, among people of all ages and backgrounds, at a variety of skill levels, and in many capacities. Most school sport experiences and contexts are defined, presented, reviewed, and critiqued primarily as they relate to the educational system or to education in general. Before this can be presented, however, I define terms here to provide clarification.

- Amateur athlete: A person who participates in formal athletic competition but who receives no external rewards
- Athletics: A term used to describe structured physical activity, games, or sports within an educational setting; internationally, the term athletics can refer to the sport of track and field
- Athletic conferences: Used to organize athletic competition between high schools and colleges according to predetermined characteristics, resulting in competition between similar institutions
- Athletic director: An administrator who is responsible for every aspect of an athletic program within a specific institution
- Athletic training: The profession that provides prevention, treatment, and rehabilitation of sport-related injuries

- Booster club: A volunteer group comprising individuals who aid an athletic program through activities and financial support
- Club sport: An organizational model of sport participation without official affiliation of a formal educational institution
- Curriculum: The goals of an educational program and the activities used to achieve these goals
- The *Education of All Handicapped Children Act of 1975* (U.S. Public Law 94-142): Federal legislation mandating equal access and opportunity for people with disabilities
- Equity issues: Issues related to the equal opportunity, access, and treatment, regardless of race, gender, age, disability, or class
- Individual sport: A sport in which the outcome is based on the performance of an individual
- Intercollegiate sport: All aspects of the system and organization of athletic competition among colleges and universities
- Interscholastic sport: All aspects of the system and organization of athletic competition among schools
- Intramurals: A program of formal sport activity in which competition takes place among members of the same school
- Lifetime sport: A sport that can be engaged in throughout the life span because of the availability of facilities and related aspects of the sport
- Olympic athletes: Athletes who compete under the authorization of a country's Olympic committee
- Olympic sports: Sports that have been officially designated for competition by the International Olympic Committee (IOC)
- Paralympics: International elite sport competition for individuals with physical disabilities
- Professional athlete: A person who competes in formal athletic competition for immediate profit or who signs a contract to compete for compensation
- Recreation: Voluntary activity done primarily for personal growth or pleasure
- Society: A system of human organization for large-scale community living
- Special Olympics: A national and international organization that supports sport participation and competition for individuals with mental disabilities

- Spectators: Individuals who observe sports for pleasure
- Sport: Institutionalized games or activities in which outcomes are determined by physical skill and strategy
- Sport aesthetics: The study of sport in the context of its visual beauty, as that of an art form
- Sport ethics: The study of the value of sport and its process
- Sport history: The study of sport in the past and how it has influenced and may inform the present
- Sport management: The study of the management of personnel, programs, budgets, and facilities in a sport setting
- Sport marketing: All activities involved in the process of increasing exposure, popularity, and revenues related to sport
- Sport medicine: The field of medicine that includes the prevention, treatment, and rehabilitation of sport-related injuries as well as the improvement of sport performance
- Sport philosophy: The study and interpretation of truth and values as they relate to sport and sport settings
- Sport psychology: The study of behavioral issues related to sport and the mental processes that affect sport performance
- Sport sociology: The study of social units and the processes of groups involved in sport
- Team sport: A sport in which the outcome is based on the performance of a group of individuals who make up a team
- Title IX: Federal legislation mandating equal access for female athletes to every aspect of the educational system for schools that receive federal funding
- Varsity model: An exclusionary model of sport involvement with the goal of providing an educational institution with the most competitive, and therefore successful, teams

SPORTS AND SETTINGS

This section provides an overview of the classifications for various sports. These classifications are needed to understand the unique benefits and problems associated with certain sports. I then cover the various settings in which sports have been established to provide readers with an understanding of the prevalence of sport participation in each setting. The specific demands of each sport and the significance of the setting, whether educational or community based, should provide additional understanding of the debates that follow in subsequent chapters.

Sports

Before specific sports can be classified, a definition of sport must be included to set the stage for what follows. I have chosen Coakley's definition because it supports the intent of this text—to present sport as it relates to educational settings and opportunities. Coakley (1994) states, "Sports are institutionalized competitive activities that involve vigorous physical exertion or the use of relatively complex physical skills by individuals whose participation is motivated by a combination of intrinsic and extrinsic factors" (p. 21). As Coakley points out, this definition may seem limiting to some, but the choice is appropriate as we attempt to examine issues of how sport participation affects youth sport and aggression; the appropriate age of initial sport involvement; and many other social issues such as gender, race, and culture.

Sports can be classified into distinctive categories, such as team or individual sport, contact or noncontact sport. There are several exceptions, however, such as gymnastics, in which the athlete competes individually against other gymnasts, but a team score is calculated. Additionally, there are many sports in which rules govern against physical contact, but serious injuries from collisions are routine and accepted. An understanding of how sports differ based on these classifications is necessary prior to a consideration of their possible benefits and inherent problems. Exceptions to the following discussions do exist; however, the most common competitive situations are presented here.

Team Sports

Team sports are those in which a group of two or more individuals work together to defeat the opponent. The outcome of the competition is most often the result of the collective effort of the group as opposed to the individual effort of a single individual. In the United States, the most commonly recognized team sports are baseball, softball, basketball, football, lacrosse, rugby, soccer, team handball, volleyball, water polo, rowing, ice hockey, and field hockey. Unique team sport issues include group or team dynamics, position play, cooperation, jealousy, camaraderie, and conflict between individual and group motivation.

Individual Sports

An individual sport is one in which a single individual participates, most often to perform to the best of their ability, and receives a score or time to reflect the level of performance. In the United States, the most commonly recognized individual sports of this nature are swimming, gymnastics, rhythmic gymnastics, running, skiing, field events, golf, archery, figure skating, speed skating, and bowling. In some individual sports, a single individual works alone to defeat the opponent. The most commonly recognized individual sports of this nature are wrestling, boxing, tennis, fencing, billiards, handball, racquetball, badminton, and table tennis. Some individual sports allow for competition of two individuals, known as doubles. Many individual sports allow for team competition by combining the individual scores or times. Unique issues related to individual sports may include alienation, self-imposed pressure, and gratification.

Contact versus Noncontact Sports

Many sports require a degree of physical contact. These sports, considered contact sports, are American football, ice hockey, boxing, wrestling, rugby, and the martial arts. Significant physical contact is required during competition; however, rules are provided to help minimize inappropriate contact that would increase the risk of injury to a player. These rules are in place to attempt to control the physical contact and minimize injuries. Serious injuries are known risk of participation in these contact sports.

Among so-called noncontact sports the risk of injury from contact varies considerably. Soccer and basketball are two sports considered to be noncontact sports with rules that penalize inappropriate physical contact. During competition, a minimal level of physical contact is unavoidable, primarily the result of defending against an opponent's offensive maneuvering. Accidental contact, which still results in a penalty, can lead to serious injury. Flying elbows in the lane of a basketball game and heading blows in a soccer game are two common concerns in these noncontact sports.

Noncontact sports in which opponents are separated from the other team, such as volleyball, badminton, tennis, and, to some degree, baseball, do include injuries as a result of collisions between teammates or with objects or equipment used during the competition. The remaining category of noncontact sports include those that either prohibit any contact, such as running and biking events, and those in which physical contact with opponents or teammates is unlikely, such as gymnastics, swimming, and downhill skiing. Participation in any sport can include risk of injury, however. The injury may not occur as a result of contact but from excessive training or when an athlete is pushed to a level that the body cannot accommodate. Overuse injuries, primarily incurred during training, are the most common injuries that athletes incur.

Settings

Sport is an established phenomenon in many settings and for nearly every age level. Clarification of these settings and the current prevalence of participation within them helps to organize discussions of whether sport is an asset or a liability to educational settings and educational opportunities.

Child and Youth Sports

Child and youth sports include all organized sport activities that take place outside the school for children and adolescents. The activities are under the sponsorship and governance of public and private agencies and organizations, whether they are community recreation leagues, parent-sponsored sport programs, or pay-for-service club sports (Siedentop 2001, 113). Why include the study of such activities in a text titled *Sports and Education*? Because it is traditionally in the name of the educational opportunities and lessons that these activities provide that they are established and promoted. In recent years, the opportunities and participation level in child and youth sport has increased at an unprecedented rate. The North American Youth Sports Institute published estimates for the number of participants in nonschool community sports programs for boys and girls at 10 to 15 million youngsters in 1975–1976, 15–20 million youngsters in 1985–1986, and 20–25 million youngsters from 1995–1996.

As professional and college sports experienced a dramatic increase in the late 1900s, society saw a need to provide settings in which children could learn sport skills and experience athletic competition. In 1939, Little League Baseball was introduced. In 1990, 2.5 million participated in Little League and the number increased to 3 million by 1997 (http://www.littleleague.org/history/index.htm). Today we see organized sports programs and league competition for young children in soccer, football, ice hockey, basketball, swimming, gymnastics, tennis, and many other sports (Polidoro 2000, 79). *The Organized Youth Team Sports Participation in the U.S.* survey, conducted in December 2000 by American Sports Data Inc., found that 26.2 million young people play on an organized team in one of eighteen sports measured—54 percent of the 48.5 million individuals aged six to seventeen surveyed. Organized basketball attracted the most participants, with slightly more that 10 million players, followed by soccer with 9.6 million, baseball with 7.5 million, slow-pitch softball with 3.6 million, and tackle football with 2.9 million.

Most recently, youth sports have grown to include an additional population: very young children. The urge to move is fundamental in young children. Physical education specialists refer to motor develop-ment theories when they espouse the necessity of physical activity for physical, social, and cognitive development. Historically, this activity has been unstructured and experimental in nature; however, organized physical activity opportunities are now provided by the private sector for children aged two to eight years. Examples of such programs are Lit-tle Gym and Fit by Five (Siedentop 2001, 6). These programs are mar-keted to day-care centers and school-based preschools. Additionally, numerous swimming and gymnastics centers across the country have provided developmental programs for preschool-age children, usually without the opportunity for competition.

As in other settings for sports participation, the benefits are doc-umented. Specifically, for very young children, enriched motor experi-ences result in more fit children who tend to participate in sports throughout their lives (Gober and Franks 1988). Sport opportunities that are highly specialized and require year-round commitment are available for children in the early elementary years, and sometimes for children as young as three years old. In response to this trend, National Association for Sport and Physical Education (NASPE; 2002) has estab-lished the first physical activity guidelines for infants and toddlers. These guidelines speak to the need for "infants to spend time with a par-ent or caregiver who provides systematic opportunities for planned physical activity." The guidelines for toddlers and preschools speak more specifically to the quantity and quality of daily physical activity.

The theme established in chapter 2 can be summarized here: as the participation in and prevalence of programs increase, the problems associated with them become more apparent. The most significant is-sues of concern for sport participation for young children are elite and championship competition, overspecialization in one sport, and poor coaching. Youth sport participation in general may be the most contro-versial aspects of our current sports culture. The proposed benefits are significant, but the problems are numerous. (See chapter 3 for a thor-ough discussion of these issues.)

Elementary School

Elementary schools, sometimes called grammar or grade schools, in-clude all K–8 schools and the variations of them. Many school districts have separate buildings for "early," "middle," and "late" elementary ed-ucation. Some school districts support K–5 buildings with separate middle schools, and many schools still maintain K–8 classrooms in the same building. The reasons for the different organizations, their advantages or disadvantages, and prevalence of each cannot be discussed in this text; however, I do discuss participation levels in school-sponsored sports programs in this section.

The elementary school is the first setting of school-sponsored sport participation. Typically this comes in the form of intramural sport programs. The term "intramural" simply means "within the walls" and refers to sport competition between the children of one school. This competition can take place before school or during free time but is usually an after-school activity. NASPE's National Intramural Sports Council (2001) prepared a position paper and guidelines for after-school physical activity and intramural programs. It states the following:

> All children should receive basic instruction in motor skills and sport activities through comprehensive physical education programs. We believe that such programs facilitate the skills and knowledge necessary to support an active, productive and healthy lifestyle. Intramural and other physical activity programs extend and complement physical education to ensure that all children are provided the opportunity, regardless of athletic skills, to participate in lifetime physical activity that can contribute to their enjoyment of leisure time. We believe that school-based programs promoting and providing physical activity should be available to students in elementary, middle, and high school years.

This position paper explains the first level of sport participation and competition that should be available in all schools.

Programs that receive more attention—and often more support—are the extramural sport programs that provide the opportunity for sport participation and competition among schools. Many describe this as the "varsity" model, in which only the best athletes, typically few in number, compete as representatives of their school. Schools at this level are typically members of a local "league" or group of schools that compete primarily against the other schools in the league to establish a champion. Statewide or national competition is not supported at the elementary level. Because competition at the elementary level is maintained at the local level, so, too, is governance of extramural sport, and no national or state organization oversees athletic competition at the elementary school level. Without state or national governance, statistics to support the level of participation are not available. Participation also varies considerably from region to region. In urban settings, private schools typically provide extensive sport programs that receive a significant amount of administrative and parental support, in contrast to public schools in urban communities that often must abandon their sport programs because of financial limitations. In rural areas across the country, sport offerings vary in response to local demand and funding opportunities.

An interesting study titled "Attitudes toward Athletic Competition in Elementary Schools" was conducted to examine the attitudes of parents, teachers, and administrators toward intensive competition (defined as a program of regularly scheduled games with other schools in the same city, which would culminate in championship play-offs) for fourth through sixth grades. Opinions from 357 parents, 508 teachers, and 234 school administrators found parents to be the most in favor of intensive competition and administrators the least. More men than women supported such competition, and those experienced in competitive sports regarded it more favorably than did those without this experience (Scott 1953). One interesting aspect of this particular study that you may have noticed was that it was published in 1953. Recent studies to examine the value of athletic competition at the elementary school and the level of participation are almost nonexistent.

Regardless of the level of participation at the elementary school level, the value of this participation is considered significant because it prepares children for participation at the high school level, where athletic programs are expected and typically well supported. If athletic opportunities are not available at the elementary school level, middle- and high-income parents often seek community-based programs and pay for their child's sport experience. This may be one reason for the recent surge in youth sport programs outside the school setting. But what about the family that cannot afford private lessons, or even the minimal fee charged for sport participation? Park districts do an outstanding job of trying to provide these services for free when possible. Should quality physical education, intramural programs, and extramural programs be available as part of the educational system to provide athletic opportunities to all children? If this is a goal, it is far from being realized.

High School

With the exceptions of Canada and Japan, the Untied States is the only country where interscholastic sports are highly valued, supported, and accepted as an integral part of the formal educational process of adolescents. In most countries, athletic programs are supported and maintained separately from the formal educational system. This fact, along with the high visibility and opposing viewpoints on the validity of interscholastic sports, has drawn the attention of researchers for many years. I now present the prevalence of programs and trends in participation. The discussion of the benefits and disadvantages of interscholastic sport and the movement to separate it from the educational setting are found in chapter 3.

Interscholastic sport, sometimes referred to as varsity sports, athletics, or prep sports, is the system and organization of sport competition between schools. These interscholastic sport programs that begin in high school and middle school provide the opportunity for only the most highly skilled students to represent their schools in athletic competition. The opportunity to participate varies according to school district. The scope of sports included may be limited or comprehensive, and the depth of competition may support only one team or several teams, based on student characteristics. Depth of competition is increased by the inclusion of "A" and "B" squads, junior varsity teams, and "light" teams for students under a specified weight in football or height in basketball.

"During the 1998–1999 school year, more that 8.6 million boys and girls participated in thirty-eight interscholastic sports in the United States" (Siedentop 2001, 118). The National Federation of State High School Association's (NFHA) Website (http://www.nfhs.org) is an excellent resource for up-to-date participation levels across the country, along with the many state organizations such as the Illinois High School Athletic Association and Ohio High School Athletic Association. As noted in chapter 2, every state currently has an athletic association that oversees its interscholastic sport programs. According to the NFHA's 2001 participation press release, "for the 13th consecutive year, the number of students participating in high school athletics increased, setting an all-time high for participation" (http://www.nfhs.org/press/participation%20surveyy02.html). This information is based on figures from the fifty state high school athletic and activity associations—plus the District of Columbia—that are members of the NFHS. Participation for the 2001–2002 school year rose by 62,292 students to 6,767,515, with participation levels numbers for both boys and girls increasing. Girls' participation rose by 22,844 students, and boys' participation rose by 39,448 (58.7 percent of the total). The biggest gain in participation was in competitive spirit squads, which ranks ninth in popularity for girls. Overall, fast pitch softball saw the largest increase, due to a decrease in slow pitch softball for girls. Basketball remained the girls' most popular sport with 456,169 participants, and eleven-player football the most popular boys' sport with 1,012,420 athletes. Texas remains the state with the most athletes, followed by California, New York, Illinois, Michigan, Ohio, Pennsylvania, New Jersey, and Minnesota.

Interscholastic sport programs are, however, being cut or dropped in many big cities and poor rural schools (Miles 1991; Swift

1991). Finances are the most prevalent reason for the dismantling of programs. Nearly all programs at the high school level are funded through a school district's allocation of tax dollars. Highest percentages budgeted to run interscholastic programs are 3 percent of total budgets, with the majority of districts actually appropriating less than 1 percent (Coakley 1994, 406). Even if an interscholastic sport program is considered part of the regular curricular offerings, the budget to run these programs will have significant limitations. Often, because interscholastic sport is seen as an extracurricular activity, programs are faced with raising money through gate receipts and fundraising. As a result, high school booster clubs have become an essential part of the whole program. Understandably, in more affluent school districts, booster clubs provide the sport programs with enough money to ensure their future. In less-affluent districts that may be experiencing overall budget shortfalls, spending cuts must occur in extracurricular programs such as athletics, music, and the arts. In these same settings, even with the most dedicated booster clubs, sufficient funding simply is not available to sustain sport programs. As a result, there is now a shift in the availability of opportunity, and therefore the optimism associated with the proceeding participation rates must be tempered by the concern for equity of opportunity that mirrors other facets of our educational systems.

Collegiate Sports

Some people literally live for collegiate sports, espousing that they are the best game in town; others consider the problems they face to overshadow the resulting athletic competitions. Some students consider collegiate sport programs the most important aspect of the college experience; others find them totally irrelevant to the acquisition of their degrees. Whatever the sentiment, there is no debate that intercollegiate sports have become a major aspect of U.S. sports culture; for the National Collegiate Athletic Association (NCAA) Division I schools, it has become big business.

Intercollegiate sports competition dates back to 1852, when a rowing competition between Yale and Harvard was held. In spite of the challenges they face, today most colleges and universities offer extensive athletic programs for their students. These programs are governed by private national organizations: the NCAA for large schools, the National Association of Intercollegiate Athletics (NAIA) for smaller schools, and the National Junior College Athletic Association (NJCAA) for two-year colleges.

As presented in chapter 3, collegiate athletics, particularly those within the NCAA's Division I, are criticized for the abuses taking place on university campuses across the nation. On its Website, the NCAA (n.d.) lists its purposes as follows:

- To initiate, stimulate and improve intercollegiate athletics programs for student-athletes and to promote and develop educational leadership, physical fitness, athletics excellence and athletics participation as a recreational pursuit.
- To uphold the principle of institutional control of, and responsibility for, all intercollegiate sports in conformity with the constitution and bylaws of the Association.
- To encourage its members to adopt eligibility rules to comply with satisfactory standards of scholarship, sportsmanship and amateurism.
- To formulate, copyright and publish rules of play governing intercollegiate athletics.
- To preserve intercollegiate athletics records.
- To supervise the conduct of, and to establish eligibility standards for, regional and national athletics events under the auspices of the Association.
- To legislate, through bylaws or by resolutions of a Convention, upon any subject of general concern to the members related to the administration of intercollegiate athletics.
- To study in general all phases of competitive intercollegiate athletics and establish standards whereby the colleges and universities of the United States can maintain their athletics programs on a high level.

The NCAA has three main divisions based on size of program and level of competition: Division I, with 321 member schools and 142,409 participants; Division III with 423 member schools and 133,611 participants; and Division II with 297 schools and 77,404 participants (http://www.ncaa.org/releases/research/2000060701re.htm). An NCAA press release dated June 7, 2000, states that nearly 20,000 more student-athletes participated in intercollegiate sports at NCAA-member institutions in 1998–1999 than in the academic year before. The highest gains were in women's sports at a 9.3 percent increase compared with men's participation increase at 3.7 percent, resulting in an overall increase of 6 percent. Women's soccer experienced the greatest increase in team sponsorship by adding sixty-six squads. Men's basketball and cross country showed the largest increase in team sponsorship with forty-two and thirty-seven, respectively. The most sponsored sport in all divisions was women's basketball.

The NAIA and its members aim to use sport informally as a vehicle for character development. They believe that because the athletic arena has become a microcosm of society, the time has come to bring a more formal emphasis to character development on every level and especially in sport. The NAIA supports more than five hundred schools in fourteen divisions for competition in men's and women's soccer and cross country, men's football, and women's volleyball in the fall; two divisions of men's and women's basketball, men's and women's swimming and diving, indoor track and field, and wrestling in the winter; and baseball, softball, men's and women's golf, tennis, and outdoor track and field in the spring (NAIA 1999).

According to the NJCAA Website,

> The idea for the NJCAA was conceived in 1937 at Fresno, California. A handful of junior college representatives met to organize an association that would promote and supervise a national program of junior college sports and activities consistent with the educational objectives of junior colleges. ... Members eligible to join the NJCAA consist of two-year colleges and institutions accredited by the appropriate state or regional accrediting agency.... The purpose of [the NJCAA] is to promote and foster junior college athletics on intersectional and national levels so that results will be consistent with the total educational program of its members. (NJCAA, n.d.)

There are approximately five hundred member colleges in the NJCAA, with memberships renewable on an annual basis. The members are divided into twenty-four geographic regions. Regional and national championships are sponsored in each sport by the NJCAA. This organization is composed of a men's division and a women's division. In the 2001–2002 school year, the men's division supported thirteen sports for 29,000 athletes, the most popular sports being basketball and baseball. The women's division supported 415 sports for 17,000 athletes, the most popular sports being basketball and volleyball. More information about the NJCAA can be found at http://www.njcaa.org/about.cfm.

Institutions of higher education that support an athletic program are faced with the decision to join a conference or remain an "independent." It is possible to be aligned with a conference for a selected sport. Conferences benefit an institution initially through the scheduling of competitions and then by providing an opportunity for championship status. Additionally, conferences can assist member institutions in controlling and addressing potential abuses. Conferences often play a major role in the development of trust among institutions and ethical behaviors through conference meetings (Bailey & Littleton 1991). Therefore, conferences are looked to as the context within which institutions comply with NCAA regulations.

There is a venue for international athletic competition for college athletes. This complementary competition is organized and governed by the International University Sports Federation (FISU). The FISU was officially formed in 1949 and sponsors international sports conferences and contests for university students every two years, called the World Student Games or Universiades. The Universiades and Championships are open to all student athletes who have not been out of college or its equivalent for more than a year and who are between seventeen and twenty-eight years old. Any association that belongs to FISU may enter a team or an individual competitor. Entries are accepted from any country that is eligible for the Olympic Games and from any national federation that is affiliated to an appropriate International Federation (http:// www.fisu.net/site/page.php?lien=R&lien_page=2&id=3). The Universiades is an international sporting and cultural festival that is staged every two years in a different city and that is second in importance only to the Olympic Games. The Summer Universiades consists of ten compulsory sports and up to three optional sports chosen by the host country. The record for participation is 6,009 participants in Palma de Mallorca, Spain, in 1999 and 162 countries in Fukuoka, Japan, in 1995.

The Winter Universiades consists of six compulsory sports and one or two optional sports, also chosen by the host country. Additionally, the FISU sponsors the World University Championships. In 1998, twenty World University Championships were organized that attracted seventy-five countries and 3,769 participants. A portion of the FISU's philosophy is included here to share a sense of the mission of this international organization.

> The FISU was formed within university institutions in order to promote sporting values and encourage sporting practice in harmony with, and complementary to, the university spirit ... With its international dimension, FISU brings together the university community in the wider sense, necessarily transcending the conflicts which divide countries and peoples, to achieve harmony between Academic Excellence and Top-Level Sport, or Competition and Leisure Sports. The World University Sporting Movement also aims to become a powerful channel of communication for bringing together the various communities whose rich diversity is all too often a source of conflict today. (FISU, n.d.)

From NCAA Division I and junior college participation through international opportunities, students participate in athletics for various reasons; some do so for pure enjoyment or educational opportunities, others seek to use it as a stepping stone into professional sports. It is this variation in motivation that causes the numerous and complicated problems associated with collegiate sports. Alternative structures for athletic opportunities that remove the academic mandates of collegiate sports have been discussed and will continue to be explored as athletic opportunities are available to all and educational standards are maintained. Baseball's minor league programs are the stepping stone to professional baseball, with players having to choose between sports and school. The "Nike" league has received attention as a similar alternative to school for those needing a stepping stone to the National Basketball Association (NBA). Variations in opportunity to participate must be explored and supported to address some of the complex issues surrounding collegiate athletics.

Club Sports

Club sports encompass several opportunities for sport training and competition. Many of the private organizations that offer elite sport involvement for young children through young adults consider themselves club sports because they are not associated with an educational setting. At the high school and collegiate level, those sports that provide training and competition as representatives of the school but that do not fall under the administration of the athletic program are considered club sports. Typically, if a school cannot support a specific sport for financial or Title IX reasons, the sport will remain a club sport until the situation changes and the team can be recognized as part of the formal athletic program. In these situations, students receive the support of a faculty member who provides general guidance, and the team members are responsible for all organizational duties. Internationally, club sports are the most typical organizational model because athletic programs are not associated with school settings.

Professional Sports

In the United States, professional sports are often the goal for athletes who play sports in the educational contexts of high school and college. For-profit corporations compensate professional athletes overwhelming sums of money for their services in the hope of providing sports entertainment to the general public. Profits are made from television and other media broadcasts, gate receipts, sponsorships, and merchandising. Typically, owners of teams are joined together and governed by a board and commissioner of their respected associations. There are hundreds of professional sport associations, from the familiar (e.g., NBA, NFL, Major League Baseball (MLB), Professional Golf Association) to the less familiar (e.g., Futsol, Professional Windsurfers, Professional Women's Rodeo Riders).

Each professional sport is organized and governed separately. League rules and policies are unique to the individual sport. For example, drug testing has been mandatory and closely monitored in the National Football League for many years. In contrast, professional baseball only recently added random drug testing to its player contracts in its September 2002 negotiations. Individual sports are governed and regulated by the respective professional associations.

It is typical for a professional athlete to be represented by an agent who negotiates the athlete's contract with a team and markets the player for sport merchandizing endorsements. Sport marketing corporations have become multimillion-dollar companies that control every aspect of the athlete's career. In some sports, athletes form a union to maximize their power against the corporate owners, but the agents and their organizations still maintain most of the negotiating power.

A brief review of some of the high-profile professional sports follows to present a sampling of the related educational benefits and problems that are presented in the next chapter. Issues associated with the formal educational setting and informal educational settings will be covered.

The NFL sponsors two conferences, the National Football Conference (NFC) and the American Football Conference (AFC) with four teams in each of the four divisions in each conference as of 2002. Competitions are scheduled with teams within and outside of a team's division, with the two conference champions participating in the Super Bowl. The Super Bowl, held on the last Sunday in January, boasts the highest television ratings of any event on television. Television networks pay millions of dollars for exclusive rights to the broadcast with commercial advertising during a Super Bowl costing a company approximately $1 million for thirty seconds of airtime. Additionally, Monday Night Football, which began in 1975, provides an additional night of weekly NFL televised game coverage. Sports fans are provided with an opportunity to watch televised football games during preseason on Thursday, Friday, Sunday, and Monday nights. The NFL supports many jobs, and millions of dollars are pumped into local and television network economies as a result of its popularity, but many question whether there may be better uses of free time for the average football fan.

Founded in 1949, the NBA has seen a rise in average attendance from 3,201 in the 1952–1953 season to 16,966 in 2001–2002 (http://www.kenn.com/sports/basketball/nba/nba_lg_attendance.html). The average player during the 1946–1947 season earned $4,500; in 1999–2000, the average player earned $2,947,000 (http://members.aol.com/bradleyrd/apbr-faq.html). Professional basketball is well established as a primary provider of entertainment to Americans in the twenty-first century. It is not without controversy, however. Issues related to player salaries receive the most attention. More specifically, concern is warranted when the national media cover inappropriate and sometimes illegal behavior of wealthy, high-profile sport figures. It is unavoidable for youth to view these athletes as heroes or role models, making problematic behavior a serious issue.

Major League Baseball, "America's sport," is the oldest professional sport in the country. The significance of its influence on the U.S. culture is immeasurable. After the September 11, 2001, terrorist attacks, MLB games were suspended, but the public outcry was that Americans needed baseball to aid the recovery process. Numerous motion pictures, such as *Field of Dreams, The Natural,* and *The Rookie,* have documented the magical allure of the sport and the power in its lessons. Yet as the popularity of this professional sport as entertainment in the United States continues to escalate, several controversial issues emerge. Most significant to the general public, and not without educational ramifications, is an issue referred to as "sportmail," a form of blackmail that sport team owners use to coerce public support from cities (Purdy 1988). For example, when the owners of the Chicago White Sox threatened to move the MLB team to Florida, the Illinois state legislature passed a resolution to provide $150 million of state funds for the facilities the owners were demanding. As a result of similar scenarios across the country, taxpayers are either forced to pay to subsidize professional sports, or the team relocates to a city where the support is more favorable. Where did the Illinois state legislature find this $150 million? One can be sure that it did not come from funds designated for education, but how might schools faced with financial hardship have benefited from a portion of that $150 million? Presently school districts across the country are facing financial shortfalls of millions of dollars due in part to federal mandates for necessary special education services that receive little federal funding, as well as faltering state economies. A review of priorities seems to be in order.

Becoming a professional athlete is the dream of many boys and girls across the country. Elite competition, rewarded with fame and financial security, is part of the American dream that millions pursue but only hundreds accomplish. A rough estimate is that of the nearly 70,000 college football, basketball, and baseball players in 1992, only 3.6 percent made it to the professional leagues (Coackley 1994, 282). Because professional sport is a primary source of entertainment in U.S. society, we must recognize it for its educational value for adults and children alike. Ideally, might we trust that continued self-imposed reform and regulations by professional organizations would continue to address this basic question?

International Competition

Education for international understanding has become one of the most insistent objectives of modern civilization. Technological advances have made the world more assessable, but cultural, political, and ideological differences around the globe have become strikingly clear in recent years. The global educational community has responded by established bodies to help monitor the process of meeting this objective, as referenced in chapter 2.

We have embraced sport to supplement this educational pursuit through international competition. The Olympic Games, held every two years, receives the most attention worldwide, with the soccer's World Cup a close second. Both these events are discussed in greater detail later. Many other international competitions, however, are held to promote humankind's common good and diminish the effects of its collective evil. Some of these games include the Central American Games, the Bolivian Games, the Pan-American Games, the Far Eastern Games, the Asian Games, the Mediterranean Games, the Pan-Arab Games, the Southeast Asia Peninsula Games, the South Pacific Games, the African Games, and the Maccabiah Games. There are also additional events that provide competition between specific countries.

The International Amateur Athletic Federation (IAAF) is a national governing body for amateur athletics (track and field) for affiliated countries. Only one representing member from each country or territory may be affiliated with the IAAF, and all members must abide by the rules and regulations of the federation. At present, the total number of countries and territories affiliated with the IAAF stands at 210—more than belongs to any other sporting organization, or even to the United Nations (IAAF 2003). This agency is responsible for approving world records in international track and field competitions and revising rules of competition. The IOC and the IAAF work together to monitor the changing nature of amateur athletics.

Olympic Games

Without question, the Olympic Games have become one of the most significant social forces of the twentieth century (Mechikoff and Estes 1998, 326). The Olympic Games are unique in that they are the world's premier sporting event. Unlike the Super Bowl, the World Series, or even the World Cup, the Olympics are a multicultural athletic festival allowing thousands of athletes to participate from almost every country on the planet. This international athletic festival enables

- Athletes from all over the world to meet and compete against athletes representing all colors, races, creeds, and political beliefs
- Athletes to travel to other countries to establish communication and dialogues with fellow athletes that will foster and promote international understanding and the appreciation of cultural diversity
- Athletes to test themselves against the best athletes in the world in the supreme physical and mental challenge
- The ideals of fair play and character formation through athletic participation to be promoted throughout the world for all the youth of the world to enjoy
- The ideals of peace, harmony, and cooperation to transcend political barriers that would allow Olympic athletes to act as a force for world peace and cooperation (Mechikoff and Estes, 326).

Despite the ideals and opportunities provided by the Olympics, the games have not been without problems and controversies. Probably the most significant issue casting a dark cloud over the games is the overemphasis on politics. Understandably, the political implications of athletic competition between countries of differing and often conflicting political and social orders cannot be discounted. It is the balance of the ideas set forth by the IOC and the political ambition of nations on the world stage that must be maintained.

FIFA World Cup

The International Soccer Federation or Fédération Internationale de Football Association (FIFA) organizes and governs the game of international football (soccer in the United States). FIFA is committed by its statutes not only to the positive promotion of football through development programs, but also to the supervision of international competi-

Olympic Timeline

Year	Location	Remarks
776 B.C.	Athens	First Olympics
1894	Paris, France	Establishment of the International Olympic Committee
1896	Athens, Greece	First Modern Olympics
1900	Paris	Olympics are held as part of the Paris World's Fair; first women's Olympic appearance
1904	St. Louis, Missouri	Gold, silver, and bronze medals are first awarded
1908	London	Official participation of forty-three women
		National teams march into the Opening Ceremonies for the first time
1912	Stockholm	The use of unofficial electronic timing devices for the track events and the first use of a public address system are introduced
1916		Games canceled due to World War I
1920	Antwerp	Following World War I, Germany and its allies are not allowed to participate
		Introduction of Olympic flag and presentation of the Athletes' Oath
1924	Winter: Chamonix, France	
	Summer: Paris	First Winter Olympic Games
		Significant increase in nation participation and introduction of Olympic Motto and flag raising at Closing Ceremony
1928	Winter: St. Moritz, Switzerland	
	Summer: Amsterdam	Winter Games held in a different country from Summer Games for the first time
		In opening ceremonies, Greece leads the parade of nations and the host nation marches last; the first Olympic flame is lit; athletes wear the ADIDAS "training boot" for the first time
1932	Winter: Lake Placid, N.Y.	
	Summer: Los Angeles, Calif.	Private land donated for bobsled run
		Record crowds attend the events; official electronic timing devises and

(continues)

Olympic Timeline (*continued*)

Year	Location	Remarks
		medal platforms are used; nations' flags are raised during medal ceremony
1936	Winter: Garnish, Germany	
	Summer: Berlin, Germany	First televised Olympics African American Jessie Owens wins four gold medals for U.S.
1940		Games canceled because of World War II
1944		Games canceled because of World War II
1948	Winter: St. Moritz, Switzerland	
	Summer: London	Germany and Japan are barred from competition following World War II First games to be shown on home television in England
1952	Winter: Oslo	
	Summer: Helsinki	First Olympic flame lit at Winter Games, relayed by ninety-four skiers The Soviet Union's first appearance
1956	Winter: Cortina d' Ampezzo, Italy	
	Summer: Melbourne, Australia	Soviet Union dominates the games; first televised in many countries The Netherlands, Spain, Egypt, and China boycott games; all athletes enter closing ceremonies together
1960	Winter: Squaw Valley, Calif.	
	Summer: Rome	No bobsled event because run was not constructed
1964	Winter: Innsbruck	
	Summer: Tokyo	East and West Germany send a combined team; lack of snow causes problems for events
1968	Winter: Grenoble, France	
	Summer, Mexico City	First drug testing by International Olympic Committee; sex testing for women
1972	Winter: Sapporo, Japan	
	Summer: Munich	First games held outside the United States and Europe; amateurism controversy Israeli athletes killed by terrorists

Olympic Timeline (*continued*)

Year	Location	Remarks
1976	Winter: Innsbruck	
	Summer: Montreal	Denver, Colorado, would not support use of public funds for games; events moved to Innsbruck
		African team boycott
1980	Winter: Lake Placid, N.Y.	
	Summer: Moscow	Underdog U.S. team beats the Soviets for the ice hockey gold medal
		Many Western countries boycott the games
1984	Winter: Sarajevo, Yugoslavia	
	Summer: Los Angeles	First games held in a socialist nation
1988	Winter: Calgary, Canada	
	Summer: Seoul	Speed skating held indoors
1992	Winter: Albertville, France	
	Summer: Barcelona, Spain	Last time that winter and summer games are held in the same year
1994	Winter: Lillehammer, Norway	Beginning of the biennial Olympics, alternating winter and summer games
1996	Summer: Atlanta, Georgia	
1998	Winter: Nagano, Japan	Men's ice hockey open to professionals
2000	Summer: Sydney	
2002	Winter: Salt Lake City, Utah	Figure skating judging scandal
2004	Summer: Athens, Greece	
2006	Winter: Turin, Italy	
2008	Summer:	

tions and the safeguarding of the sport and its good image against abuse of its rules and regulations. FIFA's mission is to see that the game is played according to a unified set of rules, the Laws of the Game, around the world. Football's ever-growing popularity; its enormous appeal, especially to young people; its expanding economic, social, and even political significance; and, not least, its importance for the media have all combined to make the sport a vital common denominator for varied interest groups. This trend means that FIFA is also obliged to deal with matters outside its immediate sporting sphere of activity (http://www.fifa.com). The scope of FIFA's roles and duties has vastly expanded in recent years, and the world body is ably supported in its coordinating task by the following confederations: the AFC in Asia, CAF in Africa, CONCACAF in North and Central America and the Caribbean, CONMEBOL in South America, UEFA in Europe, and the OFC in Oceania. There are 198 member nation associations (USA Soccer Media Guide 1999).

Apart from overwhelming tasks of organization and governance of competition for the world's most popular sport, most recently FIFA has been burdened with the inappropriate behavior of the fans it attracts to its competitions. Today, the World Cup holds the entire global public under its spell. An accumulated audience of more than 37 billion people watched the 1998 World Cup, including approximately 1.3 billion for the final game alone. Cumulatively, more than 2.7 million people flocked to watch the sixty-four matches in the French stadiums (FIFA 1994–2003). The United States hosted the 2000 World Cup, which attracted 3.5 million, the most spectators of any World Cup since the event was first held in 1930. With these enormous crowds and the political undertones of some of the competing countries, it is not surprising that violence, injury, and even death have resulted from the confrontation among "fans."

SUMMARY

This chapter has been devoted to providing information on which controversies, educational issues, and ethical debates in the context of sport can be grounded. Sport is a complex phenomenon of enormous scope. It often reflects the good and bad of the United States we have constructed. Our goal is to use what we know to understand the issues better and ultimately to find solutions to the problems apparent in sport in educational settings. Can we then use this educational force known as sport, both in and out of schools, to address some of the social problems in our society?

REFERENCES

American Sports Data Inc., Hartsdale, NY. (2000, December). *The Organized Youth Team Sports Participation in the U.S.* Retrieved July 23, 2002, from http://www.sgma.com/press/2001/press988721108-30622.html.

Association for Professional Basketball Research FAQ. Retrieved from http://www.members.aol.com/bradleyrd/qapbr-faq.html.

Bailey, Wilford, and Taylor Littleton. (1991). *Athletics and Academe: An Anatomy of Abuses and a Prescription for Reform.* New York: Macmillan.

Bissinger, H. G. (1990). *Friday Night Lights: A Town, a Team, and a Dream.* Reading, MA: Addison Wesley.

Coakley, J. (1994). *Sport in Society: Issues and Controversies.* St. Louis, MO: Mosby.

Ewing, M., and Seefeldt, V. (1997). Youth sports in America: An overview. *President's Council on Physical Fitness and Sports Research Digest* 2(11): 1–12.

Gerdy, J., editor. (2000). *Sports in School: The Future of an Institution.* New York: Teachers College Press.

Gober, B. E., and Franks, B. D. (1988). The physical and fitness education of young children. *Journal of Physical Education, Recreation, and Dance* 59(7): 57–61.

International Association of Athletics Federations. (2003). Inside the IAAF: Federations. Retrieved on October 15, 2002, from http://www.iaaf.org/insideIAAF/federations/index.html.

International Soccer Federation. (1994–2003). FIFA mandate. Common denominator. Retrieved October 15, 2003, from http://fifa.com/fgg/contents.html.

International University Sports Federation. (2003). FISU Today: Everything on the Functioning of the FISU Today. Retrieved October 3, 2002, from http:// www.fisu.net/site/page.php?lien=R&lien_page=2&id=3.

Little League online. (2002). Little League Baseball Historical Timeline. Retrieved June 23, 2003, from http://www.littleleague.org/history/index.htm.

Lumpkin, A. (1998). *Physical Education and Sport: A Contemporary Introduction.* Boston: McGraw-Hill.

Martens, R. (1986). Youth sports in the USA. In *Sport for Children and Youth,* edited by M. Weiss and D. Gould. Champaign, IL: Human Kinetics.

Mechikoff, R. A., and S. G. Estes (1998). *A History and Philosophy of Sport and Physical Education: From Ancient Civilizations to the Modern World.* Boston: McGraw-Hill.

Miles, G. (1991). Prep sports could lose budget race. *USA Today,* 30 July.

National Association of Intercollegiate Athletics. (1999). NAIA Information: Listing of NAIA members. Retrieved August 3, 2002, from http://www.naia.org/news/gen/gen/1999/12/21.html.

National Association for Sport and Physical Education. (2002, February 6). *NASPE First Ever Physical Activity Guidelines for Infants & Toddlers.* Retrieved July 23, 2002, from http://www.aahperd.org/NASPE/template.cfm?template=toddlers.html.

National Association for Sport and Physical Education. (2001, September). *Guidelines for After-School Physical Activity and Intramural Sport Programs.* Retrieved July 23, 2002, from http://www.aahperd.org/naspe/template.cfm?template=position-papers.html.

National Collegiate Athletic Association. (n.d.). About the NCAA. Retrieved August 5, 2002, from http://www.ncaa.org.

National Collegiate Athletic Association. (2002, September 26). Division I grad-

uation rates reach new plateau: First class with 13 core courses graduation at 60 percent rate [news release]. Retrieved November 1, 2002, from
http://www.ncaa.org/releases/makespage.cgi/research/2002092601re.
htm.

National Federation of State High School Associations (2003). Participating sets
record for fourth straight year. Retrieved June 22, 2003, from http://www.
nfhs.org/press/participation%20survey02.htm.

National Junior College Athletic Association. (n.d.). About the NJCAA. Retrieved
August 5, 2002, from http://www.njcaa.org/about.cfm.

Polidoro, J. R. (2000). *Sport and Physical Education in the Modern World.* Boston:
Allyn and Bacon.

Purdy, D. (1988). For whom sport tolls: Players, owners, and fans. *The World & I*
3: 573–587.

Scott, P. M. (1953). Attitudes toward athletic competition in elementary school.
*Research Quarterly of the American Association from Health, Physical Ed-
ucation, & Recreation* 24.

Segall, W., and Wilson, A. (1998). *Introduction to Education: Teaching in a Diverse
Society.* New Jersey: Prentice-Hall.

Shulman, J., and Bowen, W. (2001). *The Game of Life: College Sports and Educational Values.* Princeton, NJ: Princeton University Press.

Siedentop, Daryl. (2001). *Introduction to Physical Education, Fitness, and Sport.*
Mountain View, CA: Mayfield.

Swift, E. M. (1991). Why Johnny can't play. *Sports Illustrated* 75(13): 60–72.

U.S. Soccer 1999 Media Guide (1999), published by U.S. Soccer Communications Department. Executive editor, Jim Moorehouse; editor, Brian
Remedi. Chicago, IL.

Chapter Two

◕ Chronology

This chapter provides an overview of the evolution of sport and physical education. Because physical training was such an important aspect of education, the two are initially presented together. As the chapter's historical setting switches to the United States, the history of sport is presented independently from the development and evolution of physical education. The final section of the chapter includes a brief history of the most prominent U.S. sports. This chapter touches briefly on the topic of minorities and women in sport, a subject covered more extensively in chapter 4.

THE HISTORY OF PHYSICAL EDUCATION AND SPORT

Sport and physical training have been widely accepted as a few of the most significant factors influencing the inception of formal education. As societies began to realize the need for venues that would allow individuals to acquire knowledge, they also recognized the importance of establishing places where physical training could occur. It is widely accepted that play; the development of physical ability, physical fitness, and athletic skills; and physical competition have been significant components of most cultures since the earliest civilizations. This chapter provides a brief overview of the history of sport within the broad concept of education. Understanding how past events have shaped the present and how future events will be shaped by current events provides a foundation for analyzing problems that exist within sport and education and developing effective solutions.

A summary of primitive and early societies, ancient Greece and Rome, the Middle Ages, the Renaissance, the Enlightenment, nineteenth-century Europe and United States, along with the developments in U.S. sport and education into the twentieth and twenty-first centuries is provided. A time line of educational and sport events is also included.

Ancient Civilizations

In the area known today as Iraq, the Sumerians created the world's first civilization, recognized for having developed cuneiform writing, which supported a new means of communication, as well as for a collection of nearly three hundred laws known as Hammarubi's Code. This intellectual and orderly culture sought to retain its power, and therefore warriors were required to develop skills based on physical fitness and athletic ability. Kings who ruled the land, reported to be skilled lion hunters, were expected to develop great courage.

The land along the Nile River was inhabited more than 10,000 years ago. By 4000 BC Egypt was an established economic and political civilization. Paintings report that Egyptians enjoyed boating, swimming, and hunting. To defend itself, Egypt retained massive armies and demanded severe physical training of its soldiers. Chariot driving and archery were skills that ensured victory during battles, and contests were held to promote these skills. Physical abilities of wrestling, dancing, and acrobatics were performed for entertainment. The attention paid to sport and physical abilities in Egyptian society probably played a significant role in its becoming the birthplace of medicine.

Among the most civilized cultures of ancient times was that of the Chinese, whose civilization began approximately 2,500 years ago. Their feudal political system and the continuous claims to water routes in the area made military training a necessity. As a result, sports were prevalent in various forms, among both nobility and the lower classes. Boxing became so popular in China that by 1070 AD, a boxing teacher named Chio Yuan Shang Jen incorporated more than 170 movements in a written set of trained rules (Mechikoff and Estes 1998, 27). Board and table games, football, polo, equestrian competition, chariot racing, archery, and the martial arts were among the other activities incorporated into Chinese culture.

Greece

Regarded as the forebears of Western civilization, the Greeks are celebrated for their art, drama, history, mathematics, philosophy, poetry, science, and sculpture (Lumpkin 1998, 147). However, Greece, recognized as the birthplace of modern sport, is also the site of the earliest recorded athletic competitions. Several Greek philosophies addressed the development of mind and body, and from these works the roots developed many of the values and concepts that permeate modern Western sports and physical activity (Polidoro 2000, 1).

Greece was composed of city-states, and wars among them dictated the development of physical training. This training evolved into highly organized and sophisticated programs of competitive sports, held in honor of the gods, at funeral rituals, and in celebration of fertility (Polidoro 2000, 3). Although the Olympics are the most well known, many other "games" were established; their prevalence and significance supported the rise of the "professional athlete." In addition to the Olympic games, the Pythian games were held in Delphi, the Isthmian games in Corinth, the Newean games held in Argolis, and the Panathenaean games in Athens (Lumpkin 1998, 157). These events offered social and educational opportunities not only to the participants but to the spectators as well. Thousands would gather from all over Greece and its neighboring colonies to attend the games, which sometimes lasted for weeks.

Greek civilization, particularly as represented by the Athenians, can be thought of as a turning point in the history of education. This period marked the first time in Western civilization that the educational process had developed beyond the physical. For the first time, education had the balanced goal of developing both the mind and the body (Freeman 1992, 87). The concept of developing the physical skills necessary for competition was replaced with that of achieving "development through the physical." The attributes that could be learned through physical training and athletic competition were recognized and valued not only for the individual participant but for society as a whole. (This sentiment is still prevalent today, as discussed in chapter 4.) The study of Greek civilization as it supports education of and through the physical is extensive and interesting.

The Roman Empire

Rome conquered Greece in 146 BC. It remained a republic until 27 BC, when it was established as an empire, a status it held until its fall in 476 AD. Beginning with the significant influence of the Greeks, Rome experienced a number of political and social changes. As a republic, citizens shared in their governing and benefited from economic and political freedoms. As an empire, Rome established a professional army, allowing its citizens to enjoy festivals and games sponsored by the corrupt upper class (Lumpkin 2000, 158). The gladiator games provided bloodthirsty entertainment for the Roman public and had no connection to the nobler aspirations of Greek athletic contests. As spectators, Romans lost interest in developing their bodies, in the educational value of sport, and in the concept of mind-body balance (Freeman 1992, 89).

The importance of the Olympic and other games was maintained in the Roman Empire, but the evolution of the athlete—from an amateur to professional status—eventually led to the destruction of the Greek sport system where the athletes competed in the nude to celebrate their bodies, created harmony between mind and body, and competed in the name of religion. With professionalism, however, came the first athletes' guild during the first century BC, which negotiated time tables for events and prize structures for winners (Polidoro 2000, 22).

Initially, education in Rome took place in the home, but as the empire grew, schools were established, with Greek slaves as teachers. As a pragmatic society with no need for military training, instruction was in grammar, law, and engineering. Noticeably absent were gymnastics and music. Thus an unbalanced system of education was established (Freeman 1992, 88). Social changes encouraged the wealthy to lead sedentary lifestyles, and the ensuing moral decay contributed to the barbarian conquer of the empire. The study of the rise and fall of the Roman Empire demonstrates the position to which many sport historians and sociologists adhere: sport tends to reflect society and society reflects sport. In their 1998 book, *A History and Philosophy of Sport and Physical Education,* Mechikoff and Estes encourage readers to reflect on present-day sport in a similar light: "the various forms of sport that dominate a society's existence are emblematic of its moral health and illness" (69).

Middle Ages: 476 to 1453

The Middle Ages was a transitional period from ancient times, when a single, unified nation or civilization dominated its neighbors, to a period in which many nations experienced strength and stability contemporaneously. The feudal system was the dominant form of social and political organization throughout Europe and Asia during the Middle Ages. It offered protection to the lower classes and establishment to the upper classes and nobility. The only schools that existed were within monasteries, which restricted intellectual education to those training to serve the Church. A different career choice for sons of nobility was the chivalric system, which provided an education that was social, physical, and martial in nature. The system of chivalry, which led to knighthood, evolved from training in boxing, running, fencing, jumping, and swimming to hunting, scaling walls, archery, climbing, sportsmanship, and horsemanship (Wuest and Bucher 1995, 133).

Knights performed in jousts and tournaments that served significant recreational and social functions. Only nobility could participate, but peasants received a break from physical labor and were entertained by the display of military skills. Commoners soon began to imitate the upper class sport, however, adding democratic principles. This resulted in a variety of team ball games. One such game, similar to rugby, was called *soule* (Freeman 1992). Contests eventually included people from every social class that provided a respect for democratic practice, self-esteem, and the desire for fair play. According to Freeman, this may be one of the most significant contributions of the Middle Ages to our heritage.

Another significant contribution of the Middle Ages was the undisputed acceptance and application of the content of Galen's book *De Medicina*, which provided an understanding of human physiology and the concept of health referred to as "classical humoral medicine" (Mechikoff and Estes 1998, 103). During the late Middle Ages, both the Church and the state created laws against sporting activities for several reasons. The Church's restrictions primarily stemmed from its negative view of anything that provided physical pleasure and were also an attempt to ensure strict observance of religious occasions. The influence of the Catholic Church during this period cannot be overstated; although it supported the eventual development of formal education in schools outside the home and the establishment of the university, the chokehold with which it controlled society set the stage for much-needed change and reform.

The Renaissance: Fourteenth to Early Seventeenth Centuries

The period of transition between the Middle Ages and the beginning of modern times is known as the Renaissance. Characterized by a revival of learning and culture, intellectuals of the day used scientific research to solve problems, and artists produced works of unprecedented skill. Books were printed, and the learned once again studied the works of Ancient Greek philosophers. Education was valued for its own sake as universities, which were first established in monasteries during the late Middle Ages, were growing in number across Europe. Humanistic theory, which stressed the harmonious development of the mind and body, was widely accepted. Humanists stressed the importance of a healthy body to prepare for intellectual activity rather than stressing a dichotomous relationship between the two (Lumpkin 1998, 161).

The Renaissance concept of developing a well-rounded person (the prototypical "Renaissance man") helped contribute to the value placed on physical training and sport, and such skills were valued in harmony with intellectual skills. Team games grew in popularity, as did activities such as swimming, running, horseback riding, acrobatics, archery, swordsmanship, and wrestling. By 1600, physical education was accepted as part of the education of young aristocrats. Renaissance thinking on physical education and sport would inspire future generations as well, with scholars such as Luther, Calvin, and Elyot promoting education in the physical.

Reformation: Sixteenth Century

Within the frame of the Renaissance is a period known as the Reformation, during which many individuals sought to reform or break away from the Catholic Church, judging it to be a corrupt political institution. From social and political perspectives, the Reformation resulted in the organization of various Protestant groups as well as a reformed Catholic Church. Overall, religion was relegated to one's private life, a matter to be determined by the individual. Along with this was a rise in the status of the middle class and the eventual establishment of public education, where by the 1800s sports were used to teach desirable virtues. At the same time, some Reformation theologians argued against sport and physical training, which eventually evolved into the "Protestant work ethic" of valuing work over pleasure.

Seventeenth Century

During the seventeenth century, prominent educational theorists were responsible for advancing general education, as well as physical education and sports. Athletics, as it is know today, was in its infancy on university campuses; here it is discussed in relation to specific sports and the establishment of governing organizations. Humanistic thought gave way to realism, which changed the goal of education from "imitating the past" to a more practical approach in which students learned useful subjects to prepare them for life. Physical education played a minor role in the total educational process, but more theorists called for the use of physical activity to support the process of learning. Education for the commoner was slow to develop, but sports for the sake of recreation steadily increased in popularity. One village event that became famous was the Cotswold Olympick Games, which took place in the hills west of Oxford, England. The games included wrestling, the quintain, fighting with cudgels and pikestaffs, leaping, footraces, handball, pitching the bar and hammer, and women's smock races (Freeman 1992).

Eighteenth Century

The realism of the 1600s was replaced the following century by the Enlightenment. The work of John Locke, considered the founder of the

English Enlightenment, proceeded the theories of Rousseau, who is considered one of the most important scholars of the period (Freeman 1992). Rousseau's theories in turn influenced Basedow, who started a coeducational school where students were educated without influence of the Church. Basedow believed that children were to be treated as children, not small adults, and he reserved three hours of each ten-hour school day for recreation. Among the educators who worked for Basedow was Johann Simon, thought to be the first modern physical education teacher (Freeman 1992).

Enlightenment theories on how to educate children laid the foundation for European gymnastics programs, which were the basis for physical education programs in early America and later in the United States. This same time period can also be identified as the birth of modern sport, because standardized rules were established in response to higher levels of competition. Previously games were created spontaneously, and even if rules were written down, they were continually revised. With a transition from rural to thriving urban societies, sport was brought to the people, and spectators became a moneymaking commodity.

With few exceptions, most sports enjoyed in the United States today originated in Europe, particularly England. This section on the history of physical education and sport may be summarized with two significant concepts: (1) the necessity of physical training produced physical education and sport competition, and (2) established sport across Europe resulted in the development of sport in the United States.

HISTORY OF SPORT

Up to this point, I have combined the history of sport with the history of physical education. With the establishment of spectator sports and the institutionalization of sport, it is now more appropriate to present the history of sport independently. There are an estimated 250 sports, therefore I include significant dates and achievements only as they pertain to mainstream sports.

Colonial America: Fifteenth to Eighteenth Century

The notion that education, culture, and religion were brought to the New World by a variety of settlers with European ancestry is misleading. Well-established societies with rich cultural legacies existed in the Americas long before the arrival of Europeans, as documented by the earlier

Aztec, Inca, and Maya civilizations. What the colonists discovered were many Native American nations that had stable social structures, healthy populations, economic independence, and a structured educational system (Pulliam and Van Patten 1999). Native American education differed from tribe to tribe but typically was based on a structure that required boys and girls to master certain skills and obtain specific knowledge before they received recognition and were allowed to advance within the tribe. Physical skills for hunting and combat along with survival skills that would provide food, clothing, and shelter received the most attention. Additionally, concentric circles of people who served as teachers and taught cultural and spiritual lessons constantly surrounded Native American youth. Early settlers observed that sport was an integral part of the lives of Native Americans and acquired an appreciation for their most popular sport, lacrosse. Another game of significance was called shinney, a game similar to field hockey. As settlers began to establish societies, however, their sense of superiority prevented their acknowledgment of the rich culture and intelligence with which they were confronted. Colonial Americans were compelled to impose their beliefs on the "savages" in order to civilize them. The heritage of a great nation of people began to disintegrate.

Colonial America comprised three main areas of settlement: New England, the Pennsylvania territory, and the Virginia colony. Each had its own view on the place of sport in society based on their differing religious perspectives. The proximity to urban trading centers also resulted in differing social classes: coastal groups consisted of well-to-do traders, whereas farmers and settlers gradually moved to the frontier (Freeman 1992, 120). Multiple regions and social classes meant different levels of acceptance and opportunity for participation, and interest as spectators, in sports. In general, sport in colonial America was initially recreational and provided necessary opportunities for socialization. Colonists paid little attention to sport programs because the majority of the population received sufficient physical exercise through their work, especially in rural areas, and few hours were available for leisure. As life became easier and social structures would permit time for recreation, the colonists participated in sports recalled from their homelands.

With the tremendous influx of immigrants to America, schools were thought to be the best way to "Americanize" new arrivals, an effective way to help them attain the benefits of the new democratic society. Noah Webster is often acknowledged as the founder and facilitator of a unique American language meant to provide cultural identity and unity. His two books, *American Spelling Book* and *American Dictionary*, were used in schools, and within two generations, American English became the spoken tongue of most Americans (Segall and Wilson 1998, 62). At the time, however, only white immigrants could be refereed to as American, because of a 1790 federal law that provided naturalization exclusively to whites. This legislation prevented Native Americans, Hispanics, Asians, and former slaves, as well as indentured servants, from becoming citizens.

The Nineteenth-Century United States

In the years before the Civil War, sport began to assume an important role in burgeoning U.S. society. In relation to education, it was encouraged during after-school hours. At the time, there were approximately three hundred high schools, clustered mainly in the East and Midwest. The influence of the German gymnastics system left its most significant mark on physical education, but the establishment of German Turnverein Associations to promote the practice of gymnastics and sport was also important. By 1852, there were twenty-two Turnverein societies in the northern states—an athletic club that promoted the development of gymnastic skills on various pieces of apparatus, guided by the work of Fredrich Ludwig Jahn; the oldest, founded in 1848, still flourishes in Cincinnati, Ohio (Wuest and Bucher 1995, 140). The American Turnbund, the national association of Turnvereins, was established in 1850 and held its first national turnfest in Philadelphia in 1851. The Swedish gymnastics movement also encouraged the formation of athletic clubs in many large U.S. cities.

The 1800s saw the U.S. population shift from being a largely rural-agricultural society to a more urban-industrial one, focused in larger cities. This phenomenon had an impact on education. In 1830, 40 percent of the workforce in factories, located primarily in New England, were under the age of sixteen. Work prevented these youths from attending school, resulting in the common school movement to provide public education to all children. States began to pass laws allowing school districts to use tax monies to support education. By 1850, 45 percent of U.S. children attended school. The growth of public school attendance, particularly in high schools, was initially slow. In 1875, there were an estimated 25,000 students enrolled in public high schools; by 1890, 200,000 students were enrolled in 2,500 high schools. By 1900, there were more than 6,000 schools and more than 500,000 students (Pulliam and Van Patten 1999). Additionally, as leisure time increased within these urban settings, sport for recreation became more popular.

As sport developed, however, so did its association with gambling. Many criticized sport for this negative influence, and the idea of control within the context of sport was conceived.

In the late 1800s, during the post–Civil War period, sport exploded in the United States. Many sports became systemized with national organizations and standardized rules. This could not have occurred without the urban population's increased wealth, the greater access to transportation and communication, and the emergence of a middle class that accompanied industrialization. Sports were developed and organized for the athlete and the spectator alike.

Since the founding of the United States, Americans' enthusiasm for all aspects of sport had been obvious, but after the Civil War, the organization and programming of sport escalated. Many amateur sport organizations were established from 1868–1892. Freeman (1992) notes two significant developments during this time: teams were formed in colleges, and athletic clubs were established. These clubs led to the growth of professional sports, which produced national organizations and national championships. The prominence of sports at the college level and the mimicking of these sports at the secondary school level were remarkable. (Dates of initial competition at prominent universities are included in the timetable at the end of this chapter.)

Schools of higher education used their athletic victories for marketing purposes and to further establish an institution's prestige. Initially, the students ran intercollegiate sport competition; however, sport's effects on academic work, together with gambling and the excessive outside financial influence of alumni, drove faculty to become involved. In 1895, the Intercollegiate Conference of Faculty Representatives was held, comprising seven Midwestern institutions. Their aim was to establish eligibility requirements, control athletic financial aid, and develop guidelines for coaches. This group of schools eventually became the Big Ten Conference. Many other conferences were also created to attempt to control intercollegiate athletics across the country. Thus, at the same time that the prominence of sport in educational settings was being realized, the problems associated with the phenomena were becoming obvious. These problems are similar to those of today, which are addressed in subsequent chapters.

Physical education and sports had no association at the time, but it is important to note that as early as 1866, California became the first state to pass legislation that required physical education in schools. Physical education was still a reflection of the gymnastics systems brought over from Europe, with sports and games eliminated from the curriculum until the "new physical education" was established. However, extensive interscholastic programs did exist; a 1907 survey of 290 high schools found that 28 percent of students engaged in one or more types of sport (Wuest and Bucher 1995, 144).

Internationally, the most significant development in the context of sport was the first modern Olympic Games, held in 1896. These games, and all those to follow, were the result of the will and determination of one Frenchman, Pierre de Coubertin. Held in Athens, 311 athletes represented thirteen countries in eight sports. The United States sent thirteen athletes. Coubertin believed that these games could stimulate international goodwill. Additionally, he wanted to promote physical education in French schools because he realized the positive effect the inclusion of sport had within the English school system. His appreciation for the pure elements of athletics as factors contributing to character development was his motive for organizing the first Olympic Games. (The Olympics will be discussed in greater detail in chapter 3.)

With the expansion of sport across the country, the concept of professional sport was born. Amateur participation could not be maintained amid the financial structure that was becoming part of many sports. One of the most popular sports to develop during the post–Civil War period was horse racing. Numerous tracks were being built. The National Trotting Association was formed in 1870. Initially, horse racing was not influenced by the segregation laws of the day, and many of the first jockeys were African American. In fact, fourteen of the fifteen jockeys in the first Kentucky Derby (held in 1875) were African American (Wiggins 1997). The social conditions of the time would change this, as Jim Crow laws soon affected not just horse racing, but most professional sports. More and more white professional athletes refused to compete with or against African Americans. By 1890, more than three hundred tracks, complete with gambling, were in operation (Polidoro 2000, 60), but black jockeys had been virtually eliminated from horse racing. Segregation would continue to be a powerful force in sport for decades to come.

As Americans developed a fascination for sport, as both participants and spectators, boxing, or "prizefighting," became the major sport of the working class. John L. Sullivan, the first national sports hero in the United States, dominated this competition from 1882–1892. Sullivan is most famous for knocking out Jake Kilrain in 1889 in the last "bareknuckle" fight. Talented and successful African American boxers attempted to fight Sullivan, as well as his successor James J. Corbett, but white promoters refused to sponsor interracial fights. Interestingly, because of its violent nature, the attraction of an undesirable element of society, and its identification with gambling, boxing was outlawed in most states and territories. Fights took place in obscure locations like barns, river barges, and other remote locations (Mechikoff and Estes 1998).

Rowing and yacht racing were also popular sports in the decades that followed the Civil War. Early rowing is remembered for its concern that professionals would eliminate the amateur character of the sport. Thus, there was a formal exclusion of professionals and limited participation granted to clubs and universities. Yachting was associated with people of great wealth, much as it is today.

Affectionately known as America's sport, baseball was actually a variation of the English games of cricket and rounders. Organized baseball games began in New York in 1845 with the establishment of the New York Knickerbockers Base Ball Club (Polidoro 2000). Credited with establishing the rules, designing a uniform, and enacting a strict code of conduct, the Knickerbockers began playing the game for its recreational value and eventually played against other established clubs. The first recorded game between the New York Knickerbockers and the New York Base Ball Club was played in Hoboken, New Jersey, in 1846. Referred to as the "national pastime" as early as 1856, baseball soon became a serious element of society. Despite attempts to maintain its amateur status in order to control problems that surfaced, baseball was acknowledged as a professional sport with the establishment of the National Association of Baseball Players (NAPBP) in 1871.

Around the same time, football, volleyball, and basketball were emerging on college campuses, in YMCAs, and in high schools around the United States. In 1896, high schools in Denver, Colorado, formed the first basketball league, and in 1901 Eastern colleges formed the Intercollegiate League (Mechikoff and Estes 1998). The issues of amateurism versus professionalism and gambling dominated the sporting world as professional sports continued to emerge, becoming well established as the nation entered World War I.

1900s

With the growth of sports in schools and the replacement of amateur athletes with professionals, structures were in place to attempt to address athletics' initial problems. Reflecting larger society, however, social issues related to sport also needed to be addressed. Sports at all levels were primarily a white male activity, just as that element of society established and maintained power in every thread of American life and American institutions, notably educational systems. According to Urban and Wagoner (2000), even liberal progressive reformers like John Dewey, who had a significant impact on the course of American education, were silent on issues related to race. African Americans, particularly in the South, had to fight long, often unsuccessful battles for their right to an education. In the 1920s, there were few black high schools in the South. Although some parts of the North had initially allowed some integration, most of the nation allowed for a segregated system of schooling in which African American children received substandard educations. Yet despite their institutionalization, race and gender inequities could not be sustained indefinitely in either education or sport, just as they could not be sustained within the greater society.

Around the turn of the century, schools discouraged women from sport participation, deeming it unladylike or unsafe (Freeman 1992). Wuest and Bucher (1995) provide an interesting visual depiction of "early physical education costumes" for women from 1851–1927. Attire was a major issue to address as women attempted to participate in sport. Consider that during the original Olympic Games, men competed in the nude to glorify the male body, but it was not until 1927 that it was acceptable for women to show their bare arms and knees in "acceptable" athletic wear. It was also thought to be unsafe for women to exert themselves physically. Perspiration was considered a sign that women were overexerting themselves, and it was believed that fainting would often follow. As these myths were confronted, athletic clubs for women and associations for women's sports arrived on the scene in the early 1890s. Competitions were even held in sports such as archery, biking, bowling, fencing, golf, and tennis. Women's colleges began to offer opportunities to learn sports as a part of the physical education program, but competitive intercollegiate programs were not established until the 1950s. Women's athletics were significantly different from men's, and it was not until 1971 that an appropriate approach to women's athletic competition was established, thanks to the Association of Intercollegiate Athletics for Women (AIAW). The stage was set, but equal opportunity, programming, and finances did not follow. As a result, Congress passed Title IX in 1972, which attempted to mandate equal programming. In 1982, the AIAW became part of the National Collegiate Athletic Association (NCAA), which governs men's and women's intercollegiate athletics.

By the 1900s, the resurgence of African American participation in sports was becoming evident. Boxing and horse racing were the most significant venues, as most of the top jockeys and boxers had been of African descent. Nonetheless, because of well-established societal racism, African American participation in sports, as well as in industry and government, was not commonly supported. The Supreme Court's 1896 "separate but equal" decision had made the Jim Crow laws constitutional, and segregation was a mandated reality of American life—

including American sports. Although uncommon, African Americans had played on integrated teams before the 1890s, but white teams had demanded their removal following the Supreme Court's decision. Baseball would remain segregated until 1946. In response, African Americans established the National Association of Colored Professional Baseball Clubs in 1920. A few African American professional teams were well known, including the Chicago American Giants and the Kansas City Monarchs.

The effect of widespread racism in professional sports was most dramatic in boxing. Society could not accept the success of African American Jack Johnson as a search for a "great white hope" to defeat him resulted in scandals and injustice. Sport became an explicit vehicle that documented the racial injustices embedded in American society during the first half of the twentieth century. The accomplishments of African American athletes is presented in chapter 4.

During the early twentieth century, there remained a significant conflict between sport and education. Within college athletics, recruitment abuses and the absence of safety controls in light of the increasing number of football deaths resulted in the formation of the NCAA in 1905. At its inception, the NCAA had three basic goals: to establish high ethical standards for college sports, to develop physical education in schools, and to promote intramural athletics (Bucher and Dupree 1965). Schools were trying to take control of sport and harness its educational value. As previously noted, at the same time that the popularity of sport seemed to be meeting the needs of society, it was also providing a reflection of its problems.

Mid-Twentieth Century to the New Millennium

World War I (1916–1919) had a positive impact on both physical education and sport. As the United States called men to service by the Selected Service Act of 1917, it was also provided with the opportunity to review the health and fitness status of those men. One-third of the men were found to be physically unfit for armed service. Additionally, a 1918 survey by the National Council on Education documented that elementary and secondary school students were also unfit. In response, several prominent physical education leaders were called on to reform the area of physical conditioning. The influence of Dewey's work mandated a new way of thinking of both physical education and sport participation. By the mid-1920s the "new" physical education that focused on sports, games, and play was accepted as the country's system of physical education. Yet again, physical training for military purposes gave rise to physical education and sport. An interesting example of this relation-ship of sport and military training is the case of George W. Patton, who placed fifth in the pentathlon in the 1912 Olympic Games in Stockholm and eventually became one of the most famous military generals of World War II (Mechikoff and Estes 1998).

At the same time, changes that were occurring in the design of general education would have a tremendous impact on the develop-ment and implementation of the interscholastic program. In a 1918 re-port from the National Education Association, "Cardinal Principles of Secondary Education," the principles of health, command of funda-mental processes, worthy home membership, vocation, citizenship, worthy use of leisure time, and ethical character were stated objectives of a high school education (Urban and Wagoner 2000). This report sup-ported a movement toward a "comprehensive high school" with a phi-losophy classified as "social efficiency" and called for a revision of the school curriculum and the addition of extracurricular activities. One of the primary goals of this social efficiency was to promote social cohe-sion within the diverse U.S. population. Extracurricular activities such as athletics, journalism, and clubs would provide settings in which stu-dents from various curricular tracks could interact and learn to cooper-ate in the pursuit of a common interest, under the supervision of school staff. Thus the foundation for the development and administrative sup-port for the interscholastic athletic program as an extension of the for-mal secondary school education was laid and explains the inclusion of sports in school settings.

Interscholastic athletics skyrocketed as a result of these changes in American high schools. In 1923, the National Federation of State High School Associations (NFSHSA) was established to govern all inter-scholastic athletic programs, as it still does today (Polidoro 2000). This organization focuses on protecting high school students from exploita-tion by groups not related to the educational system and has enacted strict rules concerning college recruiting. Two years after the NFSHSA's inception, every state had established a high school athletic association. The demand for professional preparation in all areas of sport created many new areas of specialization.

On the college level, intercollegiate athletic participation in some sports was dropped; some were replaced with the Reserve Officer Train-ing Corps (ROTC). Overall, American participation in war confirmed the necessity of physical fitness and the value of sport participation. Nonetheless, the problematic aspects of athletics remained. As a result, the Carnegie Foundation provided funding to study programs at certain institutions. In 1929, the American College Athletes Report was published and documented the extent of recruitment and financial problems within intercollegiate athletics. The shame the report produced caused university administrators to become involved in the athletics-versus-education conflict; as a result intramural programs received great attention and realized significant growth.

The decade prior to World War II saw significant developments in women's athletics. At the 1932 Olympics in Los Angeles, "Babe" Didrickson won two gold medals in track and field, and Helen Madison won two gold medals in swimming. The accomplishments of these two women were significant. Despite strong opposition by International Olympic Committee directors, almost twice as many women participated in the 1936 Berlin games than had only four years before.

The Great Depression would cause significant cutbacks in education and sport programs. The effect of World War II confirmed this negative trend as forty-five percent of draft-age men were rejected for service based on physical or mental requirements. The nation once again realized the need for health and fitness; sports were strongly promoted as a means to develop fitness and were considered a positive influence on nationalism. As the war ended, another sports boom occurred, and Americans became more conscious of international competition. International sport emerged to promote peaceful competition and allow people to deepen their awareness and understanding of cultures around the world. International competition, most notably the Olympic Games, evolved into political symbols, which added an additional layer of problems to the world of sports. (Specific World Cup Competitions for international football and Olympic events will be discussed in later chapters.)

World War II also brought an official end to segregation when a 1954 Supreme Court decision, *Brown v. Board of Education,* reversed the "separate but equal" doctrine. Sports had made strides in this direction even before this, however. During the 1936 Olympic Games, Jesse Owens, an African American, won four gold medals for the United States. In 1946, Jackie Robinson became the first African American to play Major League Baseball in more than sixty years. Following the *Brown* decision, athletic teams in many parts of the country became integrated at the high school and collegiate levels. Most significant in this regard was the 1966 NCAA championship basketball game between the University of Kentucky and Texas Western, known as Texas–El Paso. Coach Don Haskins sent five starting African Americans out on the floor to face the five white starters from Kentucky. The Texas–El Paso 72–65 win over Kentucky is credited with opening the doors of universities across the country to black athletes. These issues will be discussed further in chapter 4.

During the years of international conflict, the public had viewed the value of sports and athletics in terms of their contribution to physical fitness. In times of peace, the development and focus was placed on "lifetime sports," encouraging people to pursue their choice of activities for personal benefit and to engage in them throughout the life span. From the 1970s to 1990, sport in the United States was greatly influenced by legislation that sought to ensure human rights and promote equal opportunity. Sport in educational settings was most profoundly affected by the passage of Title IX of the *Educational Amendments Act of 1972*. This legislation mandated that "no person in the United States, on the basis of gender, could be excluded from participation in, be denied the benefits of, or be subjected to discrimination under any educational program or activity receiving federal funds" (Polidoro 2000, 83). This single piece of legislation resulted in a significant rise in female sport participation. A 1995 NFSHSA survey documented the increase in female athletes participating in high school interscholastic sports from 294,015 in 1971 to 2,240,461 in 1995. At the same time, participation among male students dropped by about 100,000. That Title IX has provided equal opportunity to female athletes is without question; unfortunately, it has had negative side effects for male athletes. Because of fixed athletic budgets, often kept solvent with gate receipts from men's football and basketball games, women's programming has increased at the expense of men's. (The debate of the positive and negative effects of Title IX are covered more extensively in chapter 4.)

In 1975, the *Education of All Handicapped Children Act* (U.S. Public Law 94-142) mandated that physical education services must be available to every child regardless of disability and that children with disabilities must be educated in the least restrictive environment and be provided with individualized education plans (IEPs). This was followed in 1978 by the passage of the *Amateur Sports Act* (U.S. Public Law 95-606), which required the U.S. Olympic Committee to develop programs specifically designed for persons with disabilities. As a result, Americans with disabilities can now compete nationally and internationally in the Paralympics, the Special Olympics, the Wheelchair Games, and other events. Once sport participation became available to people with disabilities, spectators with disabilities needed to receive the same attention. In 1990, the *Americans with Disabilities Act* (U.S. Public Law 101-336) recognized them. In the area of sport, this act requires that all sport and recreational facilities provide equal access and services to individuals with disabilities. Although legislation has succeeded in providing equal rights to all citizens regardless of gender and physical limitations, sufficient funding to implement programs and reconfigure facilities is lacking. Consequently, school districts across the country are faced with financial limitations in meeting their legal requirements.

The New Millennium

A significant issue in the educational setting at the turn of the millennium is the relationship between physical education and sports. The general public continues to associate physical education and athletic programs sponsored by schools as a single discipline, although in reality the two have fought to establish their own identities with notably contrasting goals. The credibility of physical education as a profession and essential component of the educational system could not be accomplished as long as the public measured its worth by the win-loss records of its athletic teams. Sport needed to be seen as an extracurricular activity with its credibility and value being judged for the specific contributions it makes to the culture of the school and the educational process.

The over-emphasis on sports and inappropriate expectations for success of school teams are consequences of the effect of the professional sports world. At times the general public has difficulty differentiating the place of sports in school settings and professional sports big business.

Professional and amateur sports are not without their problems. As the salaries of professional athletes soar, labor disputes between players and owners have become routine, often resulting in player strikes. Major League Baseball experienced its first baseball strike in 1965, but it was the 1998 strike that dealt professional sport a major blow. Moving into the new millennium, many feel that the effects of these strikes have damaged fan support, and love of the game has been tarnished forever. Another damaging practice is the relocating of well-established professional franchises. Owners would demand assistance from state and local funding for the construction of new facilities. When the host city could not deliver, the franchise was moved to a more lucrative location. Sport tradition and fan loyalty became an acute condition of the time, replacing the enduring dedication to a team that was an important aspect of sport.

Technological advances, most notably those in sports television, also have had a tremendous impact on sport. It began at the turn of the century when William Randolph Hearst introduced the "sport's page" in his newspaper, the *New York Morning Journal* (Colfer et al. 1986). This allowed readers a better understanding of the world of the athlete and to establish themselves as sport fans in an additional context beyond attending actual sporting events.

More recently, radio, television, satellite communications, computers, and the Internet have allowed Americans to become involved in the world of sports in several different capacities. Sport events are a major component of network programming, and more than 20 percent of advertising revenues come from sport broadcasts. Cable stations such as ESPN, TNT, TBS, and Prime Sports Channel Networks use sports programming to improve their share of the viewing public by targeting a particular segment—sports fans. This transformation can be attributed to the 1978–1979 college basketball season, culminating in the NCAA tournament. As Larry Bird from Indiana State University and Ervin "Magic" Johnson from Michigan State battled in the finals, television ratings rose and networks took notice. Shortly after the season, the NCAA entered into a much more lucrative contract for television rights and established relations with a cable network. In 1979, ESPN became the first exclusive sports channel, agreeing to televise all NCAA tournament games not shown by the major networks. As a result, sport has become an integral part of U.S. culture, a vehicle for the moral, political, and social issues that Americans support.

The transition from the simple broadcast of a college basketball game to the flamboyant productions we expect should be attributed to the genius of one man and his supporting network. The late Roone Arledge is well known as the single most influential person in sports television. He is attributed with revolutionizing the industry with his pioneering vision that brought *Monday Night Football* and *Wide World of Sports* to television. He conceptualized the production of sport as entertainment and brought this concept to fruition by incorporating instant reply, free frame, slow-motion, and handheld cameras into the broadcast. His influence became global when he supervised the televised coverage of the 1972 Olympic Games in Munich, where Israeli athletes were murdered by Palestinian terrorists. To experience this transition, compare one of ESPN's classic games from the 1960s or even 1970s to a National Football League game this season.

The availability of sports television, which now includes Little League World Series, Good Will Games, major college football games, NCAA basketball tournaments, as well as professional contests that often include "up close and personal" looks into the world of various athletes, has skewed the public's perception of the role of sports in schools. Many consider interscholastic and intercollegiate sports as the professional league's training grounds.

This chronology of sport and education presents an abundance of interesting facts and themes to consider. Most significant is the theme that as sport has gained an increased presence in society, so have its problems. As Americans learn to live in an era of terrorism (one could question whether this is a time of peace or time of war) sport has never before been such a significant force in our daily lives. Currently, the effect of sport could be considered dichotomous, mirroring both the best and the worst of what our culture has to offer. The remaining chapters in this text explore this dichotomy and help the reader judge the significance of the relationship between sport and education.

THE HISTORY OF PROMINENT AMERICAN SPORTS

Baseball

Baseball is often referred to as America's pastime, mainly for the nation's devotion to the game, but also for its historical significance. The English settlers created baseball in colonial America around 1700; over time, the influences of the Irish, Scottish, and German immigrants transformed the English game of "rounders" into what we know as baseball. Although a form of the game was played during the Revolutionary War period, it wasn't truly baseball until Abner Doubleday established an accepted set of rules. Doubleday is considered the inventor of the game and is recognized for his commitment to its promotion. His efforts led a New York City sportsman named Alexander Cartwright to establish the Knickerbocker Base Ball Club of New York, which led to the first official rules for the game. The first official game was held on June 19, 1846, between the New York Nine and the Knickerbocker Club in Hoboken, New Jersey. In 1858, the National Association of Baseball Players (NABBP) was formed and included African American athletes. Following the Civil War, however, baseball spread considerably, and teams appeared in many large cities around the country. Society's influence on the game brought segregation, and by 1871 the NABBP supported the exclusion of African Americans from their clubs, leading black ballplayers to form their own teams and establish the Negro League. As the number of all-white and all-black teams grew, so, too, did the popularity of the sport. Eight professional teams comprised the first major league, founded in 1869, called the National League; by 1901 eight more teams comprised the American League. Desegregation of teams occurred, but only on a limited basis and only within the minor leagues. (Additional information about the Negro League is included in chapter 4).

The first World Series was played in 1903 between the Boston Red Socks of the American League and the Pittsburgh Pirates of the National League. In the 1940s and 1950s, television allowed the public to watch games, further increasing the popularity of the game. The Negro League continued to thrive but was overshadowed by the attention given to the majors. In 1947, however, Branch Rickey, president of the Brooklyn Dodgers, transformed baseball. Two years earlier Rickey had signed the first African American to play Major League Baseball. The player's name was Jackie Robinson. On April 15, 1947, Robinson made his major league debut for the Brooklyn Dodgers at Ebbets Field. That year Robinson was named the National League Rookie of the Year and played in the World Series against the New York Yankees. In 1949, Robinson was named the National League Most Valuable Player. During his tenure in professional baseball, Robinson, and the other African American players who followed him, was the target of racism and hatred. Nonetheless, Branch Rickey's courageous decision allowed other teams to end segregation in Major League Baseball. The Negro League folded in the 1948 (Sylvester 2003).

Basketball

Basketball is considered a truly American sport because it was created in the United States to meet the need for a team sport that could be played indoors during the winter months. James A. Naismith created the game in 1891 at Springfield College in Massachusetts. He hung two peach baskets at either end of the gym as goals. His game required two opposing teams to pass a soccer ball around while attempting to throw it into the opposing team's basket. Naismith soon realized that retrieving the ball from the basket after a goal was difficult, so he decided to cut the bottom out of the basket. The pace of the game increased immediately. The first game was played with thirteen rules, which are basically still used in today's version of the game. (The original thirteen rules can be found in the Appendix.) Backboards were installed in 1893, and in 1921 people began to call the game basketball. The sport is considered the fastest-growing game ever because it quickly spread across the nation and the world. Played by female athletes from its inception, Dr. Naismith actually married one of the first women to play the game at Springfield College.

With the exception of some segregated secondary school teams, African Americans played on all-black teams. Until the 1950s, colleges in the South were forbidden to have integrated teams due to the Jim Crow Laws. The first professional league, called the National Basketball League, was formed in 1898. It comprised four teams from New York, New Jersey, Philadelphia, and Brooklyn. In 1925, the American Basketball League was formed with nine teams.

The popularity of the game was soon evident as it began to draw large crowds. One of the reasons for this popularity was the formation of an all-black team named the Harlem Globetrotters in 1927 by Abe Saperstein. This team toured the country to promote the game of basketball as it entertained large crows with a display of unmatched skills.

Large crowds and wealthy supporters resulted in the formation of the National Basketball Association (NBA) in 1949, which replaced all existing leagues. In the decades that followed, premiere players such as Wilt Chamberlain, Larry Bird, Magic Johnson, and Michael Jordan all made unique contributions to the game. (Additional information about these players can be found in chapter 4.) At the turn of the millennium, fans' love for this great American game has been undermined by large salary demands, player strikes, and individual player scandals. At times, college basketball seems to overshadow professional games, particularly during the NCAA tournament. Coverage of this event, deemed "March Madness," has taken on a life of its own as television networks attempt to televise every game, causing fans to alter their daily routines to catch some of the action. Significant controversy surrounds the college game as well, as college athletics have become "big business."

Football

American football is a game created from the English game of rugby and an early form of soccer, also played in England. College students played variations of the game, but the running and tackling aspects of the rugby-style game proved to be most popular. Football became the contact sport of choice on most campuses. Walter Camp of Yale is credited with establishing rules under the direction of the Intercollegiate Football Association (American Football History 2001). With established rules, intercollegiate competition became popular and highly competitive. In time, the injuries incurred during football games, including a number of deaths, became severe enough to receive the attention of President Theodore Roosevelt. In 1905, Roosevelt called for a review of the sport, which set the stage for internal policing and the creation of the NCAA. Rule changes focused on safety, and the sport evolved into the highly dramatized and hotly contested game celebrated by the annual New Year's Day Rose Bowl ritual held between the Big Ten and Pac Ten conference champions.

In 1895, the first game of professional football was played in Pennsylvania. In 1920, the owners of eleven football clubs organized professional football into the American Professional Football Association. The first president was Jim Thorpe (a Native American), who at the time was thought to be the country's greatest all-around athlete. In 1922, with the association in financial distress, it was reorganized and renamed the National Football League (NFL). In 1933, the NFL split into two divisions, western and eastern, and held the first World Professional Football Title game. The Chicago Bears represented the Western Division, defeating the Eastern Division New York Giants.

In 1960, the American Football League (AFL) was formed. Television had a profound effect on the game during the 1950s and 1960s. Football's popularity put networks in the awkward situation of struggling between televising regular programming and satisfying football fans' insatiable interest in the game. The famous "Heidi" game of 1968 between the New York Jets and the Oakland Raiders is described as follows: (http://www.nfl.com/insider/story/5934055) "A seemingly innocuous decision by an NBC executive—to preempt the broadcast of the end of an AFL game for the start of the movie *Heidi*—triggered a firestorm. Better than any poll, it delivered an unmistakable message about the popularity of pro football and America's passionate attachment to the game."

The first Super Bowl was held in 1967 and today is played each January between the AFL and NFL champions. In 1970, the NFL and AFL formed one league to be called the NFL with two divisions renamed the American Football Conference (AFC) and the National Football Conference (NFC). In 1987, Arena Football, an indoor version of the game, debuted, but it has yet to reach the high-flying status of the NFL.

Professional football represents the epitome of big business within professional sports. Networks charge hundreds of thousands of dollars for a thirty-second Super Bowl commercial. More outrageous still is the sum that networks pay for NFL rights. In a deal struck at the end of 1997, Fox Television paid $17.6 billion for the right to televise NFL games until 2005. This amounts to about $75 million per team per season, a gain of $37 million per team from the previous contract (Eitzen 2000).

Golf

The origin of the game of golf has never been clearly defined. Both the Scottish and the British claim to have invented the game, with variations played throughout the Netherlands, France, and Belgium as early as the fifteenth century. Scotland is the home of the world's oldest golf course, St. Andrews, which was used as early as the sixteenth century, but was officially established in 1754. The first eighteen-hole course in the United States, the Chicago Golf Club, was built near Wheaton, Illinois, in 1893.

The United States Golf Association (USGA), founded in 1894, is golf's governing body in the United States. This organization sets ball and club specifications, regulations on hazards, and official scoring. The USGA works with the Royal and Ancient Club of St. Andrews in reviewing and revising international rules. In 1916, the Professional Golfers' Association of America (PGA) was founded. It conducts the PGA and PGA Senior tournaments, as well as the Ryder Cup competition between members of the American and British Professional Golf Associations.

What is unique to golf is that amateurs and professionals compete together in open tournaments. Among the major tournaments that have the support of the PGA are the U.S. Open, the U.S. Women's Open, the PGA, the Ladies Professional Golf Association (LPGA), the Masters, the British Amateur, the British Open, the Canadian Open, the U.S. Amateur, and the U.S. Women's Amateur.

Golf has been a popular spectator sport since the 1920s, but interest increased dramatically following World War II. Like tennis, golf has been accepted in the United States as a "lifetime" sport because it is played by people of all ages. Over the years, golf has had to contend with an elitist reputation, one supported by well-documented gender and racial segregation. For years, most privately owned golf clubs across the country prohibited minority and female members. Michael Jordan, the famous professional basketball player, brought the issue to the public's attention. An avid golfer with a true passion for the game, he was able to golf on the most prestigious private courses as a guest, but he was not allowed membership. The irony of this situation, together with the emergence of Tiger Woods, convinced most clubs to open their memberships—with one significant exception. Augusta National Golf Club, the home of the Master's Tournament, still does not allow female members.

To address this, a *New York Times* editorial called on Tiger Woods to boycott this most prestigious tournament to make a statement against the discrimination. Woods declined to boycott but stated publicly that there should be female members at Augusta. He also noted that it was not his place to make the statement against the club.

Minorities and females participate within the amateur and professional golf circuit; however, prohibition from membership at certain private clubs still exists to document the status of race and gender relations within the United States. Golfers are recognized by the number of major tournaments they win as well as the money won in tournaments within each year. In the 1950s, Arnold Palmer and, in the 1960s, Jack Nicklaus were the premiere talents of the game. Palmer was the first golfer whose career earnings passed the million-dollar mark, a feat he accomplished in 1968. Nicklaus, the only golfer to be chosen as the PGA

Player of the Year five times, was the first to earn more than $2 million, achieved in 1973; he had earned $3 million by 1977, $4 million by 1983, and $5 million by 1988.

American women were successful in professional golf as well. In 1981, Kathy Whitworth became the first female golfer with career earnings of more than $1 million; Pat Bradley reached the $2 million mark in 1986 and the $3 million mark in 1990.

Tennis

Ball games were played in ancient times as early as 1500 BC. During the eighth century, the influence of the Moors within Europe eventually gave rise to tennis. It is believed that Christian Monks, who were interested in learning the religious rites of the Moors, were the first Europeans to play tennis (Cliff Richard Tennis Foundation, n.d.). "LaSoule" was the name given this early version of the game in which players hit a ball back and forth using a stick or their hands. The game became popular in monasteries across Europe, and by the twelfth and thirteenth centuries the general public was playing the game. In an attempt to achieve better control of the ball, leather gloves and eventually wooden handled racquets were developed. In France, royalty adopted the game; from the sixteenth through eighteenth centuries the game was typically played indoor by kings and noblemen. This early version of the game was different from today's lawn tennis.

As the game gained popularity in England, it was also spreading into Spain, Italy, Germany, Holland, and Switzerland. It eventually moved outside onto grass lawns. The production of vulcanized rubber provided a ball that would be "lively" and not damage the grass (Cliff Richards Tennis Foundation, n.d.).

Official recognition of the sport came in 1877 when the name of the prestigious All England Croquet Club was changed to the All England Croquet and Lawn Tennis Club. This club sponsored the first tournament later that year with twenty-two players; some two hundred spectators observed the event that would become the first Wimbledon. With the establishment of competition and official rules, tennis gained popularity across the world. In 1905 May Sutton became the first international player who was from the United States (Cliff Richard Tennis Foundation, n.d.). The following list highlights the history of tennis in the twentieth century.

- 1940s–1950s: Several American players achieved worldwide success, including Pancho Gonzales, Jack Kramer, Ted

Schroeder, and Tony Trabert. Althea Gibson became the first African American to dominate the sport, winning the U.S. and Wimbledon titles in 1957 and 1958.

➡ 1960s: The world watched tennis on television, as it became an international sport dominated by Australians Rod Laver and Roy Emerson. Arthur Ashe of the United States became the first African American male to dominate the sport, winning the U.S. title in 1968.

➡ 1970s: International players dominating the sport include Bjorn Borg, Jimmy Connors, John McEnroe, Sue Baker, Chris Everett Lloyd, and Martina Navratilova.

➡ 1980s: The yellow ball replaced the traditional white ball to aid viewers in following the ball on television.

➡ 1990s: Wimbledon became one of the most popular sporting events of the year.

The Cliff Richard Tennis Website (http://www.clifrichardtennis. org) provides greater resources on the game of tennis and an actual glimpse into the Tennis Museum at the All England Lawn Tennis and Croquet Club, home of Wimbledon Championships.

Soccer

Soccer is an international sport played in almost every country around the world. It is considered the number one sport in countries across Europe and South America, where the game is known as football. Various soccer-style games have been played since Greek and Roman times. Soccer was played in the United States in the original Jamestown settlement of 1609 (Litterer 2001), where the game probably resembled an English game "Shrovetide." The first written accounts of soccer games in the United States were of events held on college campuses. These competitions resembled intramural play, the earliest between freshman and sophomores at Harvard in 1827.

Today's soccer originated in England in the 1830s and was played by the working class. The first established clubs were formed in Sheffield and London and led to regional competitions. Soon after it became apparent that an official set of rules and regulations needed to be adopted, and so the Football Association (FA) was formed in 1863 (Litterer 2001). In the United States, the influence of the Oneida Soccer Club of Boston in 1862 was significant. As the first official team with a roster of players—high school students from affluent Boston schools—they played pickup college teams, leading to the promotion of the game within the college community. The first intercollegiate game that used a set of official rules was played on November 7, 1869, between Princeton and Rutgers. This game is often referenced as the first official football game played in the United States (Litterer 2001). In 1880, a universal set of rules was adopted, which was influenced by the London rules of 1863. The games of soccer, rugby, and American football were evolving simultaneously, arising from the same influences. As groups of players became passionate about certain aspects of their game and unwilling to compromise, the three individual sports developed. As a result the popularity of what we call football led to the demise of soccer on college campuses. Soccer became the game of the working class and youth, an effect of the constant influx of European immigrants in the late nineteenth and early twentieth centuries.

The American Football Association was formed in 1884, which organized the first national team. Efforts to organize official leagues and competitions continued, but competition for spectators from other American sports proved to be a major stumbling block. The participation of the U.S. team in the 1904 Olympics held in St. Louis provided the necessary support for a successful professional league. At the time soccer was developing into the international game it is today. The Federation Internationale de Football Association (FIFA) was formed in 1904, but the United States was not included. Significant and continuous conflict between the amateur and professional soccer camps prevented the United States from establishing a national organization. As a result of FIFA's 1912 rejection of the Unites States, the American Amateur Football Association (AAFA) reorganized into the United States Football Association (USFA). The USFA established an official national championship tournament, the National Championship Cup, first played in 1914. Soccer grew in the 1920s with the formation of the American Soccer League (ASL) in 1921, which began to compete for European players. The women's game was significantly influenced by the 1922 U.S. tour of the famous English women's soccer team. The American teams proved to be competitive with the English, as the Americans posted a (1–1–2) record on the tour.

Until the 1970s, professional soccer was its own worst enemy. It continued to compete with other professional sports for spectators and television broadcasting contracts, but interleague fighting and the inability to work for the common good of the game led to financial difficulties for professional teams. Highlights of the time were the U.S. team's 1–0 victory over England in the World Cup and the recognition of soccer as a sport sanctioned by the NCAA in the 1950s. The 1970s saw a concerted effort to resurrect professional soccer, and in 1975 Brazil's

Pele was signed to play for the New York Cosmos. Pele, who had recently retired from soccer in South America, overwhelmed Americans with his athletic brilliance and unprecedented level of play. Attendance climbed quickly, and in 1977, more than 77,000 fans watched the professional playoff game at Giant Stadium in New York. Additionally, parents and youth were beginning to embrace youth soccer as excellent alternative to Little League Baseball and Pop Warner Football. The United States Youth Soccer Association (USYSA) and American Youth Soccer Organization (AYSO) provided well-organized youth sport programs across America. The USYSA provided a more competitive program, compared with AYSO's recreational focus in which sportsmanship and appropriate parental participation and behavior were enforced.

At the 1984 Olympic Games in Los Angeles, soccer was the most heavily attended competition, proving to the world, and most significantly to FIFA, that the United States would turn out to see international soccer matches. The 1994 World Cup was awarded to the United States on the condition that it establish a division 1 professional league. It was clear that college teams could not produce the caliber of players needed for this league, so the United States Soccer Federation (USSF) developed its National Team Training Program. Players were contracted to play full time to train for the national team and World Cup competition. This team qualified for the 1990 World Cup.

In 1991, FIFA established the Women's World Championship, which the U.S. women's team won. The success of the women's program could be attributed to the training women received at the college level. Four years after the U.S. women's first World Cup victory, the team lost to Norway in the semifinals, but this loss seemed to provide the motivation to support a national team that could regain its crown as the world's best. The 1994 Men's World Cup held in the United States proved to be an enormous financial success, providing unprecedented attention to soccer in this country. FIFA awarded the 1999 Women's World Cup to the United States. At the time, no one realized the impact this would have on American soccer. When the U.S. women's team won the World Cup that year, it

connected with youth players and the general public as no other [team] had ever done, and attracted an entire new female audience to the game. More importantly, they did so with a heavy dose of altruism, good sportsmanship, respect for the audience, professionalism and skill that is sadly lacking in so many of professional sports these days. They not only provided inspiring role models for young girls, but also more importantly to young boys, who looked across the gender divide to see a moral example truly worth following. (Litterer 2001)

U.S. soccer has had a challenging past. As the men's program fought to survive despite the negative influences of the national and international soccer communities, the women's program quietly picked up the pieces and catapulted the sport to its present level of recognition. Soccer in the United States might not be garnering the record crowds, television coverage, and financial success awarded to other sports, but more U.S. youth participate in soccer than any other sport; one might argue that no other sport deserves the respect that soccer has attained for both men and women.

Volleyball

Like basketball, volleyball is one of the few sports that has its origins in the United States. Today this popular international sport ranks second only to soccer in terms of participation. More than 46 million Americans play volleyball, and 800 million players worldwide play this exciting game at least once per week (Volleyball World Wide, n.d.). In 1895, William Morgan, an instructor at the Young Men's Christian Association (YMCA) in Holyoke, Massachusetts, decided that the businessmen needed a game for recreation that was less physically demanding and required less physical contact. He developed a game that combined elements of badminton, baseball, basketball, tennis, and handball. Using a tennis net raised to six feet, six inches, above the floor, Morgan's game allowed for teams of two or more players, who batted the ball back and forth over the net. The original game consisted of nine innings, with three servers per inning and points awarded to the team that could prevent the ball from dropping to the floor of its side of the court. Hitting lines drawn on the floor or the net was considered out of bounds.

Observers of the game commented on how the players seemed to be "volleying" the ball back and forth over the net, and as a result, Morgan changed the name from his original "mintonette" to "volleyball." At first, players used a basketball, but it was too heavy. Players tried using the bladder from inside the basketball, which proved to be too "flighty." Morgan approached A.G. Spaulding Brothers, requesting that they develop a ball that would not float but that was easier on the hands. The original calfskin volleyball is not much different from the ball used today. On July 7, 1896, the first game of volleyball was played at Springfield College. In the early 1900s the game was not flourishing when compared with basketball; it was considered a "slow, sissy" sport. This led to changes in the game. The net was raised to seven feet above the floor, and a player could no longer "dribble" the ball to oneself. The nine inning game was replaced with a winner being declared after winning 21 points. The second wave of changes to the game came in 1916 when the net was raised to eight feet; the winner was declared after earning 15 points, winning 2 out of 3 games consisted of winning the match, and the rotation of the server was implemented. The game quickly spread to other countries through the YMCA system. In 1914, an estimated five thousand courts were used to play the game in YMCAs, schools, outdoor playgrounds, and in private clubs.

In the Philippines, the game was particularly popular. As volleyball's popularity grew in that country, players further developed the game. The offensive strategy of volleying the ball with a high arch to a designated teammate, who would then "bomba" the ball over the net, was devised. Thus, a game created in the United States was revolutionized in the Philippines. In 1916, the YMCA invited the NCAA to assist in changing and establishing the rules, hoping to promote the sport in school settings. In the 1920s, the court size was established at thirty by sixty feet, and lifting, throwing, carrying, jabbing, and slapping of the ball were designated as illegal moves. The women's game evolved differently from the men's game, with eight players per team, two serves per player, unlimited hits, and a thirty-minute time limit per game. This women's version did not change to the six-man, three-hit game until 1958. The first Amateur Athletic Union (AAU) Volleyball Championships were played in 1925, and in 1928 the U.S. Volleyball Association (USVBA) was formed (Volleyball World Wide, n.d.). One reason for volleyball's popularity was the fact that it could be played both indoors and outdoors, and in 1930 the first two-person beach volleyball match took place. A study of recreation in the United States declared that volleyball was the fifth most popular team sport in 1946. In 1957, the International Olympic Committee designated volleyball as an Olympic sport, which was to be included in the 1964 games (Volleyball World Wide, n.d.). Two years later, two-person beach volleyball was added to the Olympics.

During the 1960s, the game's popularity demanded additional changes; the women's net was dropped to seven feet, the six-two offense with three hitters and quick sets was developed, as well as the "dink," "bump," and "block." In the 1970s, the United States seemed to take the game more seriously as the women's national team began a year-round training program. In 1984, the U.S. men won the Olympic gold medal, and the women won the silver. As a sport, volleyball has benefited from significant changes over the years. Volleyball is most popular at the university level, and unfortunately the professional game does not receive the attention it deserves.

NASCAR

Throughout history, racing the vehicles that transport humans from point A to point B has been a testimony to our competitive drive, but it was the efforts of the founders of the National Association for Stock Car Auto Racing (NASCAR) that truly brought it to the level of sport. At the end of World War II, as soldiers returned home and the country was on the verge of prosperity, the auto industry realized it needed to increase production to keep up with demand. Automobile manufacturers began to design cars to market to young men seeking adventure. The United States became passionate about the sports car—cars that were fast, powerful, sleek, and attractive. Once the cars hit the streets, racing promotion and organizations quickly followed. As with other sports, unifying the various factions within auto racing was vital to its success with the public. Bill France organized a meeting of the leaders of the various racing organizations to outline what would become the national automobile sport (http://www.membres.lycos.fr/binuxracing/history.html). After four days, the members agreed on a set of rules and on the name NASCAR, making it an official sport in 1948. The first races involved "modified" prewar cars. Red Byron won the first championship of fifty-two races and received $1,250 (NASCAR.com, n.d.). Soon Bill France, now the president of NASCAR, decided that people should race "the cars that people actually drove on the street" (NASCAR.com, n.d.). The idea that these cars would be more popular and elevate interest, was resurrected. Thus the "strictly stock" cars (those without modifications) became the legal cars to drive in NASCAR races. No modifications could be made to the earliest stock cars. Nine automobile makers were represented in the first official races, an event called the Grand Nationals: Buick, Cadillac, Chrysler, Ford, Hudson, Kaiser, Lincoln, Mercury, and Oldsmobile (NASCAR.com, n.d.).

The first Super-Speedway was built in Darlington, South Carolina, which is still the site of the Winston Cup; it is considered one of the toughest racetracks in the country. In 1959, the first Daytona 500 was held at the new Daytona International Speedway, and in 1960, the first televised coverage of the event took place. Throughout the 1960s and 1970s, some of the biggest names in NASCAR history emerged, including Richard Petty, David Pearson, Cale Yarborough, and later Dale Earnhardt. NASCAR had a significant impact on the auto industry and on the general public as well.

Later NASCAR decided that modifications to mass-produced cars could be made to comply with safety specifications. Therefore, as the auto companies began to see that winning high-profile NASCAR races could translate into increased sales of their cars, their efforts focused on improving the design of their car bodies and engines. Some of the advances that were then available to the general public were Monroe "air lift" shocks, high-quality Firestone and Goodyear tires, the 427-cubic-inch "high lift" engine, and the hemi engine; high-end automobiles also became available to the general public, including the Ford Thunderbird, the Chevrolet Corvette, and the Mercury Marauder.

At the start of the new millennium, NASCAR began to experience a surge of popularity with unprecedented attendance at races and increased television coverage.

REFERENCES

American Football History. (2001). Retrieved on March 12, 2003, from http://wiwi.essortment.com/americanfootbal_rwff.htm.

Bucher, C. A., and Dupree, R. K.(1965). *Athletics in Schools and Colleges*. New York: Center for Applied Research in Education.

Cliff Richards Tennis Foundation. (n.d.). The history of tennis. Retrieved April 9, 2003, from http://www.cliffrichardtennis.org/index2.htm.

Colfer, G. R., K. E. Hamilton, R. A. Magill, and B. J. Hamilton (1986). *Contemporary Physical Education*. Dubuque, IA: Wm. C. Brown.

Eitzen, D. S. (2000, March–April). Public teams, private profits: How pro sports owners run up the score on fans and taxpayers. Retrieved on March 17, 2003, from http://www.dollarsandsense.org/archives/2000/0300eitzen.html.

Evolution of the stock car. (February 6, 2002). Retrieved April 12, 2003, from http://www.nascar.com/knowyournascar/history.html.

Flashback (1968): The Heidi Game. NFL Insider Online. Retrieved June 20, 2003, from http://www.nfl.com/insider/story/5934055.

Freeman, W. H. (1992). *Physical and Sport in a Changing Society*. New York: Macmillian.

Gensemer, R. T. (1991). *Physical Education: Perspectives, Inquiry & Applications*. Dubuque, IA: Wm. C. Brown.

History of NASCAR in a few lines (n.d.). Retreived June 25, 2003, from http://membres.lycos.fr/binusracing/history.html.

Lee, M. (1983). *A History of Physical Education and Sports in the USA*. New York: John Wiley.

Litterer, D. (January 27, 2001). An overview of American soccer history. Retrieved on April 9, 2003, from http://www.sover.net/~spectrum/overview.html.

Lumpkin, A. (1998). *Physical Education and Sport: A Contemporary Introduction.* Boston: McGraw-Hill.

Mechikoff, R., and Estes, S. (1998). *A History and Philosophy of Sport and Physical Education: From Ancient Civilizations to the Modern World.* Boston: McGraw-Hill.

NASCAR.com. (n.d.). NASCAR 101: History. Retrieved June 16, 2003, from http://www.nascar.com/kyn/history.

NFHS.org (n.d.). 2001 Athletics Participation Totals. Retrieved June 20, 2003, from http://www.nfhs.org/participation/sportspart01_files/sheet001.htm.

Polidoro, J. R. (2000). *Sport and Physical Education in the Modern World.* Boston: Allyn and Bacon.

Pulliam, J., and Van Patten, J. (1999) *History of Education in America.* Columbus, OH: Prentice Hall.

Rosenthal, J. T. (1981). Dark age education: Our latest survey. *History of Education Quarterly* 21, 115–121.

Segall, W. E., and A. V. Wilson (1998). *Introductions to Education: Teaching in a Diverse Society.* Upper Saddle River, NJ: Merril.

Sylvester, M. (2003). African-Americans in the Sports Arena. Retrieved on March 17, 2003, from http://www.cwpost.livnet.edu/cwis/cwp/library/aaitsa.htm.

Urban, W. J., and Wagoner, J. L. (2000). *American Education: A History.* Boston: McGraw-Hill.

Van Dalen, D., and Bennett, B. (1971). *A World History of Physical Education: Cultural, Philosophical, Comparative.* New Jersey: Prentice Hall.

Volleyball World Wide. (n.d.). History of volleyball. Retrieved April 12, 2003, from http://www.volleyball.org/history.html.

Wiggins, D. K. (1997). *Glory Bound: Black Athletes in White America.* Syracuse, NY: Syracuse University Press.

Wuest, D., and Bucher, C. (1995). *Foundations of Physical Education and Sport.* New York: Mosby.

Zeigler, E. F., editor. (1975). *A History of Physical Education & Sport in the United States and Canada.* Champaign, IL: Stipes.

A Timetable of Educational and Sport Events throughout History

Education/ Social Events	Year	Sport Events
	2000 BC	Evidence of contact sports, wrestling, and boxing
	776 BC	First Olympic event
Plato's Republic	378 BC	
Aristotle's Lyceum School	335 BC	
Middle Ages	500–1500 BC	
Renaissance and Reformation	1300–1550	
Invention of the printing press	1445	
	1499	South Hampton Town Bowling Club in England
Martin Luther attacks Catholic Church's role in schools	1517	
	1552	First golf club in St. Andrews, Scotland
Jamestown is established in Virginia	1607	
African slaves are brought to Virginia	1619	
Harvard College becomes first college in North America	1636	
Old Deluder Satan Act: requires every town to establish a school	1647	
College of William and Mary in Williamsburg established	1692	
Age of Enlightenment	1688–1789	
	1750	Formation of the jockey club for horse owners
	1754	
American Declaration of Independence	1776	
Northwest Ordinance provides land to support education	1787	Marylebone Cricket Club is founded
	1793	First documented tennis match in England
First school for African American children is founded	1807	
	1811	German Turnfest, Berlin
	1816	
Froebel publishes *Education and Man*	1821	
First high school opens in Boston	1824	

A Timetable of Educational and Sport Events (*continued*)

Education/ Social Events	Year	Sport Events
Round Hill School requires daily physical education	1827	First competitive football game takes place
	1846	First official baseball game
Lincoln University opened for African Americans	1854	
First Young Men's Christian Association opens in Boston	1852	First collegiate competition: crew race between Yale and Harvard
	1859	First Intercollegiate baseball game between Amherst and Williams
	1861	
Physical education becomes an academic field	1861–1865	
American Civil War	1863–1865	
California state legislature mandates physical education	1869	First intercollegiate football game between Rutgers and Princeton
	1870	Pep club forms at Princeton
	1872	
Michigan Supreme Court establishes public financial support for high schools	1873	First intercollegiate track and field meet, Saratoga regatta
	1874	Tennis is introduced to the United States
	1875	National Bowling Congress forms Intercollegiate Association of Amateur Athletes of America
	1877	Wimbledon
	1878	Badminton first played in United States
	1883	Intercollegiate Lawn Tennis Association formed
	1885	
American Association for the Advancement of Physical Education	1886	Cincinnati Red Stockings Professional Baseball team is founded
	1890	First women's tennis club appears at University of California

A Timetable of Educational and Sport Events (*continued*)

Education/ Social Events	Year	Sport Events
Dudley Sargent addresses AAAPE	1891	James Naismith invents basketball at Springfield College
	1892	University of California forms a women's basketball team
National Education Association (NEA) included Department of PE	1895	William Morgan invents volleyball
		First intercollegiate hockey competition
		Intercollegiate Conference of Faculty representatives form (led to Big 10 Conference)
Supreme Court "separate but equal" decision	1896	Modern Olympic games first held
		First intercollegiate swim meet
	1900	Oberlin College hosts six-team women's basketball tournament
	1902	First Rose Bowl
Sargent College of Physical Education	1903	First baseball World Series First Tour de France
	1906	Playground Association of America is formed
	1905	Football crisis mediated by President Theodore Roosevelt
		Intercollegiate Athletic Association is founded
	1910	National Collegiate Athletic Association founded
	1911	National Park Service formed
	1913	Federation Internationale de Football Association founded
		Intramural programs established in Michigan and Ohio
John Dewey publishes *Democracy and Education*	1917	National Hockey League formed in United States
World War I	1923	National Federation of State High School Association founded

A Timetable of Educational and Sport Events (*continued*)

Education/ Social Events	Year	Sport Events
"New" physical education curriculum	1920	National Association of Professional Colored Baseball Clubs founded
		ADIDAS-designed "training boot" appears
	1929	Carnegie Foundation issues a report on college athletics
	1928	International Congress on Sports Medicine
	1930	Bobby Jones wins the Grand Slam in Golf
		First World Cup
	1938	National Junior College Athletic Association
	1939	Little League Baseball founded in Pennsylvania
		First National Football League (NFL) televised game
World War II	1941–1945	
United Nations Educational, Scientific, and Cultural Organization is formed	1945	
United Nations is formed	1946	Professional Baseball first includes African Americans
	1949	National Basketball Association is founded
	1950	American Bowling Congress ends membership restrictions against nonwhites
	1951	National Athletic Trainers Association is founded
Supreme Court orders integration of public schools in *Brown v. Board of Education*	1954	*Sports Illustrated* debuts; First College Athletic Scholarships awarded
Russia launches Sputnik satellite	1958	Baltimore Colts vs. New York Giants: greatest NFL game ever played
The Pursuit of Excellence Report	1959	National Art Museum of Sport opened

A Timetable of Educational and Sport Events (*continued*)

Education/ Social Events	Year	Sport Events
	1961	The creation of ABC's *Wide World of Sports*
Conant's book; the American High School Today	1962	Blue Ribbon Sports (renamed Nike in 1972) is founded
Congress passes the Civil Rights Act of 1964	1964	American Youth Soccer Organization is established
Economic Opportunity Act is enacted	1965	First indoor baseball game is played at Houston Astrodome
Project Head Start begins	1966	First Super Bowl played
Elementary and Secondary Education Act		Texas–El Paso beats Kentucky for the NCAA men's basketball championship
	1968	National Jogging Association is established
		First Special Olympics is held
	1970	First ABC *Monday Night Football* is aired
	1971	Association for Intercollegiate Athletics for Women is founded
Title IX of the Educational Amendments Act	1976	First Perfect Ten scored in Olympic gymnastics
	1977	HBO begins televising sporting events
	1979	The first twenty-four-hour sport network, ESPN, goes on air
	1990	*Life* magazine names Roone Arledge as one of the one hundred most influential Americans
	1999	National Association of Sport and Physical Education (NASPE) opposes national sports competition at high school level
September 11 terrorist attack	2001	

Chapter Three

☙ What We Learn from Sport

The issues presented in this chapter are organized within unifying themes: (1) Does sport participation benefit children? (2) What are the most salient coaching and administrative issues? (3) Do collegiate athletics need to change? (4) Does victory demand unethical behavior? (5) Should sport be eliminated from school settings?

DOES SPORT PARTICIPATION BENEFIT CHILDREN?

At What Age Should Children Begin Sport Participation?

The question of the best age at which to begin playing sports has received considerable attention in recent years, particularly in response to the level of organized sport and competition available to young children. It is estimated that most American children begin participating in sports between the ages of four and seven years, with most children finding the sport experience enjoyable. What are the documented effects of early participation? Research indicates that infants who have enriched motor experiences tend to be more fit and are more likely to participate in sports throughout their lives (Siedentop 2001). The National Association of Sport and Physical Education (NASPE) provided the first physical activity guidelines specifically designed to meet the developmental needs of infants, toddlers, and preschoolers as a result of their Early Childhood Physical Activity Task Force that consisted of motor development experts, movement specialists, exercise physiologists, and medical professionals. Dr. Jane Clark, who chaired the task force, is quoted in a February 6, 2002, press release as saying, "Adopting a physically active lifestyle early in life increases the likelihood that infants and young children will learn to move skillfully." She continues, "Promoting and fostering enjoyment of movement and motor skill confidence and competence at an early age will help ensure healthy development and later participation in physical activity" (American Association for Health, Physical Education, Recreation, and Dance [AAHPERD], February 2002).

Additionally, psychologists who have studied the motives of athletes believe that the drive to compete probably originates in infancy and early childhood. This viewpoint is clarified by adding that parental involvement is the key, specifically when parents reward the demonstration of new skills and developmental milestones with expressions of approval and love. The research continues to document that early motivation and stimulation have a dramatic effect on the skill development and fitness of young children three to eight years old (Gober and Franks 1988). Given these findings and statements of support from a variety of experts in sport related fields, it is understandable that parents who want the best for their children will seek early involvement in activity programs for them.

As this theme is repeated in the motor development literature, it must be emphasized that the strategies used to provide this opportunity for skill development and activity should remain exploratory in nature with adult supervision for safety. Exploration allows the child to learn through self-motivated trial and error. Children are in a continuous state of assessment and refinement of performance during activity. They learn to motor program as cognitive alterations are made when a task is accomplished. Because moving is a basic urge of young children, this process will provide the necessary foundation for children to be successful movers if they are given the opportunity. As children enter their elementary school physical education classes, the physical education specialist can then assess and focus on any deficiency that may be apparent as a result of lack of experience with a particular movement theme.

Providing the opportunity for young children to develop physically through exploration and spontaneous play has become a tragically overlooked idea, however. How many Americans can recall a day when they spent their after-school hours playing timeless games of makeshift sports or games without coaches, uniforms, organized practice drills, or spectators? Most children, and even young adults, cannot. In most areas of the United States, those days are over. It is difficult to know why the shift from informal games to organized youth sport has occurred, but some theories have been explored. Some researchers suggest that there are fewer parents at home during after-school hours, and therefore children are told to stay indoors. In urban areas, parents may believe that the streets are not safe and therefore do not allow their children to play unsupervised at any time. Additionally, references are made to growing up with television and video games designed to bring entertainment to the child rather than allowing the child to go out and create entertainment. Finally, researchers note that U.S. culture is infatuated with competition (Shields, Bredemeier, and Power 2001), something provided by organized programs. One profound theory to explain the shift from spontaneous play to organized sport is that some parents today may believe that they need help raising their children: "children need more guidance than normally can be provided by parents, relatives, and teachers" (Crosset 2000, 35). This theory may indeed be part of the explanation because many families are more mobile and therefore lose the support of an extended family to meet the needs of their children.

As a result of an obsession with competition and for a variety of reasons, adults today believe more in the enlisting of their young children in highly organized sport programs than in leaving their children's future sport careers to chance. This is where the controversy arises, because the focus becomes the development of specific sport skills in anticipation of producing a superior athlete. The focus shifts from whether children should participate in physical activity to for what reasons and in what kind of program they should participate. In *Little Winners: Inside the World of the Child Sports Star*, Greenspan suggests that well-organized youth sport programs are the outlets for parental ambition and for parents who want to get a jump on the competition. She also adds that there are plenty of programs to do so. It is without question that very young children begin their sport participation according to the interests of their parents. The lives of many successful athletes, such as Tiger Woods, Venus and Serena Williams, and Wayne Gretsky, reinforces this theory of producing a superior athlete by exposing a young child to highly specialized sport skills. But are the needs of the child taken into consideration? Most children play sports for fun, a fact that numerous studies have confirmed. Skill development, being with friends, and getting exercise are other reasons for participation. For teenagers, winning may be ranked as low as 6th to 12th place, whereas with preteens, winning is even less of a priority (Ewing and Seefeldt 1991).

In many adult-supported and organized programs, children's play is replaced with highly organized sporting events that mirror adult professional sports. It is this sentiment that produced the position paper prepared by the USA Volleyball Sports Medicine and Performance Commission on National Championship Competition for players aged ten years and under. Two of the important questions asked by the commission were "Are children ready for the elite-level competition?" and "Do children need national championships to enjoy their participation in sports?" This position paper reviews the medical, physical, cognitive, psychosocial, and motivational readiness for organized sports and competition. The authors conclude that

> Children under 10 years of age do not need national level competition
> to enjoy sport. Elite championships are highly stressful events with a
> great emphasis on winning at all costs. Coaches and parents often are
> anxious to have their children compete without understanding all of
> the specifics of young children's physical and psycho-social develop-
> ment. As a result, they promote improper values and set unrealistic ex-
> pectations for youngsters who are vulnerable at this age, both physi-
> cally and emotionally. (American Volleyball Coaches Association, n.d.)

Historically, the major forces behind such elite programs have
been parents and interested laypeople, while educators, physicians, and
psychologists have been less enthusiastic. Actually, professionals have
been fairly effective in prohibiting the interscholastic sports model at
the elementary school level and have severely restricted school sports at
the junior high level (Eitzen and Sage 1993). Professionals in various
sport-related areas have been less effective in influencing nonschool
sport programs, however.

As we consider the appropriate age for initial sport involvement,
the focus shifts to the reasons for participation and the quality of the
program. It would seem appropriate for the needs of the children to be
the driving force in any determination related to youth sport programs,
but we know that is not the case. Bob Bigelow, former professional basketball player and first-round draft pick, has been involved in youth
sport programs and makes presentations on how to keep youth sports
in perspective. His chapter (Bigelow 2000) in Gerdy (2000) provides an
account of his personal change in perspective from teaching the "pick
and roll" to third and fourth graders at sport camps to being an advocate
for sport programs that address the needs of children. He explains,

> I realized that never, during my hundreds of basketball lectures, had I
> considered whether my audience of children had the ability to compre-
> hend what I was trying to teach them. I thought of the billions of hours
> spent by adults every year in activities known as "youth sports," most of
> those hours spent teaching skills far too advanced for even the most
> mature youngsters to comprehend (Bigelow 2000, 9).

Bigelow continues to review a few aspects of youth sport that are
examples of inappropriate adult influences on programs. One of the
most dramatic is what he calls "delusions of prepubescent grandeur" as
he recounts the "cutting" of Michael Jordan from his sophomore basketball team. Bigelow's sentiments support the notion that what professionals know about children is not taken into consideration when youth

sport programs are developed and allowed to function without critique. The chapter concludes with seven steps to a "prescription for reform": (1) eliminate all travel, select, elite, all-star groupings and teams through sixth grade; (2) volunteer for the Special Olympics; (3) require training for coaches; (4) evaluate coaches based on whether they like kids, whether they are able to act like a kid, and whether they can be void of self-importance; (5) when coaching practice sessions, remember elementary school recess; (6) during games, switch coaches halfway through the contest; and (7) smile.

What Bigelow suggests is different from what actually occurs within most youth sport programs both within and beyond the school setting. This is the reason that youth sport programs are receiving so much attention, primarily in response to their negative qualities.

Nationally, there are thousands of programs that fall into the category of youth sports. They can be placed on a continuum on which we might find programs to which Bigelow would give his stamp of approval at one end and programs that border on child abuse at the other. Guidelines designed by professionals and based on the needs of children should be in place to evaluate programs, and such guidelines do exist (see chapter 6). Many programs should be commended for the quality of the educational opportunity that they provide to the youth they serve.

One such national-level program is the American Youth Soccer Organization (AYSO), which was established in 1964 and is headquartered in Hawthorne, California. This program supports developmental soccer programs for children as young as four years and has received national recognition for its efforts. AYSO's history, philosophy, guidelines, and policies can be found at http://www.soccer.org. There is probably no youth sport organization that is held in higher esteem than AYSO. To provide just one simple example of the level of dedication to its mission that this organization maintains, the rank and file members do not encourage use of the term "ASO" that has endearingly evolved over the years because they are concerned that focus on the "youth" aspect of what they do will be overlooked. A June 10, 2002, NASPE press release described AYS0 as having 625,000 players nationwide and about 80,000 coaches. The intent of the press release was to notify the public that this program is among the first organizations in the United States to receive accredited status for its coaching education programs by the National Council for the Accreditation of Coaching Education (NCACE). Drew Zwald, president of NCACE, acknowledged, "AYSO has once again shown that it is a leader among youth sport organizations. Its coaching education programs will serve as prototypes for other organizations seeking to promote excellence in coaching preparation. This, in turn, will play a major role in ensuring positive, healthy, and enjoyable sport experiences for all athletes" (AAHPERD June 2002).

When discussing the appropriate age for participation in youth sport, the quality of the program and respective philosophy will determine the answer. Involving very young children in the local AYSO program is not only appropriate but in most cases can be viewed as an extremely positive aspect of the development of an athlete. I make this statement based on involvement with AYSO as a coach and as a parent with two children who participated in the program. My experience was undoubtedly a blueprint for other coaches across the country. Teams were developed to provide for an equal level of competition, only appropriate parental conduct was tolerated at games, any coaching behavior that merely hinted at "winning-at-all-costs" was addressed by the officials, all players received equal playing time, and coaching a team that was headed for a one-sided victory was felt to be an embarrassing situation.

In summary, physical education and sport professionals have established the benefits of involvement in physical activity at a very young age. This can be done at home and within the educational setting, but within American society the shift has moved the provision of this beneficial activity to organized youth sport programs. Supporters of these programs cite the personal-social attitude and character development as well as skill and health benefits. Critics refer to the excessive physical and psychological demands placed on participants and the encroachment of adults that replaces spontaneous play with organized competition conducted for the self-serving needs of the adults. Program evaluation seems to be one major step toward ensuring that youth programs meet the needs of the youth that they serve. The educational implications of not addressing the problems that exist may have a profound effect not only on today's youth but also on American society in the future.

Is Competition the Problem?

Is competition in sport that portion of the equation that generates most of its problems? More specifically, is the "winning at all costs" attitude that is pervasive at all levels of sport detrimental to the educational values attached to it? As one might imagine, and justifiably so, there is an abundance of information regarding these questions. One might argue that it is the competition within sport that creates the powerful opportunities for educational lessons. Others argue that it is the competition itself, or the way we as a society deal with competition, that is detrimental to the sport experience. First, competition as a possible necessity within sport will be discussed and then the attention it receives.

The term "competition" can be used in many ways. People compete against another person or group of people, themselves, the clock, a statistic, an element (mountain), or even a situation or disease (cancer). Within the context of sport and education, competition should be considered as a social process "that occurs when rewards are given to people on the basis of how their performances compare with the performances of others doing the same task or participating in the same event" (Coakley 1994, 78). In addition, when defined this way, winners and losers are identified and participants are ranked based on who does better than others; and the competitive process focuses on outperforming or defeating opponents. Coakley goes on to say that competition involves the use of a reward structure where a set of rules is in place for distributing rewards among the participants. That stated, it would be helpful to distinguish this concept of competition from the concept of cooperation. Consistently using Coakley for defining terms, "cooperation is a social process through which performance is evaluated and rewarded in terms of the collective achievements of a group of people working together to reach a goal" (p. 79). Cooperation does not necessarily result in winners and losers. Nor does cooperation evaluate performance in relation to the performance of another. It is appropriate to point out here that there is an area of the physical education curriculum that is receiving overwhelming support and attention for its focus on cooperation, problem solving, communication, and trust. "Challenge education," which many people often refer to by other titles, is included in areas of adventure education and experiential education. The activities included in all three require cooperation among participants to successfully accomplish a challenge. To accomplish the "challenge" at hand and win or finish before other teams, cooperation, communication, and problem solving are essential elements of the process. Sports teams and corporations have incorporated these activities into their practices and training programs to increase the productivity of their respective groups. The National Collegiate Athletic Association (NCAA) has promoted the inclusion of these activities into its "life skills" programs.

Both competition and cooperation are aspects of sports. So why has cooperation taken a backseat to competition? Using the definition cited in chapter 1, sport always involves some form of competition and should be considered a necessary part of the sport experience at every level. In this context, where do the problems arise? Many argue that in life there are winners and losers and that the sport experience can teach participants the stark realities that they will face in the future. But is this argument a stretch? How often in life is winning or achieving a goal the result of defeating another individual? One might suggest that this occurs in a courtroom where attorneys argue against each other to win the judgment of the judge or jury. Another example of competition would be when sales associates are competing against each other for "salesperson of the year." But are these forms of competition appropriate? Corporate American has long known the benefits of and has shifted its focus toward a more cooperative approach to business operations and strategies. This was supported by school systems as they incorporated cooperative learning experiences into their educational strategies so students would be better equipped to function in the corporate world. Sport sociologist Harry Edwards confirms a lack of evidence to support this preparation for life theory and explains that the transfer of lesson learned from sport to life probably does not occur. He explains, "the human psyche has a way of ordering past events and rendering them amenable to interpretation consistent with current attitudes, values, and personal circumstances" (1973, 324). Moreover, Edwards reviews the work of others and concludes that there are many cases in which participation in athletics was detrimental to adjustment in the greater society. We have seen this played out in the lives of successful athletes at the collegiate, Olympic, and professional levels. Sport, as an opportunity for socioeconomic mobility, is discussed in chapter 4.

If we accept that competition itself may not teach strategies or lessons necessary for becoming a productive member of American society, why is it so valued? The answer is simple: Americans are obsessed with winning. Cooperation and individual development often receive lip service, but being "number one," the best, having the most, and having it first infiltrates much of American society. This becomes most apparent when Americans and foreigners alike compare our culture to others. It seems the concept of a "land of plenty" has become a driving force with a disregard for hard work and the freedoms we receive.

Siedentop (2001) refers to this obsession with competition as it relates to the economic world as "zero-sum" competition. In this degree of competition, whatever is gained by one competitor must be lost by the other; to the extent that I win, you lose. This is the aspect of competition that may not be fully realized by many of today's youth who participate in sports and their university counterparts. The drive to compete and its related behaviors are undertaken without any regard for the consequences of this behavior. Most often there are consequences for the opponent or opponents that are not realized and therefore never considered. Within this situation, athletes appear to lose their sense of empathy for others, and the values of sportsmanship seem to become an old cliché. Is this sense of competition a learned behavior? Have athletes lost their ability to be empathetic as a lesson learned from American society or from the program they find themselves in? Many coaches respond negatively when their players show regard or concern for the opponent as if this will somehow negatively affect performance. Sounds like a good idea for research!

Coakley (1994) suggest that it is the competitive reward structures imbedded in American society and therefore in sport that have created the obsession with competition within this country. This sociological explanation of why winning is becoming the only thing in every setting and at every level is both fascinating and somewhat discouraging. Coakley provides this explanation from the understanding of power relations in American society. It is undeniable that our society provides and promotes the extreme inequities that exist in relation to power and wealth. Within this democratic society, the position of privilege that power and wealth provides is often judged as legitimate by "merit." What this implicitly teaches is that those who are privileged have earned it through hard work, persistence, or overcoming obstacles and those who are without wealth and power somehow lack the moral character to better themselves (Coakley 1994). Certainly one can argue against this explanation, but the important element within it is that those who are privileged with wealth and power are driven to maintain it, which results in the focus on competition to win, to prove that one is better and rightfully deserves his or her position and all its benefits. Coakley states that "one way to promote the idea that rewards in a society are based on merit alone is to emphasize competition and get people to accept that competitive reward structures are not only fair but that they are a 'natural' part of social life" (Coakley 1994, 84).

Yes, it is this aspect of competition that receives the most scrutiny. The "win-at-all-costs" approach to competition seems to be steamrollering through the world of sport and at every level. Some of the sport clichés that reflect this attitude are "Winning isn't everything, it is the only thing," "Winning isn't everything, but it beats anything that comes in second." "Defeat is worse than death, because you have to live with defeat." When this overemphasis on winning is the philosophy of the coach and supported throughout the program, it is likely that negative attitudes and inappropriate behaviors will follow and be accepted. Winning-at-all-costs coaching has been linked to increased intimidation and violence. The use of supplements and even illegal drugs becomes an acceptable means to achieve success. Learning how to "bend" the rules is taught to players, and they are led to believe that cheating is only cheating if you get caught. These are just a few of the potential pit-falls of competition within sport when winning becomes the primary focus. Cumulatively, all these behaviors produce an atmosphere in which the pure joy of competition is lost. From an educational stand-point, children, adolescents, and young adults should be taught that the process is what is most important and not the outcome. Appropriate lessons are learned when the participant is allowed to reflect on the process and feel a sense of accomplishment. We should reward athletes for putting forth their best effort, following rules, and maintaining re-spect for their opponents.

Many in the sport community, especially in educational settings, argue against this position. From their perspective, athletes are taught that nothing but the best is acceptable and therefore whatever it takes to be the best is forgiven in this quest. These coaches believe that allowing athletes to accept second place or a loss will stifle the drive to work harder.

Sportsmanship

So in America, where competition is part of our culture and winning in overemphasized, what happens to sportsmanship? And just what is sportsmanship? Is sportsmanship following the rules as best one can and participating in the compulsory hand shake after the competition? Is sportsmanship voluntarily admitting an overlooked violation by an official and the spontaneous "hand-up" assist given to the opponent on the floor? Who draws the line between sportsmanlike and unsports-manlike behavior? Where is it discussed and exemplified? Where is it ig-nored and often demonized? Siedentop (2001) suggests that "fair play" is a better term. He explains that ethics, or "moral philosophy," is actu-ally a study of just how individuals should behave in situations where there is the opportunity to behave "bad" or "good." We have always looked to sport as a place that allows participants the opportunity to learn about this good and bad moral behavior. Historically, amateurism and fair play could describe British sport, in which American sport has its roots. Thomas Arnold, headmaster of the Rugby School, believed that sport and fitness were important activities of the educational process that produced courage, patriotism, moral character, and team spirit. What followed was the first term to describe sportsmanship: "Arnold-ism" (Siendtop 2001).

"Sportsmanlike behavior—playing by the rules and not taking unfair advantage of competitors" is how Eitzen and Sage (1993, 86) ex-press this concept of sportsmanship; they believe that even though it is universally admired, it sometimes conflicts with the quest for victory. These authors maintain that even though the research on this topic has significant weaknesses, the findings are consistent, that those with more experience in organized sport do not display sportsmanship as much as those with less sport experience. This point will be expanded on as we consider whether sport builds character.

Coakley (1994) would explain that a good sport might be one who exhibits cooperative behavior at the expense of competitive success. Examples of this are often seen in sporting events, but not often enough. It can be argued that as the setting for sport becomes more competitive or the rewards for winning become greater, the amount of sportsmanlike behavior diminishes. This brings up the point of competitive reward structures presented in the previous section. Understanding that competition and its rewards are actually aspects of the American cultural ideology helps us to realize why Americans place such an importance on competition and winning. Sport is the forum, the stage, and the process that confirms this aspect of our society. It is important because it confirms what people think the world should be, how people should behave, and what behavior should be rewarded. Thus, there is a societal contradiction between competition and sportsmanship, yet many people sincerely value sportsmanship. I would go as far as to say that I thrive on displays of sportsmanship. I attribute a portion of this aspect of my value system to a great philosophy of sport teacher, Kathleen Pearson. I was taught to see and understand the true value and beauty of sport. Empathy among competitors, acknowledgment of opponents as equals in the pursuit of a goal, respect for the process of competition, and respect for every level of participation are most often overlooked. I delight in the explicit acknowledgment and support of such displays and am saddened because it occurs so infrequently. This approach to sport can be considered incompatible with the American value system that embraces competition and winning over sportsmanship. For those like me who have been taught to value sportsmanship, we do so in contradiction to this American ideology embedded in our society. So, why do we? Because individuals do not always internalize the dominant ideologies. Coakley (1994) explains that personal orientations often do not match cultural ideologies. Those with strong competitive orientations do not question the competitive reward structures within our society. Those lacking such an orientation might question, challenge, and even resist the dominant cultural practice.

Sportsmanship or "fair play" presents an interesting discussion point. As it becomes acceptable to "bend the rules" or "cheat" but not get caught, how does this behavior change the competition and the victory or loss? Do the victors actually win the contest if they did not follow the rules? If they change the rules of the game, by not following the rules, don't they actually change the game, and therefore what game did they actually win? Do things that are considered illegal or unacceptable during the preparation of the game complicate this discussion? Olympic sport has struggled with this question. How can the field of competition be equal if supplementation or blood doping is used to gain advantage? One might even consider the funding and time allocation that some athletes receive in contrast to others. Nowhere did the issue receive more attention than here in the United States, where some argued that we continue to send our amateur athletes to compete in the Olympic games against what our system would classify as professionals. This resulted in allowing American professional athletes to participate in the Olympic games. Taking advantage of the opponent's weaknesses in contrast to the emphasis on one's own performance is a change in philosophy from the sport of the past. There may not be a clear distinction between victories earned and victories stolen, but the issue should receive more attention if we anticipate using the word "sportsmanship" in years to come.

Rick Wolff (2002), the chair of the Center for Sports Parenting at the Institute for International Sport, speaks to the issue of sportsmanship in maintaining the integrity of the game. He recounted a specific event between Green Bay Packer's Brett Favre and San Francisco 49ers Steve Young at the completion of a hard-fought football game that ended with Green Bay ahead. Immediately after the game, Young worked his way through fans and reporters on the field to find Favre. He wanted to congratulate him on the win and for having played so well. The encounter was caught on tape. Wolff believes that this valuable display of sportsmanship, as well as the many others he describes, must be pointed out to young people: "Such graciousness should be part of any game, and you can tell kids about many other such shining examples." Wolff goes on to explain, "Real athletes understand that they must maintain the integrity of the game. That's what counts above all else, and integrity always starts with sportsmanship" (p. 54). Wolff also makes reference to the IT PAYS—I Teach Positive Attitudes in Youth Sports organization, created by Dan and Jay Bylsma (who play for the Anaheim Mighty Ducks hockey team). In its first year, this organization received the enthusiastic endorsement of the National Hockey League (NHL). More information can be found at http://www.hockeyitpays.com.

To expand on how participating within the rules of the contest is emphasized over winning regardless of the rules, I refer again to the "challenge education" model that physical education teachers, guidance counselors, and people involved in the amateur and professional sport world use. Within this curriculum, activities or challenges are presented to a group along with a set of rules. Along with the rules specific to the challenge, "No put-downs," "No swearing," and "No arguing" are added. If any rule is broken, the activity is stopped, and the group must begin again. These activities or challenges place an emphasis on the process of accomplishing the task without breaking the rules. While facilitating a group through one of these challenges, I have clarified this point by saying, "Yes, it would be easy to do this if you didn't have to follow the rules, but the challenge is to accomplish the task while not breaking any rules." Most challenges are designed so that cooperation is the focus and must be explicitly planned. Respect for others as integral members of the group is an additional focus. Karl Rohnke, who is considered the founder of this model, began his work within Project Adventure. His 1984 book, *Silver Bullets*, is widely used within the profession as a guide to these activities. Additional recourses in this area appear in chapter 6. This model is included here to bring attention to the movement toward cooperation and sportsmanship and away from the winning at all cost and lack of sportsmanship that are acceptable aspects of sport today. Will the American cultural ideology that supports competition continue to move sport in the wrong direction or can an emphasis on fair play and cooperation be revisited?

What is interesting is that cooperation, as opposed to competition, is highly valued in many other countries. An abundance of research highlights other cultures in which competition is not valued or is even discouraged. Coackley (1994) and Kohn (1992) are excellent resources that present and discuss cooperative cultures around the world and how this affects sport in those countries.

I have discussed sportsmanship in relation to competition to encourage readers to question where they stand on related issues and to gain an appreciation for those who might have a different perspective. I now provide readers the opportunity to take the "Sportsmanship Self-Test," designed by David Hoch (2001). Hoch explains that because sportsmanship is a focus of high school athletics, his program uses the test to get the sportsmanship issue across to parents at their preseason parents' meeting. The test asks parents whether they agree or disagree with each of the following statements.

1. It is normal to complain about officials' calls.
2. Yelling at an official is OK if he [or she] makes a very questionable call or one with which you don't agree.
3. Taunting is just part of the game. It's part of the gamesmanship that goes on and is not a big deal.

4. Ignoring a negative comment by an opponent or fan is the thing to do in a heated contest.
5. When an opponent reacts to a great play or a score by one of his [or her] teammates, you do not react. You stay calm.
6. Sincerely congratulating an opponent on a good play or victory is the way it should be in sports.
7. Cheering should be done for your team, not against your opponent.
8. Both participants and fans should walk away from confrontations or potential fights.
9. During or after a contest, if you can't say something nice or positive, you really shouldn't say anything at all.
10. If a player is injured, you should be supportive and cheer for him [or her] when it has been determined that the injury is not severe.
11. Inappropriate language during a contest is natural because of the intensity and emotion involved.
12. This push for sportsmanship is important for high school athletics.
13. It's important to exhibit good sportsmanship, even when your opponent and their fans do not.
14. If pushed, provoked, or attacked, one should retaliate. It is always important to stand up for your rights.
15. It's OK to gain the edge in a game anyway you can.

Refer to the article (Hoch 2001) to calculate your score. Find out where you rate on sportsmanship and then pass a copy of the article on to a coach or athletic administrator. The statements are very interesting and deciding whether you agree or disagree should help you decide just how much of this American cultural ideology that supports a competitive reward structure is internalized through your behavior and approach to sport? How will the level of accepting this cultural ideology affect people in coaching and administrative positions? If sport is an aspect of our cultural hegemony, how can it promote sportsmanship and measure up to the assumption that it builds character?

Does Sport Build Character?

The notion that schools can use organized, competitive sports to supplement the educational development of students originated in England in the early 1800s (Stoll and Beller 2000). The theory behind this was that if boys were involved on the playing field in competitive activities regulated by rules, they would be less likely to engage in other inappropriate behaviors. The objectives went further to include the development of sportsmanship, discipline, and leadership. Over the past two hundred years, these sentiments have progressed to what most would consider a universal acceptance of the notion that "sport builds character." This profound statement is receiving much attention from both sides of the debate and is the catalyst to an abundance of research, position statements, journal articles, interviews, and books.

What we really want to understand is whether sports participation hurts or helps children. If you ask a dozen people, you are likely to get a dozen answers, or at least variations of several answers. So we must look to the research to see what the carefully designed and documented studies have found. Not surprisingly, the general consensus of research findings support the notion that "it depends!" Research has not provided us with an abundance of clear-cut answers, but does indicate that whether participation is good or bad depends on many factors; I would add that it can be based on the individual's unique perception of a given situation. Some of the factors include the specific sport, the age of the participants, the coach's philosophy and training, the parent's philosophy and involvement, the specific group dynamics, and the level of competition. Experts in the field, such as Shields, Bredemeier, and Power (2001), have provided a set of generalizations:

1. When kids enter sport, having fun is their top priority. When asked to rank the values of having fun, playing fair, and winning, having fun tops the list. But the longer the kids stay in sport and the higher the level of competition, the more they adopt what has been labeled a "professional" value orientation in which winning becomes the dominant value.
2. Participation in high contact sports—such as football and ice hockey—seems to carry particular risks for younger participants. Young participants have a difficult time distinguishing between forceful, physical contact intended to further a game-related goal versus that intended to hurt someone. One behavior is assertive, and the other is aggressive.
3. The competitive process itself can discourage the development of such vital social and psychological skills as empathy and compassion.
4. Coaches largely determine the quality of the sport experience. Good coaches can create an environment and experience that promotes social and psychological development; bad coaches can do the opposite.

Shields et al. conducted more than twenty years of study to investigate the relationship between sport participation and a person's moral reasoning development. Their research is based on the theory that as children develop "increasingly sophisticated and complex understanding of their physical world" they also develop more adequate understandings of social relations and morality as they progress in age and experience. Additionally, this moral development varies from person to person and is affected by the quality of the experience. Hopefully, we can understand how complex the answers to questions regarding sport participation are and how significant the factors are in determining whether the sport experience will be positive or negative.

More adequate understanding of social relations and morality implies that there is a progression from the beginning to a higher level of functioning. One therefore might want to address the starting point. Perhaps sport settings are merely particularly good opportunities for allowing persons to exhibit preexisting character traits (Sage 1998). Edwards stated similar sentiments in his 1973 publication, *Sociology of Sport*: "Available evidence indicates that athletes do not necessarily generate fortitude, but they may provide a situation wherein an individual can gain positive experiences that may sustain or heighten existing self-confidence and reinforce an already positive self-image. ... Athletics may also provide the situation wherein the individual experiences failure, and as a result, his courage and self-confidence may be diminished or its development may even be precluded" (Edwards 1973, 323). Some researchers would continue to support the notion that attributing the display of culturally valued personal and social characteristics of some athletes wholly to their sport experiences would depend on an enormous leap of faith (Shields and Bredemeier 1995). What we can all agree on is that the sport experience will have an effect on personal and social development of participants. The socialization that sport demands, the cooperation required, the interactions of individuals from diverse cultural backgrounds, the adherence to rules and authority, and the emotional outcomes of the competition must affect the participant. The specific factors surrounding each individual sport experience will play a role. The question that remains is how significant is a participant's initial character development in determining if character development will occur and to what extent.

When we speak of culturally and socially valued characteristics, we assume that there is such a thing. Has society as a whole agreed on a certain set of characteristics as being acceptable? Will this set of characteristics change depending on the situation? From whose culture has this set of characteristics developed and as a result whose does it support? Somewhat in jest, I refer to the phrase "moral majority." If there is a set of moral characteristics that are accepted, are those who espouse them still in the majority? What happens to sport if immoral people become the dominant authority figures? In some programs, this might already be the case. How would we evaluate the moral character of a high school football coach whose team beats the opponent sixty to zero? What could be said for the moral character of the high school football coach who has his team "take a knee" on their opponent's five-yard line with twenty-eight seconds to go in the game because they are already winning by two touchdowns? I know how I felt as a parent whose son plays in the conference where both these situations occurred. Personally, I could not bring myself to condone the sixty-point victory regardless of any reason the coach could present to defend his actions. In contrast, words could not describe the admiration I felt for the coach who had his players take a knee instead of scoring one more time. What profound lessons both these coaches taught their players. One could only hope that the character development they brought to these situations provoked shame for the sixty-point victors and an overwhelming sense of pride in those who took a knee.

It is direct observations such as these, stories the sports media provide, personal experiences, books written by famous athletes, and many other bits of "evidence" that the general public uses to support the notion that sport builds character. Just as the research has failed to prove the link between sport participation and character development, however, studies suggest that sport participation actually decreases a person's moral reasoning level. Stoll and Beller are the leading researchers in this area and have collected data from more than 40,000 individuals from a variety of populations at several levels of sport. They primarily looked at levels of moral-reasoning as measuring by the Hahm-Beller Values Choice Inventory (HBVIC), explaining that "the higher the HBVIC score, the more impartially, reflectively, consistently, and ideally an individual reasons" (Stoll and Beller 2001, 20). A summary of their findings includes the following: (1) male team sport athletes generally scored significantly lower than individual team sport athletes; (2) female team sport athletes scored lower than their individual sport counterparts, and female athletes score significantly higher than male athletes; (3) nonathlete's scores are significantly higher than team sport athletes but not significantly higher than individual team sport athletes. In interpreting the findings of this and similar studies, researchers have suggested that an athlete's moral-reasoning becomes "masked" the longer they participate in competitive athletics. This "masking" of moral-reasoning in athletics is the direct result of how sport is conducted in the United States. Winning at all costs is the fundamental principle upon which athletic competition is based today. This notion is termed "moral callousness," and it minimizes feelings of right and wrong (Stoll and Beller 2001). Kretchmar (1994) has developed common symptoms of moral callousness:

•• Frequent appeals to the fact that "everyone is doing it" (therefore, how could it be wrong?)
•• An inability to distinguish between what is part of the game and what is not (there is no penalty for a certain behavior, therefore the behavior must be part of the game)
•• Difficulty in telling morally sound strategy from win-at-all-costs trickery
•• A sense that if one is not caught, nothing wrong happened

Despite the stated findings and explanations, sport advocates continue to espouse sport for its character-building capabilities. Whether sport builds character is based on many factors, and the philosophy of the program and coach are among the most important of these. Contact sports, other team sports, and individual sports each provide a unique situation. Gender is a determining factor. The level of character a participant brings to the sport experience will affect the development and in fact becomes masked the longer the involvement in competitive activities. So to return to the question of whether sport builds or corrupts character by teaching participants to bend the rules and take advantages of opponents to win, Siedentop (2001) offers this answer:

> Sport Teaches! It has the capacity to teach positive lessons and it has the capacity to teach negative lessons. Sport when done well and properly, can raise the individual and the group, transcend the ordinary and mundane in life, and teach valuable lesson of perseverance, teamwork, and loyalty. Sport can also corrupt ... those who compete. Whether any sport experience is more likely to build character than to corrupt is up to those in control of that experience and what they do. (p. 107)

COACHING AND ADMINISTRATIVE ISSUES

What Training Do Coaches Need?

With the dramatic increase in youth sport programs and competitive sports at the junior high and interscholastic levels, the need for additional coaches becomes obvious. Every program, parent, and participant wants the best coaches possible, but there are not enough quality coaches to meet the demand. When programs are forced to depend on volunteers—and most do—the "take what we get" approach becomes sadly acceptable. In many instances these volunteers, whether parents or others, are highly qualified, having professional teacher training or previous involvement with high-quality programs. But the reality is that many coaches are neither qualified with professional training nor screened to determine if their philosophical approach to coaching is in alignment with the program and age level with which they will be working. Coaching issues, as with most sport-related issues, are complex. When the aspects that affect the role of the coach are better understood, it might lead to a system that better prepares individuals to have a positive impact on all the children with whom they are entrusted.

Coaches fill an extremely unique role in the lives of their players and their parents. Barker stated that "Coaching is the only job in which we hand over our 18-year-olds and expect them to be turned into not just winners, but better people" (Barker 2002, 11). For many athletes, a strong emotional bond develops with this authority figure. When a player has the same coach for several years, that coach often becomes a "significant other," having tremendous impact on the player's development and self-esteem. One reason for this is that athletes evaluate themselves personally based on the feedback from and interaction with the coach. Watching any youth sport or school-related athletic team practice session would provide a vivid picture of this. Research in this area suggests that coaches provide too much evaluation and too many corrective-feedback statements and initiate too many negative interactions (Smith, Smoll, and Curtis, 1978). One reason for this may be that the model of "how to coach" is the visible, televised intercollegiate or professional coach (Siedentop 2001) who is under tremendous pressure to win and is probably receiving a substantial salary. Tailoring one's coaching style to these high-profile coaches is probably not explicit, but it is unlikely that it has no influence. Another model for coaching are one's own former coaches. When many of our coaches were young athletes, most of the qualified coaches were physical education specialists. These specialists were highly trained in technique but too often were extremely authoritative and sometimes used militaristic strategies for classroom management. Controlling their students and players was a high priority and had a tremendous influence on the characteristics they presented.

Whatever model was available to a coach, Coakley (1994) explains that his or her behavior reflects three sets of factors: (1) the personality traits and ideas of the coaches themselves, (2) what happens within the occupational settings in which coaches work, and (3) general cultural beliefs about what coaches should do and how they should act (p. 193). In addressing cultural beliefs about coaching, would Americans be supportive of autocratic coaches who use a strong aggressive leadership style, or would they be more inclined to support a coach who attempted to espouse the democratic principles on which the country was founded? When Coakley questioned students in a sociology of sport class regarding the use of democratic principles while coaching, the students argued that "being a coach and being democratic are incompatible" (p. 193). The students provided the following reasons for this:

- Coaches have more experience and know more about sports than athletes do.
- Athletes cannot be trusted to make responsible decisions.
- Coaches must make decisions if they are to be respected.
- If athletes made the decisions, it would destroy the basis for disciple and authority.
- Athletes look to coaches for decisions and answers and would be lost if they had to make the decisions.
- Coaches have the right to make all the decisions because their jobs are on the line.

These reasons are included to elicit reaction. I was surprised by the amount of control and authority that college students were so eager to insist a coach maintain. Even Coackley questioned these reasons and found it strange that so many students felt that democracy and sport were not compatible. The concluding point should be well taken: in this society it is widely believed that sport participation prepares people to live as democratic citizens. What portion of our democratic society would agree with these students, and are proponents of sport for the same reason stated above? It appears that even though sport in the United States is seen as an expression of our society, when it comes to the role of the coach and his or her subsequent behavior, there may be a double standard.

To address the second factor that affects the behavior of the coach, we must agree that in the vast majority of programs in which coaches function, accountability for the performance of the team or athletes is primarily theirs. The resulting pressure is often overlooked. Athletic events are highly visible, often reported through the print and televised media. The outcomes can often depend on unpredictable and uncontrollable factors followed by serious scrutiny and debates. Americans expect and often demand winning at all levels, and the pressure on the coaches and the effect on their behaviors will rise proportionately. It is not surprising that the general public is generally more accepting of the winning-at-all-cost coaching style.

To address these factors and the complexity of the role of the coach, appropriate training for and evaluation of coaching is creeping into many of our youth sport and school-based programs. Several national programs endorse the supporting sentiment, both informally and officially. Ten years ago, when my husband volunteered to help coach the eighth-grade boys' basketball team for our local parochial school, he was welcomed with open arms void of any questions or screening. This year, at the same school, for the same level team, he was asked to read and sign a coaching statement that addressed the program philosophy, and he was formally screened for criminal behavior. The "taken for granted" assumptions of the past seem less acceptable as issues within youth sport are presented and discussed.

Explicit efforts to address coaching concerns are flourishing. For soccer, the AYSO coaching education program that was described earlier is one example of an organization that ensures its philosophy is maintained by training quality coaches. In fact, a national council exists to support and acknowledge such programs. The National Council for the Accreditation of Coaching Education (NCACE) was founded in 2000 and is committed to seeing that the NASPE Quality Sports through Quality Coaching program, which developed the National Standards for Athletic Coaches, is used to establish and maintain coaching education programs. This council grants accreditation to educational programs that meet or exceed established requirements determined to be essential in the preparation process of well-qualified coaches. It includes representatives from single and multisport programs, science, medicine, and educational fields, as well as colleges and universities concerned about the availability of coaching education at all levels. (More information can be found at http://www.aahperd.org/naspe/programs-ncace.html.)

Another widely recognized coaching education program is the American Sport Education Program (ASEP). The mission of ASEP is to help improve the sport experience for youth by providing quality instructional resources, workshops, and courses for coaches, administrators, officials, and parents (see http://www.asep.org). Prominent sport psychologist Rainer Martens initially founded the American Coaching Effectiveness Program (ACEP) in the 1970s as he attempted to provide a vehicle to improve the sport experience for youth by training better coaches. ACEP evolved into ASEP, and in 1981 the first Level 1 course package was released. In Marten's words, "ASEP is committed to improving amateur sport by encouraging coaches, officials, administrators, parents, and athletes to embrace the 'athlete's first, winning second' philosophy, and by providing the education to put the philosophy to work" (ASEP, n.d.). Most significant about this organization is its affiliation with the National Federation of State High School Associations (NFHS). In 1990, NFHS joined with ASEP to offer coaching education of high school athletic coaches by providing a special version of its Leader Level courses to be called the NFHS Coaches Education Program. ASEP continues to play an active role with the NFHS in maintaining Interscholastic Coaching Requirements across the United States. More than twenty years after the first course offering, ASEP provides three levels of courses for coaches, administrators, and parents. They estimate that more than 1 million people have used their courses and recourses to help prepare themselves to offer the best possible sport experience to the youth of this nation.

To continue to addresses Coakley's second point, which asks what happens within the occupational settings in which the coach works, program administrators should receive considerable attention. Probably the most difficult task of the athletic director of a university program in consultation with the university administration is to hire the right coach. The right coach is one who will bring success to the program in terms of a winning season and at the same time can uphold the academic integrity of the program and the institution. This objective needs to be met at all levels of sport and within every context. The program administrator, or the athletic director, is responsible for this daunting task. In recent years, the vocational specialization area for these professionals has come to be called Sport Management and Administration. The primary career focus of this vocational area is not coaching or teaching but in the day-to-day operations of a program. These professionals can work in a variety of settings: sport for leisure and recreation, competitive sport, sporting goods and fitness industries, hostelries and travel settings, agency settings, and college and university teaching (Siedentop 2001). Undergraduate and graduate degree programs in this area can receive accreditation from the Sport Management Program Review Council, through compliance of standards developed by NASPE and the North American Society for Sport Management (NASSM). (More information about NASSM can be found at http://www.nassm.org.)

As the administration of sport programs receives more attention for governance, it becomes apparent just how critical the role of the administrator becomes in attempting to provide quality programs based on the needs of the organization or institution as well as the sport participants. At the youth sport program level, the administrator may be a volunteer or a paid employee of the organization.

At the junior high and high school level, an athletic director typically administers the sport program. This person must know, understand, and keep the program philosophy the focus of their professional behavior and decision making. This philosophy and its bylaws are often written by a group of individuals associated with the school and serves as the framework for every decision from hiring to funding. Athletic directors should be members of an organization within their respective state or at the national level for athletic directors. The National Federation of High School Athletics (NFHS) supports the National Interscholastic Athletic Administrators Association (NIAAA). This organization supports athletic directors in the areas of growth, leadership potential, publications, continuing education, conference opportunities, and more. One important area is to set standards for ethical behavior. The NIAAA has established an ethical code for the interscholastic athletic administrator. The NIAAA states that this administrator

- Develops and maintains a comprehensive athletic program that seeks the highest development of all participants and that respects the individual dignity of every athlete.
- Considers the well-being of the entire student body as fundamental in all decisions and actions.
- Supports the principle of due process and protects the civil and human rights of all individuals.
- Organizes, directs, and promotes an interscholastic athletic program that is an integral part of the total educational program.
- Cooperates with the staff and school administration in establishing, implementing, and supporting school policies.
- Acts impartially in the execution of basic policies and in the enforcement of the conference, league, and state high school association rules and regulations.
- Fulfills professional responsibilities with honesty and integrity.
- Upholds the honor of the profession in all relations with students, colleagues, coaches, administrators, and the general public.
- Improves the professional status and effectiveness of the interscholastic athletic administrator through participation in local, state, and national in-service programs.

➡ Promotes high standards of ethics, sportsmanship, and personal conduct by encouraging administration, coaches, staff, student-athletes, and community to commit to these high standards. (http://www.niaaa.org).

This ethical code is included to provide an overview of the comprehensive enterprise that falls on the shoulders of the athletic director. This position is responsible for the quality of the program and to be a check on coaches, staff members, or any other person associated with their program. Because this is such a powerful position the athletic director becomes the most important person in the sport program. Without a strong administrator, committed to maintaining the educational focus of the program, doors are left open where power struggles surface and the overall philosophy of the program becomes jeopardized.

At the collegiate level the organization that provides support for its athletic directors is the National Association of Collegiate Directors of Athletics. It serves as the professional association for those in the field of intercollegiate athletic administration, providing educational opportunities and serving as a vehicle for networking, the exchange of information, and advocacy on behalf of the profession (http://www.nacda.ocsn.com/nacda-admin.html). The NCAA also provides opportunity for support, networking, and decision making through its many committees to address the issues that challenge collegiate athletics. Attempting to function isolated from other professionals, be it coaches or administrators, places those individuals and their programs in vulnerable situations. Discussing similar challenges and possible solutions, comparing how and to what extent other programs live their philosophies, and sharing concerns regarding stress and burnout are activities that will be beneficial to professionals in sport.

Sport is a fascinating profession with no room for complacency. All coaches and administrators should remain committed to being lifelong learners. Decisions should be made based on knowledge of the concepts related to the issue not on empirical evidence or because "that is the way it has always been done." One such example of this is what Bigelow (2000) refers to as "delusions of prepubescent grandeur." He describes the most famous example of this concept: "In December 1978, a 15-year-old, 5'11", sophomore basketball player was cut from the varsity. By his junior year, Michael Jordan was 6'3" and, as a senior, 6'5" (Bigelow 2000, 12). As a 6'6" freshman in college, he made the final basket to win the NCAA championship for North Carolina. At age 21, he skipped his senior year and entered the National Basketball Association draft. He is known today as the greatest basketball player of all time.

Understanding and using the knowledge of adolescent growth and development in a junior high or high school "tryouts" protocol will help ensure that all athletes are given a fair chance and that the decisions are the right ones. Likewise, attending seminars and conventions as well as reading professional journals will help ensure that the program benefits from state-of-the-art concepts, equipment, and facilities. The fields of sport nutrition, sport medicine, sport psychology, sport sociology, and sport pedagogy are dynamic and receive considerable attention from researchers and experienced practitioners. Appropriate answers to problems and understanding the best way to address challenges are available to those who are open to learning from other professionals committed to the educational aspects of a quality sport program.

Struhar (2002) complements this section on lifelong learning well. He declares, with thirty years of coaching experience, that a few things will always be vital to the success of a coach, but that no one ever taught them in a formal setting. He shares ten things he has learned:

1. Not everyone will like you.
2. Try to play everyone.
3. Never run up the score.
4. Be on time everywhere.
5. Make sure you and your team look good.
6. Improve yourself.
7. When bad things happen, go back to fundamentals.
8. Minimize your pep talks.
9. Never criticize the officials in public.
10. Spend time with the average players.

If you find yourself not agreeing with all of them, fine. But just don't dismiss them—discuss them with other professionals, your coaching staff, or read more on the topic. The world of sport will be better because of it.

Are Injuries Just Part of the Game?

It is widely accepted that physical injuries are part of sports, but I question which and how many are *really* part of the game. We accept so much of what we encounter in our daily lives (at school, at work, or within the family structure) without question. This is particularly true in schools settings, and most notably in sports. We often see things the way they are and assume that this is the way things should be. At this time in our history, questioning the status quo is no longer considered bucking the system, but a conscientious way to work, teach, or parent. Race and gender issues typically top the list of inequities in our society. We should all be advocates for social justice issues as they relate to American society in general, but in relation to sport-related injuries, I ask us to begin to question our routine and immediate social settings. For example, when I teach, I routinely ask my students to look with a critical lens at what they hear, see in schools, and even believe. I use the word "critical" as a way to ask students to critique a situation.

To dramatize with a more specific example, I once had a student report his observations of a freshman swimming class of male high school students. We had been discussing policies and procedures within the physical education setting and how they can affect students' feelings toward physical education classes. The student reported that he observed the policy requiring students to remove their "school issued" swimsuit and place it in a bin before they left the pool area. This bin was positioned at the opposite end of the pool deck from the door to the locker room where they were then issued a towel. My immediate response was, "Does anyone see something wrong with this picture?" After a passionate discussion, I believe that I succeeded in developing a critical sense of observation in some of my students as opposed to turning out a herd of mindless "lemmings" willing to follow policy that will be detrimental to our profession and to students. I must editorialize that I do not espouse confrontation, revolution, or even inappropriate complaining but hope to teach that a critical lens will help each of us to evaluate the world within which we live for our collective benefit. The world of sport needs us to put on this critical lens at times particularly when it comes to the safety of the participants and specifically the level and extent of injuries that occur.

The benefits of regular exercise are not limited to adults. Participants of youth, high school, and collegiate sport programs realize motor development, fitness, as well as psychological and social benefits. In general these benefits significantly outweigh the "risk" of injury. In rare cases, however, acute traumatic or catastrophic injuries are seen at all levels of sport. Therefore, it is important to realize that the safety of participants and the prevention of injuries should be the primary objective of participants, parents, coaches, and administrators. Do you believe it is? What information is available to help you make this decision?

Several classifications of sport-related injuries are used. Catastrophic injuries are defined as a severe injury and further classified as fatal, nonfatal with permanent severe functional disability, and serious but with no permanent functional disability. All injuries are further classified as direct or indirect. Direct injuries result directly from participation in the skills of the sport. Indirect injuries are caused by systemic failure as a result of exertion while participating in a sport activity or as a complication of a nonfatal injury (Mueller 2001, 312). Most injuries are classified as overuse injuries, which occur when a tissue is injured as a result of repetitive submaximal loading (DiFiori 1999) during training for sport competition. In a study of children aged 5 to 17 who sought attention at a sports injury clinic, 49.5 percent of 394 injuries were classified as overuse (Watkins and Peabody 1996). Whatever the classification or severity of injury, sport participants and their families should be able to trust that measures to decrease the risk of any injury are designed and followed without hesitation.

This increase in overuse injuries may be the result of the change in youth sport participation that has taken place over the last decade. Children and adolescents are choosing to dedicate themselves to one sport and training year-round at it. Obtaining that college athletic scholarship is most often the motivation for becoming a "one sport athlete." When this training increases in quantity, an increase in quality or a more extensive training program is often adopted. This change in training requires repetition of a limited number of sport-specific skills and will increase the occurrence of overuse injuries. Without adequate recovery time, these simple aches and pains often develop into chronic degeneration. In contrast, involvement in a variety of sports will provide the opportunity for children to develop total body fitness and increase the scope of motor skill efficiency. Just because the trend to specialize in one sport is observed more frequently does not mean it must be accepted. Increase in injuries is just one negative aspect of this change in sport participation. The American College of Sports Medicine (ACSM) is the leading authority in the field of sport related injures. This organization estimates that 50 percent of overuse injuries in children and adolescents are preventable (ACSM 1993). One way to prevent these injuries is to evaluate the preparticipation screening that is required by most schools and should be a part of all youth sport programs.

Typically children must receive medical clearance from their family physician prior to participation. This part of the medical screening should not be eliminated but most often does not assess participants' risk for incurring sport-related injuries if they become involved in strenuous training. DiFiori (1999) believes that is an excellent opportunity to identify the sport-specific injury risk factors, which might include a critique of children's level of skill and maturity and their motivation for participation. Most parent and coaches do not explicitly consider these factors when beginning a season with many new faces, but they can provide vital information in assessing the risk of injury.

DiFiori (1999) explains that these factors that contribute to overuse injury can be classified as intrinsic or extrinsic. He considers intrinsic factors to be growth, prior injury, inadequate conditioning, anatomic misalignment, menstrual dysfunction, and psychological factors such as maturity and self-esteem. Factors considered extrinsic are the following: too-rapid training progression or inadequate rest, inappropriate equipment or footwear, incorrect sport technique, uneven or hard surfaces, and adult or peer pressure. These factors represent an aspect of the sport experience of which participants, parents, and coaches should be mindful if prevention of injuries is a primary objective. As these factors have been presented, consider the extent to which the young participant is actually in control of them. A review of these factors prior to and continuing throughout participation can be the vehicle by which participants and parents can take control of and critique the situation to assist in the prevention of injuries. I believe that if parents and coaches focus on just two of DiFiori's (1999) factors, inadequate conditioning and adult or peer pressure, participants will not only be able to avoid unpleasant injuries, but they will also be able to enjoy their participation more. If children are generally unfit or lack core strength and flexibility, they will be more susceptible to injury but will not be able to meet the demands of what otherwise could be a positive practice experience. Athletes who have developed a higher level of general fitness will be more successful in practice and feel better about themselves and their participation. Additionally, inappropriate pressure from others, particularly adults, will affect the athlete's ability to make appropriate decisions about discomfort and pain. Ignoring early warning signs of pain and even general muscle soreness after practice sessions seems to be acceptable behavior, but it may lead to overuse injuries. Matheson (2001) believes that we must lose the bigger, faster, and win-at-all-costs image that casts a negative influence on the field of competition. From his medical frame of mind, he believes that the assumption that injury is implicit to sports does not fit the current health model. Evaluating the sport experience with a critical lens will probably help decrease the participants' risk of injury and make participation more positive and enjoyable.

In relation to sport injuries, we have learned most from the medical community. In fact, physicians have often been the leaders in the establishment and evaluation of playing conditions that have had a direct impact on decreasing the amount and seriousness of injuries. As our attention has been on overuse injuries, serious or catastrophic injuries do occur and have also been reviewed with a critical lens. Universal reaction of a fatal or disabling injury is, "How can we ensure that this does not happen again?" It is impossible to ensure that these kinds of injuries will not occur, especially with advances in training, increased use of supplements, and the winning-at-all-cost approach to the game that has developed. But the sports medicine community should be commended for what they have learned and implemented from the painful lessons of serious injuries.

Roberts (1998) explains that primary prevention involves strategies that can be placed on a continuum from passive to active. He explains that passive strategies do not require the cooperation of the participant and comparatively are the most reliable for preventing injury. Examples of passive strategies include breakaway bases in baseball and softball and changing the start time of races to allow runners to compete in the least dangerous conditions (e.g., during cooler hours rather than at midday). Roberts explains that active strategies require the participant to cooperate or make changes and therefore are not reliable. Examples of this type of strategy include recommendations for adequate fluid intake and using individual water cups to prevent spreading illness to teammates. In between the active and passive strategies are "blended" strategies that incorporate both approaches, still requiring some degree of cooperation from participants. Examples of these would be the rules of the game, which are the fundamental strategy for prevention of injuries. Required interventions such as the mandatory protective equipment in football and helmets in bicycle races are included as blended strategies (Roberts 1998). As a participant or spectator, have you realized that the rules of the game, the enforcement through penalties, and even the code of conduct that are taken for granted during competition are there to decrease the risk of injury to the participants? Would appreciating the rules of the game and the resulting penalties from this perspective change the way we respond to the competitions we watch?

An additional point that Roberts (1998) brings to our attention is the unintentional consequences of safety measure. He explains that even though safety innovations are well founded, they have unintended consequences that dilute their effectiveness, citing ice hockey as an example. Helmets and face shields have decreased the risk of eye loss, facial laceration, dental injury, and contusions, but these improvements "have apparently increased the risk of serious head and neck injury. ... The aggressive nature of the sport has been heightened by the false sense of security that added protection gives players, especially young ones" (Roberts 1998, *Unintended Consequences of Safety Measures*, paragraph 2). This concept is likely apparent in other contact sports, such as football. Roberts is a proponent of eliminating intentional body contact in ice hockey for juveniles because he feels it may be the only strategy that could provide a solution to the risk of neck injury for these athletes. I often wonder why intentional body contact is not eliminated at all levels of ice hockey? Would the fans enjoyment of the resultant skating finesse overshadow their unmet need for violence?

We have learned a considerable amount of valuable information from the field of sports medicine, and this knowledge has saved the lives of athletes and decreased the risk of catastrophic injuries and overuse injuries. Roberts considers the physicians who have conducted the research and worked hard for reforms in sports heroes. These physicians generally have gone unnoted by the general public, so I include a few of them here. I encourage readers to learn more about their accomplishments.

- Thomas Pashby, MD, and Paul Vinger, MD: The work of these physicians led to the use of facemasks in ice hockey.
- David Janda, MD: Janda's work led to breakaway bases in softball.
- Fredrick Mueller, PhD: Mueller's work led to a ban on spearing in football.
- Charles Tator, MD, PhD: Tato's work led to the outlaw of checking from behind in ice hockey. (Roberts 1998, *Leaders in Prevention*, paragraph 1)

Sports medicine is not without its challenges and controversies. Probably the most prevalent concern is one that includes the decisions around when an injured player should return to competition. Years ago, when the positions of the team doctor and the athletic trainer were not given their appropriate respect, coaches thought they should make the decision. Battles erupted, and often the coach made the decision to have an athlete return to competition despite the medical professional's belief that competition was not in the best interest of the athlete. Hopefully those days are gone, and a certified medical professional is given the responsibility for making the decision with the athlete's safety their first concern. Even in this ideal situation, however, the decisions become controversial, result in emotional and political fallout, and place the medical professional in a challenging position. Rubin (1998) explains that the team physician should be considered an integral part of the team, but that being the athlete's doctor on the sideline can produce a conflict in goals. For example, keeping a star athlete out of a game because of the injury, particularly when the return to competition is controversial as with minor concussions, being "conservative" to protect the athlete can have a negative affect on the outcome of the game. The team physician can be made to feel that his or her actions are in conflict with the goal to win. Therein lies the conflict between the team physician, whose goal it is to win, and the athlete's personal doctor, whose goal is to protect the player regardless of that player's value to the team. Rubin warns against being caught up in the "winning-is-the-only-thing" mentality that is a priority among coaches and players. He also encourages the public to view the team physician as the one who picks up the pieces after an injury, who gets the player back into action and tries to keep the athlete playing. The public has learned the value of these professionals; now we need to respect their decisions when they are made with the athlete's safety in mind.

Sports medicine is a fascinating profession. Career choices are numerous, with professionals specializing in different levels and sports. *The Physician and Sports Medicine* is the most respected journal in the field and includes an abundance of valuable articles for professionals, athletes, parents, coaches, and administrators. Additional resources are provided in chapter 6.

DO COLLEGIATE ATHLETICS NEED TO CHANGE?

Athletics versus Education

I have included participation rates for youth sport programs, as well as reasons for students to participate in elementary and interscholastic athletics in an attempt to provide a better understanding of their espoused benefits and the challenges that they face. Issues related to the educational value of these programs as a part of the American educational system are certainly of major concern. If we determine that a conflict of interests undermines our present sport programs and challenge the place of sports in the educational setting, than it is extremely fitting that we address the issues related to collegiate athletics.

Sport in the American educational setting was first realized at the college level. A rowing race between Yale and Harvard took place in 1852 and the first intercollegiate football game was played between Rutgers and Princeton in 1869. Much of what has occurred between then and now has significantly changed the culture and attitude toward higher education in the United States; it has also had significant influence on developments within youth sport programs, elementary school sports, and interscholastic athletics.

The marriage of athletics to higher education occurred as colleges attempted to bring in additional sources of revenue. The general public was proud of their state colleges, and sports as entertainment were in high demand. The formula certainly paid off. Athletic programs at many universities generate revenue from gate receipts and apparel sales, and successful teams stimulate alumni giving. However, collegiate athletics are receiving considerable scrutiny specifically for the financial aspects of their programs. Eitzen and Sage (1993) provide ten examples of the "intrusion" of money into collegiate sport and an additional eight examples of the intrusion by way of compensation for coaches in big-time programs. I include an abbreviated list here for review:

- In 1990, the total revenues generated by college football bowl games exceeded $63 million.
- In 1992, the total amount paid to schools with teams competing in postseason college football bowls exceeded $68 million.
- Beginning in 1991, CBS agreed to pay $1 billion over seven years for the television rights to their NCAA's men's basketball tournament.
- In 1991, the athletic budget at the University of Michigan exceeded $21 million.
- The University of North Carolina constructed a $35 million arena during a time in the 1980s when there was a faculty pay freeze.
- In 1991, Jerry Tarkanian, basketball coach at the University of Nevada at Las Vegas, was a tenured member of the faculty with an annual salary of $203,976, which made him the highest salaried state employee. (pp. 128–129).

These examples document the issue that is under scrutiny here and across the country: college athletics is "big business."

In business, the bottom line is traditionally profit versus loss. Does the existing business practice generate enough money to result in profit for the company or shareholders? This is one of the major contradictions to the big-business aspect of collegiate athletics. With few exceptions, college athletics programs do not pay for themselves, producing a financial drain on the academic institution that has an obligation to provide the best possible education for the vast majority of their students, a sentiment decreed by every institution of higher education. The NCAA documented this financial situation in a 1997 survey indicating that only 28 percent of Division I programs and only 46 percent of Division I-A programs reported profits (Gerdy 2000). An additional dark cloud that Gerdy (2000) suggests should enter into this discussion of finances is the actual accounting practices of athletic programs. He cites *The Financial Management of Intercollegiate Athletics Programs*, conducted in 1993 by the National Association of College and University Business Officers, which suggests that it is the institution that is actually paying many indirect or overhead costs generated by the athletic programs. Interestingly, Edward (1973) provides an example of student criticism of this inappropriate financing practice; increasingly, student governments and student bodies are working to restrict or eliminate the flow of funds to athletic programs from mandatory student fees. He cites several institutions with high-profile athletic programs where such action has taken place.

So why do colleges maintain such programs? It seems as though these institutions have created a structure for visibility that infers both viability and a quality product (academic degree of value). Americans have come to accept this structure and often assign value in choosing an institution based on the accomplishments of the athletic program. Athletics has become the window through which Americans critique a university. Eliminating oneself from the visibility structure might be considered a fatal decision for recruiting efforts—not in terms of student athletes, but for students in general. Additionally, administrators have serious concerns about the continuation of alumni financial donations if the athletic program were to be discontinued. It seems that colleges have created a system that they believe they cannot live without, but it is also a system that many believe they can no longer live *with*. Dr. Cynthia Patterson, who was looked upon to salvage Southern Methodist University's football program from NCAA violations, supports this sentiment:

> Many presidents, administrators, and faculty view college sports as a necessary, if often problematic, component of university life. Whether a fan or critic, many college officials appear to have made an uneasy peace with intercollegiate athletics, accepting it as an unnatural intruder protected by forces beyond the institution's control. (Patterson 2000, 120)

Gerdy (2000), through a review of the research regarding this myth, concluded that there is no evidence that a successful athletic program will necessarily result in alumni giving or applications. He cites examples of programs that have dropped athletic teams. At Tulane, donations increased by $5 million in 1986, the year after the basketball program was eliminated after a point-shaving scandal. Wichita State raised $26 million during a 1987 financial drive the same year it dropped football (Wolf 1995, cited in Gerdy 2000). Stakeholders are diverting more and more attention to the effect of athletics on the educational efforts of institutions of higher education, but as long as the value of athletics is based on undocumented beliefs instead of the facts and realities of big-business programs, a meaningful dialogue cannot take place.

Identification of some of the major problems associated with collegiate athletics will provide a better understanding of how big-business college athletic programs have come to the problematic state where they find themselves. At the end of this section, I review the effects of some of these problems on programs at the high school level to further the discussion on the educational value of sport in schools.

Recruiting

Understanding the connection between intercollegiate sport participation and academic performance is complex, but it must be understood to discuss the relationship between sport and education. To develop a winning program, coaches traditionally recruit talented athletes to play for them. An athletic scholarship is given to the athlete, either covering all expenses (tuition, room and board, and books) or providing partial financial assistance. This practice is under scrutiny; many argue that the scholarship is actually payment for the athlete's services, which by definition would give the athlete "professional" status. At this point, the scholarship is called a "grant-in-aid" for educational purposes, and the student athlete retains an "amateur" status. This specific situation places considerable restrictions on the athlete and the institution.

The recruiting practice is virtually eliminated at the interscholastic level, as public high school students must attend the school within their geographical district. Some recruiting at this level occurs by private schools to increase the success of the program, but for the most part recruiting and the awarding of scholarships is not a major concern. In contrast, at the collegiate level, many feel that recruiting and payment for services in the form of scholarships is actually the element that results in additional problems for programs and encourages other violations. Analysis of NCAA abuses "demonstrates that it is in the recruiting of prospective student athletes that the structure of intercollegiate athletics is most vulnerable to abuse" (Bailey and Littleton 1991, 117). To address this, the NCAA's recruitment policies are under continuous review and revision. The principle that governs recruiting specifies that recruiting regulations shall be designed to "promote equity among member institutions in their recruiting of prospects and to shield them from undue pressure that may interfere with scholastic or athletics interests of the prospects or their educational institutions" (NCCA 2002, 5). It is explicit that the NCAA attempt to protect the scholastic interest of the student-athlete. Recruitment of some athletes into Division I revenue-generating sports often occurs when there is minimal scholastic interest on the part of the athlete, however. It has become accepted practice among coaches supported by their programs to recruit students into an institution of higher education when the athlete is not academically prepared to participate in the educational aspects of the school. In many of these cases, the athlete has no intention of meeting the requirements necessary to receive an academic degree from that institution. Two aspects of big-time collegiate athletics generate this contradictory behavior. The first is the winning-at-all-cost attitude of the coach and program, and the second is the transformation of collegiate athletics from a viable component of the total college experience into a training ground for professional athletes.

It is the winning-at-all-cost attitude that brings the ill-prepared athlete to an institution, places unreasonable demands on the athlete's time and physical and mental abilities, and then fails to support the athlete in the pursuit of the academic degree. As a faculty member of a Division I university who maintains a close relationship with the athletic program, I can and am compelled to confirm two points. First, there are countless exemplary programs across the country that work hard to avoid the practices just described. The NCAA's review process, which places considerable demands on the institution, identifies and acknowledges these programs. The second point is that it is undeniably the philosophy of the coach and resulting practices that are the driving force behind these inappropriate situations in which programs find themselves. The most difficult position with which university administrators are faced in relation to athletics is attempting to hire a coach who will uphold the academic standards espoused by the university and at the same time produce a winning team for the athletic program. It must be recognized that the demands placed on high-profile coaches often place them in a situation that makes it nearly impossible to achieve both objectives. It can be done, however. At Duke University, basketball coach Mike Krzyzewski, often referred to as "Coach K," is an exemplary model that every collegiate coach should attempt to emulate. In 2001, *Time* magazine and CNN named Coach K America's Best Coach; in the same year he was inducted into the Naismith Memorial Basketball Hall of Fame. In 1992, the *Sporting News* named Coach K the Sportsman of the Year, making him the first college coach to ever receive this honor. Josh Tyrangiel of *Time* magazine hails Coach K with these words: "No college coach has won more in the past two decades, and Krzyzewski has accomplished all this with a program that turns our real-deal scholar athletes—kids who go to class, graduate and don't mind telling everyone about it" (Tyrangiel 2002). The Duke University basketball team truly qualifies for the term "student athletes" and sets the standard. During Coach Krzyzewski's tenure at Duke, all but two Duke basketball players that played four seasons have graduated. This graduation rate was achieved during a period of elite rankings. Since 1986, fifty of the fifty-four players who complete four years of eligibility played in the Final Four and at least one NCAA Championship game. Although recognizing that Coach K is an outstanding coach as well as a unique individual, one is compelled to question why other coaches who often post outstanding records on the field of play post dismal records for graduation.

This winning-at-all-cost attitude and the training ground of professional athletes are most often addressed by the dismal graduation rates of athletes from high-profile, revenue-producing sports. Graduation rates of all student athletes should be looked at first. A review of the latest data collected by the U.S. Department of Education produced the 2002 NCAA report, which found that 60 percent of all student athletes who entered Division I colleges and universities in 1995–1996 graduated within six years. This figure compares to 58 percent for the entire full-time student body at those same institutions. These rates for both groups are two percentage points higher than in 2001. On a sport-by-sport basis, however, Division I football student athletes graduated at a rate of 52 percent, and male basketball student athletes in Division I-A are only graduating at a 36 percent rate. The most disappointing rates belong to African American male basketball student athletes, of whom only 28 percent graduated. All three rates fall below the general student body rates. These data do not appear to provide the dismal picture they initially suggest because it considers all athletes competing for the school who receive financial aid. The data need to be looked at more closely, specifically for high-profile programs with successful teams. Eitzen and Sage (1993) cite a 1991 *USA Today* article that reported that ten men's basketball programs graduated less than 10 percent of their athletes, schools in the Big Eight conference graduated 25 percent of their players, schools in the Big West graduated 27 percent of their athletes, and that six of the perennial basketball powers across the country failed to graduate 20 percent of their freshman recruits within five years (142). The problem continued, as documented in a May 1, 2000, *USA Today* article that states, "There's a good reason that academic feebleness sits at the core of the many problems—unethical payments, illegal payoffs, conflicts of interest, exploitation and miserable graduation rates—that continue to bedevil men's college basketball. A system that values winning and revenue above learning and graduation can never be free of fast-buck, quick-shot seductions" (17). *USA Today* provides many viewpoints on college athletics and accompanied graduation ranks. The NCAA reports graduation rates for Division I, II, and III member institutions. Actual rates and corresponding reports can be found at http://www.ncaa.org/eligibility/cbsa/indexl.html.

There is good reason for the defense of the athletic scholarship aspect of higher education. The graduation rates cited in the previous paragraph document that athletes graduate at a higher rate than the general student population. This may be because finances need not be a major concern for the student athlete, as they can be for the student at large. When athletic scholarships were debated in one of my classes at the university level, working students passionately expressed their views. As athletes complained about the long hours of practice and lack of spending money, nonathletes expressed how challenging it was to attend the university full-time and hold down a full-time job to pay tuition and living expenses.

Additionally, collegiate athletic programs generally provide the student athlete with considerable academic and social support. These programs have a variety of names, one example being the Athletic Academic Assistance program. These programs are established to help student athletes succeed in the classroom in view of the tremendous demands that practices and games place on their time and energy. Edwards estimates that these demands are significant: during the season, basketball players spend fifty hours and football players as much as sixty hours per week preparing for, traveling to, participating in, and recovering from competitions. Academic assistance programs monitor a student athlete's progress in classes, provide tutoring services, and require "study table" hours for freshman and those who need the structured study time. These programs also provide additional support as required by the NCAA in "life skills." The efforts of these programs are in place to avoid "exploitation" of the student athlete and more specifically to provide the additional assistance needed to those athletes who have received special treatment in the admissions process. It is common for good athletes who are marginal students to be admitted to an institution even though they did not meet the admission requirements for the general student population. Admission requirements are based on a combination of scores on the Scholastic Aptitude Test (SAT), the American College Test (ACT), and the student's high school grade point average. The *Chronicle of Higher Education* documented questionable admissions practices, noting that "football and men's basketball players in big-time sports programs are more than six times as likely as other students to have received special treatment in the admissions process—that is, be admitted below the standards requirements" (Eitzen and Sage 1993, 139).

Of highest support for the recruitment of athletes and the awarding of scholarships is that scholarships often provide the opportunity for students to attend college who would otherwise not be able to do so, either for financial and or academic reasons (or both). This is particularly true for students from areas of the country, both urban and rural, where elementary and high schools do not provide students with an adequate education that will allow them to be successful in college. This absence of educational equity has been well documented, but is dramatically presented in Jonathan Kozal's 1992 classic, *Savage Inequalities*. White privilege, which is embedded in the American educational system, results in the disproportionate percent of minority students not academically prepared for the rigors of many of the top universities of the country. An excellent resource on this topic is Wise and Fine's (1993) *Beyond Silenced Voices: Class, Race, and Gender in United States Schools*. Within this text, Mickelson, Smith, and Oliver state, "African Americans and other minorities suffer because most lack the sustenance of initial privilege. They often suffer severe difficulties conquering personal and institutional barriers in their quest for academic success" (p. 15). The economic implication of white privilege also results in the inability of many minority students to pay for the necessary undergraduate and graduate degrees necessary for upward social mobility. It might be argued that through financial aid, as the result of need or to acknowledge academic or athletic capabilities, the inequities in the educational system can be addressed. Of course, an athletic scholarship does not ensure an academic degree and the advantages that it might offer; however, access to institutions of higher education through these scholarships may increase the opportunity for minorities to achieve significant academic success, which may result in upward social mobility.

Is there truth to the notion that athletics is a vehicle for upward social mobility? Many Americans believe that the class system in the United States is an "open" one that allows members of one social class to move freely between classes, regardless of social origin. In theory, this is correct; however, nonwhites and those in lower socioeconomic classes realize that the word "open" is relative in this context. Ideally, positions of wealth and power should be available to those who have the talents and abilities to obtain them. However, opportunity to develop talents and abilities, obtain the necessary education, and be accepted into a higher social class even if one obtains it are factors not realized equally in U.S. society. Because of the institutionalized inequities for marginalized people in this country, upward social mobility can be difficult. As a result, sport has become an avenue to facilitate upward social mobility, particularly for young African American men from poor urban areas. For this particular group, sport has provided an abundance of visual evidence to support this belief. Former NBA superstar Isaiah Thomas is an excellent testimony to the opportunity that athletic ability provides for the elite. Thomas, the youngest of nine children, grew up in a west-side ghetto in Chicago. After receiving a full scholarship to play basketball at Indiana University, he led his team to the NCAA championship in 1981. After his sophomore year, he was drafted by the Detroit Pistons; following a successful career as a player, he entered the coaching and management ranks. His is a true "rags-to-riches" story, as is vividly recounted in his 2001 book, *The Fundamentals: 8 plays for Winning the Games of Business and Life.*

Despite the documented examples of upward social mobility that some athletes attain, the percent of those who accomplish this dream is astonishingly small; many have suggested that dedicating one's time and energy to developing athletic ability at the expense of academics is damaging. The issue of role models will not be presented here in depth; however, if we consider what young, vulnerable, highly skilled male athletes learn from watching professional sports on television, we must realize that they can acquire a distorted picture of what athletic participation is capable of providing. Eitzen and Sage (1993) document the inability to attain the "professional dream": "There were 1,892,475 American boys playing high school football, basketball, and baseball in 1984–1985. That same year 110,000 men were playing those sports in college, and 2,261 participated at the major professional level ... only one in 837 high school players will play at the major professional level" (p. 314). Despite these eye-opening statistics, researchers conclude that college athletes are generally upwardly mobile, probably because of the expanded social network that typically results from participation in collegiate athletics. Likewise, employers often select people who have demonstrated the ability to participate in a variety of activities and assume that athletic participation has developed characteristics that would be beneficial to the institution (Eitzen and Sage, 1993). So, is it appropriate for young high school athletes to spend their high school years dedicated to the attainment of being awarded an athletic scholarship to play collegiate athletics? Do the benefits outweigh the potential costs? Is the recruiting aspect of collegiate athletics a diversion from the realities of upward social mobility that is the dream of most Americans?

Another controversial aspect of the recruiting process is the issue raised when an athlete and his or her family are forced to use the educational system as the training ground and stepping stone to professional athletics. The financial and social allure of professional sports results in an appropriately high percentage of athletes chasing the professional dream, a dream that progresses from being a star high school athlete, being awarded an athletic scholarship to play for a high-profile athletic program, to being seen by professional sport recruiters, and being drafted from college into the professional sport world. This model has been criticized for undermining the educational mission of the educational institutions it uses. This acknowledgment of collegiate teams acting as the "farm system" for professional teams is so prevalent that it prompted well-established author Michael Novak to make this proposal: "Professional teams should pay for the services so provided. A mandatory contribution to the NCAA sports fund of, say, $250,000 by each professional team every year would go a long way in many of the more modest college athletic departments" (Novak 1994, 289). This is an interesting idea, one that has not yet been implemented. At this time, however, there are few alternative opportunities to play after high school. Professional baseball's minor league system is an example of a structure that provides development of the athlete in preparation for a major league career. But this system often places the athlete in a position to choose between the chance to play in professional baseball or continuing his education. The "Nike" league is an experimental system in place to allow exceptional basketball players to continue to train and play outside of the collegiate system. The collegiate athletic system does provide athletes with the opportunity to continue to develop their athletic abilities, mature both physically and emotionally, and continue their education. This system may appear to be one that works, but for those exceptional athletes who have not received the prior education necessary for success in college and will not make it to the professional league, the system can be exploitive. Colleges recruit them, give them a scholarship, and place them in a situation in which the social and academic demands are overwhelming. Some athletes who were not successful in high school find themselves in college classrooms with the academic elite of the country. They often must compete with these students for grades and participate in classroom discussions with them. This situation results in an athlete's withdrawal from working to fulfill the academic requirements of a course and taking easier classes, a situation that does not support the attainment of an academic degree.

The Failure of Eligibility Requirements

As noted in chapter 2, the first significant statement regarding the abuses of collegiate athletics came in 1905 when President Theodore Roosevelt warned the educational community of the negative consequences of big-time intercollegiate sports programs, responding to eighteen deaths that had occurred in college football that year. The Carnegie Corporation report on college sports in the 1920s and the Knight Foundation Commission on Intercollegiate Athletics in 1991 continued to address the need to review and reform college athletic programs. As a result, the NCAA, prompted by the American Council on Education, has established and maintains a close check on requirements for athletic eligibility. In 1983, the NCAA passed Proposition 48, which established minimum standards for a first year athlete to be eligible to play on a Division I team. This rule specifically stated that in order to play, the student athlete must have entered college with a 2.0 grade point average (GPA) in eleven stipulated core subjects in high school and a score of 700 or greater on the SAT or 15 or greater on the ACT. These eligibility requirements went into effect in 1986, but this ruling allowed students who met only one of the requirements (test score or GPA) to enter the school and receive financial aid, but lose their first year of eligibility. These student athletes were nicknamed "Prop 48," and if they demonstrated their ability to meet the academic requirements of the institution by maintaining the established GPA, they played for three years. Proposition 48 was meant to place responsibility on high schools to better prepare prospective college athletes. Additionally, it began to discourage the recruitment of athletes who had no reasonable chance to succeed in college-level courses and provided the first year of college as an academic year for the student athlete. The consensus is that Proposition 48 is working, and as a result even higher eligibility standards have been implemented. Nonetheless, there are those who believe that elevating the standards discriminated against athletes from low-income areas whose educational opportunities are limiting and that the standardized test standards are inappropriate because the SAT and ACT tests have built-in cultural biases (Coackley 1994).

As some of the abuses in recruiting have been addressed, abuses in eligibility have become scandalous. Despite the NCAA's efforts to maintain the integrity of institutions of higher educational and their athletic programs, student athletes at many institutions are treated inappropriately. Not attending classes, having others complete their assignments (often athletic program personnel), and receiving passing grades despite poor performance on tests and assignments are a few of the examples of abuses of a system that attempts to establish a minimum academic performance in the classroom. Sperber (2000) discusses the widespread acceptance of cheating on college campuses, confirming that staff members write papers and take-home exams for undergrads, particularly intercollegiate athletes, citing a former tutor for the University of Minnesota who revealed that she had written four hundred papers for twenty varsity men's basketball players between 1993 and 1998 (Sperber 2000, 130). That many institutions tolerate cheating has been documented, and the NCAA has handed down harsh penalties and sanctions. Consider the negative visibility and incurring financial liability of the athletic programs that have been placed on NCAA probation. Thus, what we have before us are athletic programs that are established and managed as an entertainment enterprise catering to external constituencies (alumni, fans, and television networks) being driven by market forces rather than educational priorities (Gerdy 2000).

Despite the apparent negative aspects of big-time athletics, the positive influences on the institutions that support them and the participating athletes are both tangible and immeasurable. Academic degrees awarded to graduates from Big Ten and Ivy League schools are among the most prestigious in the country. Most can only imagine what opportunities accompany a bachelor's or master's degree from the University of Notre Dame, for example. The words of James Delany, commissioner of the Big Ten Conference in 1996, support this reality: "Big Ten institutions provide more that 6,400 young men and women opportunities to play on 250 intercollegiate teams. These young people receive in excess of $42 million annually from Big Ten institutions in grant-in-aid. While receiving the opportunity for a world-class education, they compete with and against some of the finest amateur athletes in the country" (http://www.umich.edu/%7mrev/archives/1996/9-18-96/13.htm). For those who have participated in Big Ten athletics, or any collegiate athletic program, the experience was probably among the most memorable and valuable of their lives. The opportunity to be coached by some of the most highly acclaimed professionals in intercollegiate sports, the relationships forged between teammates, the life lessons learned, and the moments in victory and defeat are priceless to the individuals involved.

The opportunities that participation in collegiate athletics provide have a significant influence on all levels of sport participation prior to it. In the United States, many parents worry about the cost of a college education from the day their children are born, aware that the costs may be in excess of $100,000 for four years. As a result, parents often structure their financial plans to ensure they will have sufficient money to send children to the college of their choice. The reality is, however, that many families struggle to meet everyday expenses and simply do not have the money to meet the financial demands of college. A college scholarship or "full ride" becomes the goal of many families when they see athletic ability in their children at a young age. This may be one significant reason that inappropriate parental involvement has become a reality in many youth sport programs. The college scholarship becomes a driving force behind the private lessons and year-round involvement in a specialized sport. College recruiters from the best teams typically visit high-profile "winning" teams to see the top players. Therefore, the success of the team or the athletic reputation of the high school becomes vital, placing additional pressure on administrators, coaches, and players. Because of what is known about the recruiting and eligibility practices of some of these high-profile collegiate programs, academic achievements take a backseat to the athletic accomplishments of the athlete. These college aspirations or dreams are why many believe that sports have a negative effect on the educational process at the high school level. The influence of the collegiate programs does have a powerful implicit effect on what happens at the high school level. Knowing the realities of the college system and how few players receive the "full ride" to a high-profile program should help high school athletes understand that the true value of high school is getting the education they will need to succeed academically at the next level. The dramatic increase in media coverage of college football bowl games and the NCAA "big dance" basketball tournament only perpetuate the myth that athletics is an easier way to succeed than academics.

CROSSING THE LINE

Is Drug Use Really a Problem in Sports?

Schools are but one social setting within which drugs have become an issue of major concern. The America 2000 Program included a goal of "safe, drug-free schools," which has yet to be realized. It should be understood, however, that pervasive social problems such as drugs and violence cannot be solved within the school setting until they are addressed in the larger social context. Schools can only try to control their environment by keeping weapons and drugs out of schools. With this understanding, we can begin to consider whether sports in schools help to control violence and drug use or if sports may actually foster unacceptable social behavior.

Athletes may take drugs for several reasons, two of which I discuss in this section. Drugs are used to enhance performance and in social settings. These two approaches to drug use are different and must be considered separately.

Nutritional supplements are a multibillion-dollar industry in the United States. Supplements are available from a variety of places, from retail stores to the Internet; with a few exceptions, they are legal. Consumers are entering into a new era, however. Many substances that are advertised and that the public uses extensively are not safe. No more can we assume that if a substance is legal, easily available, and widely used, then it is safe. Consumers—athletes included—must become educated about the substances they are taking and be critical of the proposed benefits when considering the side effects. Those substances that should receive the most scrutiny are performance-enhancing supplements.

Performance-enhancing drugs actually belong to a larger category of substances called ergogenic, or "work producing," aids. These supplements are any physical, mechanical, nutritional, psychological, or pharmacological substance or treatment intended to improve exercise performance (Wardlaw 1997). Therefore, ergogenic aids include sufficient water, carbohydrates, vitamins, and even a well-balanced diet. This concept is presented to point out that to perform at maximum capacity, athletes need to do many things. Physical training receives the most attention, but good nutrition and hydration should be key components of the training efforts of any athlete at any level. Sometimes, however, athletes realize that their dietary choices may not be as beneficial as they would like, or they simply want to get the necessary nutrients the easy way, so they choose supplementation. This supplementation can range from what many would consider appropriate behavior (taking a multivitamin, hyperhydrating, and "carbo loading" before a game or race) to illegal and life-threatening behavior (taking amino acid supplements, anabolic steroids, or ephedrine) and everything in between. What most athletes do not know or will not accept is that there is no scientific evidence that supports the effectiveness of most of the substances touted as performance enhancing. In addition, many of the widely used substances pose serious health risks. For example, ephedrine is a substance used in many over-the-counter products that are sold as energy boosters and weight loss aids. It is a powerful stimulant to the central nervous system that increases metabolism, provides more energy, and increases caloric expenditure. Because it is a natural substance, many erroneously believe it is safe. As of October 2002, it was reported to be responsible for forty-one deaths and 1,400 heart attacks nationally.

The attention paid to these substances probably rose most significantly in response to the deaths of four college football players and one professional athlete during the 2001 season, all suspected of taking a sport supplement. The federal government does not regulate most of these substances because they are not considered a food or drug, although a movement is underway to ban many of them. The NCAA currently bans the use of ephedrine, as do many other national and international sports governing bodies. According to a 2001 Blue Cross and Blue Shield survey, almost 1 million American teenagers have taken a "sport supplement," with the most common ingredients being androstenedione, creatine, and ephedrine.

One of the most popular substances in the sport world is the anabolic steroid, which is taken to increase muscle mass and strength. The sad commentary on this substance is that it works. It is effective, and athletes at all levels have taken it for decades. It is illegal in the United States, however, because of its numerous potential side effects. The side effects include premature closure of growth plates in bones, resulting in reducing the adult height a teenage athlete will reach; bloody cysts in the liver; increased risk of heart disease; high blood pressure; and reproductive dysfunction (Wardlaw 1997). Psychological side effects, such as increased aggression and mood swings, have also been documented. Despite these serious side effects, steroid use is common at all levels in sports, although steroids are not widely abused among the general youth population. Only about 2 percent of eighth-, tenth-, and twelfth-grade students have ever used steroids according to the 1996 National Institute on Drub Abuse–sponsored study, Monitoring the Future. Current surveys estimate that steroid use among high school boys is up to 4 to 6 percent, with one study reporting 12 percent. The estimate for girls is about 2 percent.

Charles Yesalis, professor of exercise and sport science at Penn State University, suggests that steroid use could be at an all-time high, and his 2000 work found that usage by eighth-graders was similar to that of high school seniors (Manning 2002). Steroid abuse occurs more often among young people who are involved in physical training, however, because anabolic steroids can increase muscle mass, strength, and stamina. The influence of professional sports cannot be overlooked as researchers attempt to determine the cause of the increase. Professional athlete Mark McGuire's admitted use of androstenedione during his 1998 home run record season taught young athletes that steroid use works. Additionally, according to the 2001 Monitoring the Future Study, among high school seniors, disapproval of steroids dropped from 91 percent in 1997 to 86 percent in 2001, and the belief that steroids pose a significant risk dropped from 67 percent in 1997 to 59 percent in 2001. Society cannot ignore the fact that young players model themselves against their professional sports heroes.

In response to high school athletes' use of steroids, a program designed to provide an alternative to use of this drug was developed by Dr. Linn Goldberg of Oregon Health Sciences University in Portland. He states, "The Adolescents Training and Learning to Avoid Steroids (AT-LAS) program uses a team-oriented educational approach that motivates and empowers student athletes to make the right choices about steroid use." The program consists of classroom, weight-training, and parent information components. Together, they give student athletes the knowledge and skills to resist steroid use and achieve their athletic goals in more effective, healthier ways (see http://www.drugabuse.gov/prevention/program.html).

To return to our initial question of whether sport participation increases the likelihood of drug use, most studies show that the drug use rate for the general college population is much higher than that of the varsity athlete (Schwenk 2000). This might be due to the decrease in leisure time, cost, and effect on performance. In the NCAA Study of Substance Use Habits of College Student-Athletes, only 29.2 percent of the 21,225 respondents indicated that they were currently using some type of supplement other than a multivitamin; at least 4 percent of the student athletes reported using a nutritional supplement that contained a banned substance. For high school athletes, the research is scarce and plagued with conflicting findings. Some studies report that high school athletes use illegal substances less than the general school population (Carr, Dimick, and Kennedy 1990), and in larger national studies, alcohol use appears about the same as non-athletes. The findings suggest that for the high school athlete, athletic involvement is only one of many factors that might influence or deter drug use, and the issue is complex. Drugs include anything from Tylenol to Vicodin, caffeine to heroin. They can be considered legal or illegal, harmful or safe, socially acceptable or unacceptable. It is important to know the level of documented use of illegal substances at different levels, even though these can only be considered best estimates. Such information is additionally important because established use at young ages often leads to increased use at higher levels, thus making programs to discourage it in the junior high and high school level a priority.

Besides the use of supplements to improve performance or lose weight, drug use for social reasons or in social settings is a serious problem for students and student athletes alike. We should focus our attention on alcohol, the most widely abused drug in the world, which remains the number one substance abused by teenagers and athletes alike. The rate of drug use among teenagers is higher in the United States than in any other industrial society. Among college student athletes, as with the general public, alcohol is the most widely used drug (predominantly beer), with 80 percent reporting that they have had alcohol in the past 12 months. Consistent findings to determine whether high school athletes drink alcohol more than nonathletes are lacking, but a survey of 215 high school athletic directors in North Carolina reported interesting findings. Of these athletic directors, 59 percent reported that they have dealt with intoxicated student athletes and that they consider alcohol to be the drug of most concern (Shields 1995). Let us not forget that nearly half of all traffic fatalities of adolescents are alcohol related.

Because of documented and perceived drug use, drug testing has become an issue for all regulating agencies—from state high school athletic associations, to the International Olympic Committee, to professional sports teams. Each is responsible for regulating drug use among its participants. The NCAA requires drug testing, which resulted in loss of eligibility for 96 athletes in the 1999–2000 academic year (Mazur 2001). Regardless of the results, the testing itself seems to be having a positive effect on preventing use of illegal substances. According to the 2001 drug testing survey, "The 2001 NCAA drug-use study showed that 17 percent of the athletes surveyed said that the threat of NCAA drug testing discouraged them from using banned substances (31.2 percent said they would not have used banned substances regardless; 45.5 percent did not answer the question)." In another section of the survey, "56.5 percent of the athletes stated that they agreed that the NCAA should test all college athletes and 55 percent stated that drug testing by the NCAA has deterred college athletes from using drugs." The National High School Athletic Association does not require or suggest drug testing for athletes; however, many high schools across the country have a code of conduct for their students athletes and promote zero-tolerance for any use of an illegal substance. Athletes' documented drug use usually results in suspension from a portion of their season. Repeated offenses result in removal from that team and possible prohibition from participation on any team. When student athletes realize they have a drug problem, however, they can typically present their situation to their coach or athletic director and take part in a drug treatment program and may continue to participate on the team as long as they continue with the treatment program. This approach is intended both to reward the student athlete for recognizing the need for help and to continue offering the support system that a sport team often provides.

This issue of drug testing among high school athletes is extremely controversial. In 1995, the U.S. Supreme Court ruled that high school athletes can be required to undergo drug tests if they participate in sports, but few districts test their athletes. Taylor (1997), in a theoretical investigation, suggests the need for "careful empirical studies" in view of the "compensating behavior factor" suggested in much of the literature. What this review of the literature suggests is that drug testing may in fact increase drug use in those not tested and in those athletes who terminate participation as a result of drug testing. The model of "compensating behavior" that Taylor (1995) presents suggests "individual responses to a government regulation diminish or even reverse the regulation's intended effect" (p. 355). The research in this area specifically reviewed the use of seatbelts, child-resistant safety caps, and security enhancements at airports, which respectively produced an increase in pedestrian deaths, analgesic poisonings, and an increase in people choosing to drive (a far riskier mode of transportation) rather than fly (Taylor 1995). This model is interesting and, when related to drug testing of athletes in high school, stresses that a given regulation (e.g., drug testing) may not produce the intended results.

What might be learned from this issue is that drug use of any kind, including the use of legal supplements, can be dangerous for athletes. Illegal drug use, most notably alcohol and steroids, will continue to be a problem for school athletic programs, but should be addressed within the larger context of the school and the level of use among the general student population. Drug testing is used successfully in sports from the college level through the Olympic Games, but at the high school level it becomes problematic.

Violence On and Off the Field

Does sport provide an outlet for aggression and violent tendencies, or does it teach that aggressive behavior and acts of violence against an opponent are appropriate in the pursuit of victory?

Curry (2000), in *Sports in Schools: The Future of an Institution,* provides an entertaining review of several of his memories from his tenure in the NFL. As he contemplates the lessons learned and the values taught to others, he addresses this question by providing what he believes are the conflicting results of participation in his beloved game. He begins by stating,

> If football condones violence, it also rewards compassion and empathy … If it has shattered bones and snapped ligaments, it also has strengthened muscles and shaped young bodies to be lean and fit for life. … If is has promoted unhealthy violence, it has also been the only place many aggressive youngsters could find expression and catharsis … It is magnificent, terrible, beautiful, hideous, pristine, and corrupt. It is … well, football. It is life. (p. 159)

His sentiment, which supports the view that contact sports provide players the opportunity to let off steam, release feelings of aggression, and learn to cope with stress, is accepted by many in the world of sports. But the theory that grounds this position is that all forms of aggressive behaviors are instinctive rather than a learned behavior. Because many prominent figures in the sport world espouse this belief, it is interesting to note that Coakley has concluded the instinct argument provides no valid support for the notion that sport participation can serve as a cure for violence. One weakness in this theory is that it cannot explain the variability of rates of aggression from one group to another, why aggression is highly correlated with specific social conditions, and that most humans have to be coerced to harm others. In addition, several studies are cited to link contact sport with aggression and violence in societies around the world. Findings suggest that contact sports seem to be expressions of the same orientations that underlie warfare, as well as high rates of murder and assault. Specifically, contact sports were popular in 90 percent of warlike societies and in only 20 percent of peaceful societies. Yet another study documents that homicide rates in the United States increase immediately after television broadcasts of high-profile boxing matches (Coakley 1994).

This position suggests that the use of violent behaviors and intimidation are often learned as a strategy to dominate the opponent, win at all costs, promote an individual's value on the team, or increase the profits of the organization. This coaching mentality teaches that the use of violence is permissible, and at some levels actually rewarded. No example of this is more dramatic and regrettable than Jack Tatum's paralyzing blow to Daryl Stingley in a 1979 National Football League (NFL) game. Known as an intimidator in the league, Tatum was proud that his "best hits border on felonious assault." After he learned the consequences of his hit to Stingley, however, he explained, "It was one of those pass plays where I could not possibly have intercepted, so because of what the owners expect of me when they give me my paycheck I automatically reacted to the situation by going for an intimidating hit" (Tatum 1979). One might feel that professional athletes belong in a different class because of the high salaries they receive and the dollars associated with the entertainment factor of the game. In November 2002, however, the NFL commissioner established the first warning to address this situation. He warned that coaches and programs that support "cheap hits" on defenseless players will be fined. This was an unprecedented move by the commissioner in an attempt to curtail the escalation of injuries incurred by "overly" aggressive hits in the league. The implicit lessons that the visibility of such violence teaches to players at younger levels, and their subsequent imitation of it, also suggest that to use violence in sports is a learned behavior. The question that follows is whether violent strategies learned from sports carry over to other aspects of life.

Another interesting question is whether violence in sporting events has a connection to fan violence, something that has become a major concern in recent years. Internationally, fan violence has received the most attention among fans of football (soccer). The term given to violence in the football setting is "football hooliganism," said to have originated in England in the early 1960s. It has been linked with the televising of and with the "reclaiming" of the game by the working class. Both the extent and the nature of football-related violence are influenced by the differing historical, social, economic, political, and cultural factors in various European countries. Problems related to social class have been a significant factor in the United Kingdom and have found their way into the football arena as well. In fact, Great Britain is perceived to have the most severe problems with fan violence. No other nation has received a blanket expulsion from all European football competitions, a ban imposed following the Heysel Stadium tragedy in which thirty-two Juventus (an Italian team) fans died when a wall collapsed after clashes with Liverpool fans. Italy, Germany, the Netherlands, and Belgium also experience a significant level of hooliganism, with incidents occurring at approximately 10 percent of the games.

Researchers, government agencies, and the private football organizations collectively have attempted to address the issue. One project that originated in Germany is called the "fan project," the primary function of which "is to turn supporters away from hooliganism by means of concrete street-work activities ... to help the adolescent fan find his personal identity and to show various possibilities of coping with life" (http://www.sirc.org/publik/fvhist.html). This approach documents that efforts to date have acknowledged the problem is a social one that is larger than sport, the area in which it is manifest.

Fan violence is not new; in Ancient Rome, 30,000 fans were killed during a spectator riot at chariot races. Nor is fan violence unique to Europe. In 1969, during the World Cup soccer series between El Salvador and Honduras, fan violence was routine and resulted in a riot following the third game. This riot severed political and economic relations between the two countries and eventually escalated into a war that has been called the "soccer war" (Eitzen and Sage 1993).

In the United States, fan violence has erupted in all professional team sports, trickled down to the university campus, and resulted in strict regulations imposed at many high school athletic contests. This problem alone may be one of the most significant aspects of the debate to remove sports from schools. The fear that competitive athletic events may promote aggression, confrontations, and acts of violence has many in the athletic world concerned. But the question remains as to whether the sport itself supports violence or are the events merely settings within which fans participate in behaviors that are aspects of the greater social context in which they live.

Fan violence in the United States was elevated to a new level on September 19, 2002, after an incident at Comiskey Park in Chicago. During the ninth inning of a game between the Chicago White Sox and the Kansas City Royals, a fifty-four-year-old man and his fifteen-year-old son jumped a low wall to enter the playing field and attacked the Royal's first-base coach, Tom Gamboa. The entire Royal's dugout emptied as the players rushed to their coach's aid. Royal's players and White Sox security overpowered the two men, who were eventually handcuffed, arrested, and charged with aggravated battery. Gamboa escaped with a few cuts and a bruised cheek, but the event is no less disturbing for its lack of serious injury. A folded-up pocket knife, which had fallen out of one of the two fans' pockets, was found on the ground near the scene; this compels the professional sports world to take the matter seriously.

One of the saddest details of this story is that the fifty-four-year-old man had brought six children to the ballpark that day. Some were his children, and the others were relatives. It can only be estimated how many parents and their children were in attendance that day to share in the American ritual of Major League Baseball. For the parents who remained in their seats and enjoyed the game with their children, the lessons learned from the confusing experience probably would be difficult to describe.

The *Chicago Sun Times* (Ginnetti and Kiley 2002) reviewed the history of similar incidents, beginning in 1886.

> July 11, 1886: A beer mug strikes umpire George Bradley during a riot in the sixth inning of the second game of a double-header in Cincinnati.
>
> October 9, 1934: The Cardinals' Joe Medwick slides hard into Mickey Owen at third base for a triple during game seven of the World Series in Detroit. Fans throw tomatoes at Medwick when he takes his position in left field for the bottom of the inning.
>
> September 16, 1940: After an argument at Ebbets Field that re-sults in the suspension of Dodgers' manager Leo Durocher, a fan punches umpire George Magerkurth.
>
> April 25, 1976: Cubs center fielder Rick Monday rescues the American flag from two fans who are trying to set it on fire in the outfield at Dodger Stadium during the fourth inning of the Cubs' 5 to 4 10-inning loss to Los Angeles.
>
> August 27, 1986: California Angel's first baseman Wally Joyner is hit in the arm by a knife thrown from the upper deck at Yan-kee Stadium but is unharmed.
>
> April 30, 1993: A spectator stabs Monica Seles, the top-ranked woman tennis player, in the back during a changeover at the Citizen Cup in Hamburg, Germany; she misses the rest of the tennis season.
>
> September 28, 1995: Cub's reliever Randy Myers is charged by a twenty-seven-year-old bond trader who runs out of the stands at Wrigley Field in Chicago. Myers sees the man coming, drops his glove, and knocks him down with his forearm.
>
> December 23, 1995: Fans at Giant Stadium hurl dozens of snow-balls at the Charger's sideline, interrupting a game between San Diego and New York. One snowball knocks San Diego equipment manager Sid Brooks unconscious.
>
> September 24, 1999: A twenty-three-year-old fan attacks Hous-ton right fielder Bill Spiers at Milwaukee Stadium. Spiers ends up with a welt under his left eye, a bloody nose, and whiplash.
>
> October 3, 1999: A metal object thrown from the stands at Mile High Stadium in Denver hits Broncos cornerback Dale Carter in the cheek, causing blurred vision and a bruise.

Note that 50 percent of the incidents cited here happened within the last ten years, which might suggest that these kinds of incidents are becoming more common. Whatever the reason, the professional athletes or coaches involved were briefly transformed from entertainer to victim—victims of inappropriate fan behavior, often classified as violence.

To leave the professional realm for a moment, it seems that coaches in particular have become the victims of violence more than other participants. Mike Davenport reports in the *Washington College Press* that many dark examples of violence toward coaches finds them unprepared for the hazards they may be facing:

- A high school football coach is knocked to the ground and severely beaten by the father and uncle of one of the high school players. The coach's sin: his team lost the game.
- An athlete's parent beats a forty-year-old ice hockey coach unconscious, in front of the coach's children, after practice. The coach later died.
- A rowing coach is stabbed to death at practice. His killer, a twenty-three-year-old athlete, was one of thirty rowers at a training camp. The killer tried to escape, but his car plunged into a lake. Fellow rowers caught him, and he was subsequently arrested.
- A Virginia high school basketball coach was shot in the stomach by a fourteen-year-old student at school.
- A professional basketball player chokes his coach at practice; he returns fifteen minutes later to attack the coach again and threatens to kill him.

It is clear that the disappointment, frustration, and anger that can result from athletic competition are often not dealt with appropriately. One study considered predictors of verbal intimidation, physical intimidation, and physical violence by male high school athletes. Among the most significant findings is that the coaching component clearly was associated with all three problem areas. More specifically, the author suggests that factors involved in staging the event, "like pep rallies, team cheers, and school atmosphere, coupled with a coach who berates officials throughout the game, may create a context in which intimidation and violence are viewed by athletes as appropriate" (Shields 1999, 517). Intimidation and violence are often perceived to be a "part of the game," but recall that these are learned behaviors—most often learned implicitly and part of a hidden curriculum, but learned never the less. If sport is to be recognized for its educational value, we must encourage young athletes to respect authority figures and enforce discipline, moral development, and good sportsmanship. Perhaps the question becomes this: can all these lessons be learned collectively, good and bad? Can a coach implicitly teach that violence is appropriate while explicitly espousing character development?

The issue of fan violence cannot be presented without addressing the alcohol consumption at sporting events. Most agree with and support the position that any alcohol consumption should be prohibited at sport events or related programs where adolescents are involved. This includes youth and high school sport programs. Nonetheless, many believe that adults have the right to consume alcoholic beverages responsibly at sporting events at the college and professional level. The selling of alcohol during college athletic events is not prohibited at most schools, yet the selling of alcoholic beverages on campuses is. Therefore, tailgating before and after college football games has become popular for several reasons, of which drinking is just one. When a sporting event takes place off campus, when private stadiums and areas are rented for use by a college team, alcohol is usually available. Because of the availability of alcohol before, during, or after sporting events, abuses often take place and present problems both for other fans and for security. In some recent incidents, not unlike the Comiskey incident, the problems are serious. In the December 22, 2001, issue of *Pittsburg Post Gazette*, Mark Madden reviews one such incident. During an NFL game at Heinz Stadium, fans began to throw snowballs at the officials following a few controversial calls. This quickly escalated to the throwing of beer bottles as the officials ran for safety. Madden's take on the situation suggests that "when fans pelted the field with bottles Sunday at Cleveland—and Monday at New Orleans—the problem wasn't bad calls by the officials. The problem wasn't lax stadium security. The problem wasn't a few deranged individuals. The problem wasn't selling beverages in bottles. The problem was the beverage itself. The problem was alcohol" (Madden 2002). Many share the belief that alcohol abuse, which results in intoxicated fans, is the source of the problem, but the controversy continues. Should all alcohol consumption be eliminated at sporting events? Should the consumption be strictly regulated, as is now the policy at English soccer matches? Should alcohol consumption remain the same with the burden of control remaining with event security? The issues are important within the context of sport and education because young fans learn about violence and alcohol use when they attend sporting events.

Jennifer McGurgan, staff writer for *Orion,* provides an example of lessons to be learned at NFL games in the March 29, 1995, issue. First she documents the violence at a 1994 Rams versus Raiders game: "Fourteen people were arrested, 55 people were ejected, and police counted at least 26 altercations." Her interview with a Chico State senior who was in attendance drives home the point, and she includes this quote from the interview: "I love to grab my dad's binoculars and watch all the fights going on during the fourth quarter. ... My dad would get mad [more appropriate word choice inserted] that I wasn't watching the game, but the fights were so great. You would see 25 people all over each other and five cops trying to break them apart" (McGurgen 1995, 1). Some might argue that for a college senior, the experience may not be that detrimental, but a large number of adolescents attend college and professional sporting events. Don't parents have the right to take their children to such events and be assured that these negative scenarios are the exception instead of the rule?

SHOULD SPORT BE ELIMINATED FROM SCHOOL SETTINGS?

Sport as Religion

As an introduction to this section, and as a means to counterbalance what might appear to be my bias against many aspects of sport, I now present the "sports creed," "Great Sport Myth," or "Sport as Religion" phenomenon.

> The Great Sports Myth ... is a fiction sustained and built up by ... the news-gatherers and other professional sports uplifters ... who tell us that competitive sport is health-giving, character-building, brain-making and so forth ... They imply more or less directly that its exponents are heroes, possessed of none but the highest of moral qualities; tempered and steeled in the great white heat of competition; purified and made holy by their devotion to ... sport. Thanks to (coaches and sportswriters), there has grown up in the public mind an exaggerated and sentimental notion of the moral value of great, competitive sport spectacles. ... Why not stop talking about the noble purposes which sports fulfills and take them for what they are? In short, let us cease the elevation of sport to the level of a religion. (Tunis 1928, 24)

I include this extract to document that it was about eighty-five years ago that the notion of sport as a religion was first presented. Admittedly, when first reading similar accounts I assumed that this reference of sport to religion was a modern agenda item in our ideological society. Tunis's words regarding the elevation of sport, written in 1928, humbled me. Who was I to speak about, and often against, many of the most popular tenants of this "religion"? And don't think that this Tunis was a lone nutcase. Edwards and other current sports writers and theorists are proponents of this position as well. In this text, I attempt to present facts, research findings, various organizations' positions, and documentation against which readers can weigh current perspectives. It may seem like a one-sided argument against many of the aspects of sport that are held most sacred, but the ideological character of a creed that claims "sport is a religion" is embedded both explicitly and implicitly in every discussion on the nature of sport, and I would add justifiably so.

Edwards (1973) reminds us that the majority of social beliefs are, to some degree, ideological and normative-expressive of what should be (including desires, wishes, needs, and hopes). Therefore, these beliefs are not true or untrue but are largely symbolic—they express or stand for something other than what is reality. Therefore, to attempt to dismantle or merely confront such belief systems often does not accomplish much. We must come to accept that the fundamental approach to the institution of sport has been one that "attributes consequences to beliefs without much consideration of the correspondence between these beliefs and objective reality" (Edwards 1973, 318).

Furthermore, these beliefs are grounded in the culture of American society. Edwards presented the aspects of sport that have allowed us to compare it to religion in 1973; Novak did the same in 1994 in his book *The Joy of Sports*. The following is a compilation of their work as well as examples provided by others. The comparison is compelling.

- Sport is based on a formal body of beliefs, accepted by faith by great masses of people from every socioeconomic level, that are primarily stated in the form of perceived attributes (sport builds character, competition is good, there is no glory without pain, winning is the ultimate expression of success).
- Sport has its "saints." Mostly men who have achieved virtual immortality in the world of sport, and often in society, enshrined in a "hall of fame" (Jim Thorpe, Knute Rockne, Vince Lombardi, Bath Ruth, Babe Didrikson Zaharias).
- Sport has its patriarchs in the form of coaches, managers, and administrators who have a controlling influence over the or-

ganization and delivery of sport (Pat Riley, Bobby Bowden, Pierre de Coubertin).

•» Sport has its "gods"—those stars and superstars who have tremendous influence over the masses (Michael Jordan, Tiger Woods, Mia Hamm).

•» Sport has its scribes—sport reporters, broadcasters, and writers have an overwhelming responsibility to record its history and present the day-to-day developments, both the accolades and the crises (Howard Cosell, Dick Vitel, Al Michaels).

•» Sport has its "true believers" in the form of fans (fanatics). Fans emerge from the masses; some ex-athletes or alumni are among the flock that attends sport events, "hoping not only to share vicariously in the thrill of victory but to find reaffirmation of the values that give meaning to their own personal struggles" (Edwards 1973, 262).

•» Sport has its shrines, the various halls of fame dedicated to specific sports.

•» Sport has its "houses of worships" —stadiums, arenas, gyms, pools, tennis complexes, and Olympic venues are places where millions congregate to bear witness to the manifestation of their faith.

•» Sport has its "symbols of the faith." From the trophies to the various pieces of equipment and clothing that bear the symbols of the various teams, these symbols can spark emotion by their sheer presence.

•» Sport involves rituals and celebrations. There are various organized sets of procedures to follow, often unspoken, while watching or participating (the coin toss, the announcing of the starting line-ups, the organ-led chants).

•» Sport, like a religion, can be intensely personal as well as communal in practice.

•» Sport has the power to teach. As has been pointed out, many lessons are explicit and many are not.

Taken as a whole these aspects of sport compel all of us, not just those of us who consider ourselves "members of the faith," but society at large to accept that sport is a force, a power, a phenomenon that most often is taken very seriously—and should be. As Sheed (1995) points out, sport is not necessarily a force for good, but it is indeed a force. It is such a powerful force that it tells people not only about themselves as individuals but also about the society within which sport is pursued.

Overemphasis on Sports in Schools

In the United States, sport and education have been through the process of dating and marriage. Initially, the union was energetic, supportive, and favorable to all. Years ago, the marriage allowed some of the union's unfavorable realities to surface, which precipitated research efforts (counseling) in an attempt to isolate the problems and promote solutions. Most recently the question of divorce has been raised. Should sport be eliminated from the school setting? This question speaks specifically to high school, secondary school, and interscholastic programs. It is without question that the union is strong. Virtually every secondary school in the country provides an interscholastic sports program for its students. But can the marriage survive the seemingly insurmountable problems that continue to increase in intensity? Most would argue that the sport program, along with other school-sponsored extracurricular activities and clubs, complements the school setting by providing the opportunity for its students to learn life lessons that they cannot learn in the classroom. Yet a growing number of critics believe that sport and education are incompatible. The most specific aspect of the criticism is that sport detracts from the educational goals—the academic achievement—of the school system. Are high school students obtaining a quality education that ensures their success in American society and provides them with the foundation to be successful at the college level? Many of our American high schools are failing to meet this basic goal. For those that do, one can ask whether academic achievement could be further enhanced without the powerful distraction and competition for resources that sport brings to the learning environment.

It should be made clear that the critics of sport in the educational setting are not critics of sport per se. To the contrary, many are strong advocates of sport for its social and educational value but question its place in the educational setting, citing the significant problems that have resulted. In fact, many critics believe that more children and young adults would benefit from the sport experience if it were separated from the formal educational system. Remember that the interscholastic "varsity" model is elitist, supporting participation for only the best. The "best" usually translates into about 10 percent of the total student enrollment.

Eliminating the interscholastic sport program would not eliminate sport. Programs in the community could replace it, allowing access for more students, a model that many nations around the world support. Siedentop (2001) provides an overview of the Sport of All movement, introduced in 1966 by the Council of Europe. In 1978, the council created a document that outlined its principles. Article One states, "The practice of physical-education and sport is a fundamental right for all" (Siedentop 2001, 158). The goal of this movement is sport participation within a structure funded by government. In the United States, our public schools are funded by the government, where access to sport participation is reserved for the elite. One could argue that U.S. community programs and private organizations allow for participation for all; however, cost becomes the prohibiting factor for many. The private sector does provide endless opportunity for participation in sport, but in a for-profit structure it becomes a system that provides participation primarily for the privileged. The Sport for All movement is being realized by many nations throughout the world. The Norwegian system, called Trim, has been adopted by Germany, Japan, the Netherlands, Sweden, and Switzerland, and Australia and Mexico are developing similar programs (Siedentop 2001).

The acceptance of this movement in other parts of the world is understandable because interscholastic sport as we know it is for the most part exclusive to the United States. Canadian and Japanese schools are moving toward the American model, but community athletic clubs that are most often funded by a combination of the state and private sector provide organized sports for adolescents and young adults in most countries. Therefore, the problems within the U.S. educational system in relation to the influence of sport upon academics are unique. Our model lacks a corresponding system to allow for comparisons and necessary improvements.

Probably the most significant aspect of sport at the high school level, used both to support and contradict the union of sport and education, is the emphasis that sport receives within this particular setting. It is without question that sport has a tremendous impact on school culture. In fact, sociologists have recognized for decades that varsity sports are among the most important social activities that high schools sponsor (Coakley 1994). Consider the athletes when you were a high school student. How were they treated? What level of recognition did they receive? What status were they granted? Few could honestly dispute that being a varsity athlete generally rewards students with membership in the highest social circle. Eitzen and Sage (1993) refer to the athlete as having high status in the school system and tending to have the "conservatism of the privileged class." Recognition from peers, faculty, staff, administration, and community members is often accepted without question, especially for male varsity athletes in high-profile sports.

This phenomenon, which most of us have witnessed either first-hand or as observers, has been well documented and studied for years, and Coakley (1994) provides a review of the research and the significance of this issue. A 1985 study specifically asked male students how they would like to be remembered after graduation. Most frequently, they chose "athletic star" over "brilliant student." Studies including female students did not offer such compelling results. The research suggests that the relationship between being popular and being an athlete is most significant for male students. A similar study of Canadian high school students found that they are similarly concerned with popularity among their peers; however, Canadian students place academics before athletics in their hierarchy of values (Eitzen and Sage 1993). These findings are significant in addressing the overemphasis placed on sport in U.S. high schools.

The status athletes enjoy affects the entire school culture in that it typically provides other, non-sport-related benefits within school as well as social settings. Other students may perceive that, because of the ways that athletes act and are treated, they are allowed special privileges or even that they "run the school." Herein lies the controversy. Has this status, which directly or indirectly affects every student in the school, been earned, or is it a privilege imposed and perpetuated by those who value athletics over academics? Many might argue that these elite athletes, who are hardworking and dedicated and who make considerable sacrifices for the school deserve this status. Opponents would argue that within the educational setting of the high school, athletic accomplishments should not be awarded over academic achievement. In fact, what resentment can surface and divide the student body in response to the perception of this unearned popularity? One should not easily dismiss that the primary targets of the Columbine School shootings were athletes and popular students. The impact of sport on the school culture is significant and not without problems. From a sociologist's viewpoint, this impact raises questions related to values, morals, and behaviors. Coakley (1994) asks, "Do they influence how students evaluate one another or how they think about social life and social relations?" (p. 390) If being an athlete or even associated with athletics, like cheerleaders and poms, results in higher social status within the high school, what implicit message does this teach when athletic achievement is awarded over academic achievement? One might suggest that the award system is a student construct, that adult and administrative award systems would be more appropriate; but to the adolescent, the student construct will generally take precedence.

The U.S. interscholastic sport system is widely supported and has become an accepted aspect of the high school experience. For most, the pure experience of being part of team, being with friends at practice and games, working toward a common goal, attaining high levels of fitness, and experiencing competition that results in joyful victories or painful losses is the value attached to sport participation. School administrators and board members support sport programs because of their social values, believing that schools should teach individuals to be disciplined, follow rules, work hard, set goals, and respect others. Realizing these values is not guaranteed, but sport provides an additional opportunity to achieve them. Nonetheless, it is the collective good experienced by the entire school that is most often discussed in relation to the educational setting. School spirit is the first benefit that comes to mind. This cohesive force that is created within a school and its community around the varsity team is seen as an invaluable asset. It is apparent that regardless of race, occupation, religion, or gender, members of the school and the community coalesce in their support for the high school team against the opposition. Eitzen and Sage (1993) also believe that sports can be a cohesive force between generations, making reference to the opportunity for adults to empathize with youth in their struggles during competition and to take pride in victories.

Aside from the impact of sport on the school culture, finances have become a significant issue in considering whether sport should be eliminated from the educational setting. In 2002 and 2003, the most significant problems facing schools at all levels, but particularly the high school, are projected budget deficits. School districts across the country are fighting losing battles as they attempt to pass referendums that would increase property taxes to more appropriately address the financial needs of the schools. Throughout the United States, schools receive their funding through local property taxes. Schools in the most affluent areas, serving the highest socioeconomic groups, have the most money to operate. It has always been a reality that our urban schools routinely attempt to provide quality education to their students with half of the money per student that suburban schools have available to them. This financial crisis has penetrated suburban schools as well, however. Property tax caps and mandated programming, imposed by the federal government, have resulted in a structure that forces schools to spend money on programs without financial assistance from the forces that imposed them while facing freezes in local financial support. This is occurring at a time when the U.S. economy is weak and unemployment is rising. Average Americans are uncertain about future finances and are reluctant to vote to increase property taxes, even though they believe in supporting local schools. Without the increase in property taxes, schools are faced with significant budget deficits. Cutting expenditures is the only answer, and this most often means cutting programs. What programs should be cut? School districts are asked to decide to increase class size or eliminate band, decrease the number of advanced placement classes or make cuts in the athletic program. This situation asks administrators, faculty, parents, and students what they most value. What budget cuts in the athletic program will a town like Odessa, Texas, allow, a town where "football stood at the very core of what the town was about. ... It had nothing to do with entertainment and everything to do with how people felt about themselves" (Bissinger 1990, 237)?

In schools across the country where athletics receives overwhelming support from the community and administration, what cuts have been made in the academic programs available to all students in an effort to maintain a highly competitive athletic program? In response to this situation, some schools are considering taking money from private sponsors. Vernon Hills became the first Illinois school district to sell the naming rights to their stadium. This Chicago suburban school district sold the rights to Rust-Oleum for $100,000 (Your Turn 2002). Proponents of such activity realize that it provides the much-needed funds for cash-strapped districts, but critics are against the advertising and implications of endorsement (Your Turn 2002). Where else can a school district get the $1.8 million to build a stadium? It is unfortunate that Americans are faced with these complex questions, which have far-reaching implications.

Finances aside, research to address whether academics and athletics can coexist, conducted by the Brookings Institute as well as the University of Oregon, suggests that sport does not appear to undermine academic success within the high school setting. Specifically, the Brookings Institute researchers found that at top-ranking sport schools, students score about the same on state reading and math tests as students at other schools. The researcher, Tom Lovelace, cautions school districts, "Think twice before you eliminate sports. There could be a benefit in team sports in building an ethos of excellence at the school" (in Schouten 2002). These findings are encouraging, but additional research should be conducted to document the benefits and detriments of high-profile interscholastic programs at the high school level.

To underscore the scope of the issues high school sport programs face, I refer to Polidoro (2000), who discusses pivotal social forces and their relation to "persistent and historical problems" that have directly or indirectly influenced physical education and sport. Ten problems have been identified as persistent professional concerns. It is number eight that speaks most specifically to the issue of sport in educational settings because it addresses the relationship of the different levels of sport to each other. It states, "The eighth professional concern is the perplexing matter of amateur, semiprofessional, and professional sport.

The relationship of these three subdivisions of sport to one another, to the educational system, and to the entire culture must be fully understood before improvements can be made in the light of changing circumstances" (Polidoro 2000, 169). The U.S. structure that supports the development of the professional athlete, particularly at high-visibility sports, through the public educational system is not fully understood. As this and previous chapters have attempted to illustrate, the levels of U.S. sport are significantly interrelated. The professional system drives the collegiate system, which in turn drives the interscholastic system. The problems of the interrelationship between these levels were actually realized in 1927 when Amos Alonzo Stagg stated, "The day boys start playing football with one eye on the college and the other on professional careers, the sport will become a moral liability to the schools" (in Koehler 1995, 159). In a four-part series on high school sports, *Sports Illustrated* (Wolff 2002) discusses the "changing world of our young athletes." Part one speaks to the overspecialization that athletes who are focused on that college scholarship are forced to endure. The three-sport athlete is becoming rare as boys as well as girls give up a sport they love to train year-round in one they believe will get them noticed by college recruiters (Wolff 2002). Koehler (1995) believes that high school coaches and counselors are an important part of the developing liability and that they can work together to steer students away from abusive college programs. In the end, external-level influence and the problems it creates for our educational system must be better understood.

Role Conflict: Coach versus Teacher

One significant liability of including sport in the educational setting, particularly in high schools, is the resulting role conflict that often plagues the varsity coach who is also a member of the faculty. This situation evolves for several reasons. Most states mandate that the varsity or head coach at a public high school must hold a state teaching certificate and be a full-time employee of the school. This mandate is in place to ensure that the coach has the necessary qualifications and training and that he or she be held accountable to the school district. The school district therefore hires coaches to teach, and they are paid a significant salary to fulfill this primary role. A full teaching load can require the teacher to prepare for and deliver lessons for up to five hours of the seven-hour school day. Coaches receive a stipend to compensate them for the responsibilities and resulting demands of selecting, training, preparing for the competitions, and numerous additional duties for the team they are assigned. In essence, one person is taking on the responsibilities of two full-time positions. It is not uncommon for coaches to spend twelve hours per workday at school. On game days, their schedule demands even more hours. The time demands are typically not the most controversial aspect of the dilemma, however. The teacher-coach must prepare both for teaching classes and for practice or competition. Developing engaging, creative lessons that provide current material is a daunting task in itself. Analyzing the skill level and capabilities of players and strategizing offenses and defenses can be equally overwhelming. When and how is this accomplished? Conflict arises between fulfillment of the two roles, and the result is what has been termed "role conflict." One might consider it obvious that the primary responsibility of the coach-teacher should be that of teacher, the role in which he or she interacts with a greater percentage of the student body. Within our culture, however, coaches at all levels are intensely scrutinized for the performance of their team on the playing field. In comparison, their teaching performance remains virtually unnoticed. Coaches do teach a variety of subjects at a variety of levels, but because of the nature of the discipline, many teach physical education. A stereotype of the teacher-coach plagues the secondary school physical education professional. Siedentop (2001) describes this stereotype as

> the teacher-coach who "throws out the ball" during physical education class and spends his or her time on the sidelines working on plays for that afternoon's interscholastic team practice. Then, at 3:30 P.M., this unenthusiastic teacher turns into a dynamic coach, with a well-prepared practice plan. During the physical education class, our stereo-typical teacher-coach does little interacting, except to reprimand students who misbehave. During the afternoon practice, the same person is highly interactive, providing specific skill feedback and encouragement to players. (p. 276)

It goes without saying that this stereotype is unfair to the many teacher-coaches who do an excellent job meeting the demands of both roles. Unfortunately, many do live up to the stereotype.

There is an abundance of evidence and research that documents the existence of "role-conflict" (Chu 1981; Sage 1987). This is not a new phenomenon, nor does it seem that a resolution to the situation is at hand. Consider the additional demands of today's youth, elementary, or high school coach. Parents and students expect more from teachers and coaches than they did in the past (Coakley 1994). We expect these professionals to be experts in their specific sport, but today they must have at least adequate knowledge of nutrition, supplementation, weight management, pubescent strength training, eating disorders, and a variety of emotional and psychological concerns. Considering the serious situations confronting these professionals, it is no wonder that the number of teachers who wish to coach has decreased. To support those that remain, volunteers from the community are often called on to assist with the demands of the programs. Many do an excellent job, but the situation increases the likelihood that children are placed in the hands of less-qualified, even inappropriate adults.

The teacher-coach role does permit the regulation of qualifications and screening of these individuals for behaviors that are unacceptable for working with children. Professionals in schools settings are screened for drug use, psychiatric problems that may affect their abilities, and criminal activity. These safeguards are important when considering the potential employment of any individual in a school setting, but may be particularly critical when one considers the enormous responsibility and autonomy that coaches have in both elementary and high schools.

Teacher-coach role conflict takes place within the confines of the school setting, but another problem that these professionals face—family-role conflict—may be another reason we lose quality professionals from our coaching ranks. Coaches who are spouses and parents often work evenings and weekends, missing out on the normal activities of a traditional family. It is not unusual for coaches to miss their own children's athletics events, school plays, and musical recitals. One might argue that it goes with the job, just as other adults work grueling hours in the corporate world, but the strain that results and the pressures placed on the marriage and family cannot be dismissed. The coach-family conflict is probably one of the reasons female high school coaches drop out of coaching more frequently than their male counterparts (Mathes 1982, as cited in Coakley 1994). Spouse support and negotiated family time is essential as the teacher-coach tries to manage the demands of the profession. The reality is that something has to be sacrificed within the current system. Obviously, a system that allows teachers to teach their classes without the additional coaching responsibility would be a better system, but is the price of eliminating sport from the school setting too high to pay?

The overemphasis of sport in the high school setting, its financial implications, as well as the role conflict that results from asking teachers to take on coaching responsibilities are among the most significant issues that should encourage consideration of whether our educational system would benefit from the elimination of sport. The majority of Americans would likely support continued efforts to resolve the problems embedded in the present system rather than eliminating sport from our schools. Resolving the issues is a goal for many of us who realize the value of youths' sport participation.

REFERENCES

American Association for Health, Physical Education, Recreation, and Dance. (2002, February 6). Press release. Retrieved from http://www.aahperd.org/naspe/template.

American Association for Health, Physical Education, Recreation, and Dance. (2002, June 10). Press release. Retrieved from http://www.aahperd.org/naspe/template.cfm?template=ayso.html.

American College of Sports Medicine. (1993). "Current comments from the American College of Sports Medicine: Prevention of sport injuries of children and adolescents." *Medicine and Science in Sport & Exercise* 25(8): 1–7.

American Society of Exercise Physiologists. (n.d.). http://www.asep.org.

American Volleyball Coaches Association. (n.d.). Retrieved from http://www.avca.org/sportmed.

Bailey, W., and T. Littleton. (1991). *Athletics and Acaademe: An Anatomy of Abuses and a Prescription for Reform*. New York: Macmillan.

Barker, S. (2002). The personality theory in coaching. *Coach and Athletic Director* 72(1): 11–12.

Bigelow, B. (2000). Is your child too young for youth sports or is your adult too adult? In *Sports in Schools: The Future of an Institution*, John R. Gerdy, editor. New York: Teachers College Press.

Bissinger, H. G. (1990). *Friday Night Lights: A Town, a Team, and a Dream*. Reading, MA: Addison Wesley.

Carr, C., Dimick, K., and Kennedy, S. (1990). Alcohol use among high school athletes: A comparison of alcohol use and intoxication in male and female high school athletes and non-athletes. *Journal of Alcohol and Drug Education* 36: 39–43.

Chu, D. (1981). Origins of teacher/coach role conflict: a reaction to Massengale's paper. In *Sociology of Sport: Diverse Perspectives*, S. L. Greendorfer and A. Yiannakis, editors. West Point, NY: Leisure Press.

Crosset, T. W. (2000). Role Model: A Critical Assessment of the Application of the Term to Athletes. In *Sports in Schools: The Future of an Institution*, John R. Gerdy, editor. Williston, VT: Teachers College Press.

Curry, B. (2000). The Pedestals Are Vacant. In *Sports in Schools: The Future of an Institution*, John R. Gerdy, editor. Williston, VT: Teachers College Press.

Difiori, J. (1999). Overuse Injuries in Children and Adolescents. *The Physician and Sportsmedicine* 27: 1.

Edwards, H. (1984). The collegiate arms race: Origins and implications of the "Rule 48" controversy. *Journal of Sport and Social Issues* 8(7): 195–209.

Ewing, M., and Seefeldt, V. (1991*). Participation and Attrition Patterns in American Agency-Sponsored and Interscholastic Sports.* East Lansing: Michigan State University, Institute for the Study of Youth Sport.

Ginnetti, T., and Kiley, M. (2002). Attack prompts changes. *Chicago Sun Times,* September 21, p. 110.

Gober, B. E., and B. D. Franks. (1988). Physical and Fitness Education of Young Children. *JOPERD.*

Greenspan, E. (1983). *Little Winners: Inside the World of the Child Sports Star.* Boston, MA: Brown & Benchmark.

Hoch, D. (2001). A sportsmanship self-test. *Coach and Athletic Director* 71(4): 6–7.

Koehler, M. (1995). Student athletes and high schools: Let's shift the focus. *Clearing House* 69(3): 158–159.

Kozal, J. (1992). *Savage Inequalities.* New York: Harper Collins.

Kretchmar, R. S. (1994). *Practical Philosophy of Sport.* Champaign, IL: Human Kinetics.

Madden, M. (2001). Alcohol is the root of fan violence. Retrieved on October 2, 2002, from http://www.post-gazette.com/sports/columnists/20011222 madden1222p6.asp.

Mangan, J. (1981). *Athleticism in the Victorian and Edwardian Public School.* London: Cambridge University Press.

Manning, A. (2002). Teenagers' steroid use "at all-time high." *USA Today.* Retrieved December 17, 2002, from http://www.usatoday.com/sports/bbl/2002-97-11/special-steroids2.htm.

Matheson, G. (2001). Are we losing the injury-prevention battle? *The Physician and Sportsmedicine* 29: 6.

McGurgen, J. (1995). Athletic events, alcohol have fans fighting in the stands. Retrieved October 2, 2002, from http://orion.csuchico.edu/Archives/Volume34/Issues9/sports/Aeahffistst.html.

National Collegiate Athletic Association. (2002, July). *NCAA Division 1 Manual, 2002–2003.*

Novak, M. (1994). *The Joy of Sports: Endzones, Bases, Baskets, Balls, and the Consecration of the American Spirit.* Lanham, Maryland: Madison Books.

Patterson, C. M. (2000). Athletics and the Higher Education Marketplace. In *Sports in Schools: The Future of an Institution,* John R. Gerdy, editor. Williston, VT: Teachers College Press.

Polidoro, J. R. (2000). *Sport and Physical Education in the Modern World.* Boston: Allyn and Bacon.

Roberts, W. (1998). Keeping sports safe: Physicians should take the lead. *The Physician and Sportsmedicine* 26: 5.

Rohnke, K. (1984). *Silver Bullets*. Dubuque, IA: Kendall/Hunt.

Rubin, A. (1998). Team physician or athlete's doctor? *The Physician and Sportsmedicine* 26:7.

Sage, G. (1987). The social world of high school coaches: Multiple role demands and their consequences. *Sociology of Sport*. 4: 3, 213–228.

Sage, G. (1998). Does Sport Affect Character Development in Athletes? *JOPERD* 69: 1, 15–18.

Schouten, F. (2002). Academics, Athletics Can Co-Exist: Studies Point Out Benefits of Sports. Retrieved December 16, 2002, from http://www.arizonarepublic.com/news/articles/0903edusports03.html.

Schwenk, T. (2000). Alcohol use in adolescents: The scope of the problem and strategies for intervention. *The Physician and Sportsmedicine* 28: 6.

Sheed, W. (1995). Why sports matter. *Wilson Quarterly* (winter): 11–25.

Shields, D., Bredemeier, B., and Power, F. C. (2001). Can youth sport build character? *Zip Lines* 43: 20–23.

Shields, David, Brenda Bredemeier, and F. Clark Power (2001). Can Youth Sport Build Character? *Zip Lines* 43 (summer): 20–23.

Shields, E. W. (1995). Sociodemographic analysis of drug use among adolescent athletes: Observations-perceptions of athletic directors-coaches. *Adolescence* 30: 189–861.

Shields, E. W. (1999). Intimidation and violence by males in high school athletics. *Adolescence* 34: 503–521.

Smith, R., Smoll, F., and Curtis, B. (1978). Coaching behaviors in Little League Baseball. In *Psychological Perspectives in Youth Sports*, F. Smoll and R. Smith, editors. Washington: Hemisphere.

Sperber, M. (2000). *Beer and Circuses: How Big-time College Sports Is Crippling Undergraduate Education*. New York: Henry Holt.

Stoll, S. K., and J. M. Beller (2000). Do Sports Build Character? In *Sports in Schools: The Future of an Institution*, John R. Gerdy, editor. Williston, VT: Teachers College Press.

Struhar, C. (2002). Ten things you don't learn in coaching school. *Coach and Athletic Director* 70(10): 28–29.

Tatum, J. (1979). *They Call Me Assassin*. New York: Everest House.

Taylor, R. (1997). Compensating behavior and the drug testing of high school athletes. *The CATO Journal* 16: 3, 351–364.

Thomas, I. (2001). *The Fundamentals: 8 Plays for Winning at Business and Life*. New York: Harper.

Tunis, J. (1928). *$port$*. New Haven, CT: Quinn and Boden.

Tyrangiel, J. (1992). "Not-so-dumb Jocks. *Time*, April 20.

Watkins, J., and Peabody, P. (1996). Sports injury in children and adolescents treated at a sports injury clinic. *Journal of Sports Medicine and Physical Fitness* 36(1): 58–70.

Wise, L., and Fine, M. (1993). *Beyond Silenced Voices: Class, Race, and Gender in United States Schools.* New York: State University of New York Press.

Wolff, A. (2002). The high school athlete. *Sports Illustrated,* November 18, 74–78.

Your Turn. (October 2002). You Say: Keep Athletics at All Costs. *American School Board Journal* 189(10). Retrieved December 16, 2002, from http://www. asbj.com/2002/10//1002yourturn.

Chapter Four

●◆ Significant Issues and Individuals in Sport

This chapter presents an overview of the significant issues of race and gender, most specifically as we consider their relation to formal athletics in our educational systems. Additionally, I present the history of inclusion of minorities and women into the world of sport, focusing on the major profile sports in the United States. With regard to race, I focus primarily on African Americans because they represent the most predominant minority group in sport and best illustrate the broader societal issues surrounding race and sport. My hope is that the information included in this chapter encourages the reader to think about what specific events have taught us collectively and individually about our society. It is my intent to push readers toward an examination of their beliefs and perspectives regarding race and gender. Each of us recognizes that an individual's beliefs are unique, resulting from their culture and life experiences. Therefore, there is no single right answer or best practice scenario, but a journey that will affect each reader differently—and hopefully move America toward a more just society.

Included in this chapter are lists of prominent African American and female athletes of the twentieth century, as well as a brief list profiling some of the most significant individuals in the world of sport. Athletes or individuals who have had a significant impact on the world of sport are included as well as those who are considered activists for racial or gender equity and those considered advocates for reform that have changed sport. These individuals are included regardless of the context of their sport involvement (youth, high school, college, Olympic, or professional sport) or their type of participation (athlete, coach, teacher, administrator, or fan). The list is not complete but attempts to provide the accomplishments of a select group of individuals who have influenced sport as well as society in general.

RACE

The two major themes that emerge in the literature regarding racial issues and sport in educational settings are (1) educational opportunities versus exploitation of African American athletes and (2) the stereotyping of minorities. Desegregation of sport provided minorities with the opportunity to participate in the sports at which they excelled. This inclusion has not led to the elimination of racism and prejudice, however, with many suggesting that it has led to stereotyping and exploitation. Those courageous athletes, particularly African Americans, were pioneers in the world of sport and did so at a great expense. All experienced inequity, discrimination, and personal insults. Some paid with their lives.

Educational Opportunity or Exploitation?

Most Americans would find it difficult to imagine what the world of sports would be like without African American athletes, but it was not so long ago that the first African Americans "broke the color barrier" and officially joined the rosters of professional teams. When we consider Jackie Robinson's 1947 contract with the Brooklyn Dodgers, integration occurred within the lifetime of many Americans alive today. What we must realize is that sport participation for the African American was only one aspect of the long and painful process in the struggle for civil rights. During the civil rights movement, breaking into the world of sports made a point about the worth, character, ability, and dignity of African Americans in the face of prejudice and imbedded racism. Yet were the doors of opportunity in professional sports and on college campuses opened to African Americans because society realized the self-worth, moral character, and dignity of African Americans? Or was the recruitment and inclusion of these gifted athletes steeped with mere tolerance as owners and coaches considered the potential impact of including minorities on their win-loss records?

It is shameful to acknowledge the circumstances within which college teams initially became integrated. As one courageous coach included an African American on his team, the opposing coach, after observing the physical and mental talents of the athlete, would declare, "We have to get us one of those." Implications for the individual athlete were typically not considered as integration of teams occurred at a surprising rate. In 1948, only 10 percent of college basketball teams had one or more African American on their rosters, in 1962 the percent had increased to 45 percent, and by 1975 92 percent of teams had African American players (Eitzen and Sage 1993). Previously, African Americans competed on historically black college teams and in black conferences, but as predominantly white universities with high-profile teams were looking to boost their rosters with African American talent, visibility and television exposure was a consideration that African American athletes who dreamed of making it to the pros could not ignore. This provided the incentive to attempt the transition into a world where they might find themselves in the extreme minority and attending classes with mostly white students who were privileged to receive a quality K–12 education. The ability of the African American athlete to succeed academically at the institution of higher education was typically not a consideration. Exploitation of these athletes was a serious problem from the day integration of teams occurred.

Predictors of college performance are the Scholastic Aptitude Test (SAT), the American College Test (ACT), and the student's high school grade point average (GPA). Admission to a university of a non-athlete is contingent on a review of these records to determine the plausibility of the student being successful in obtaining the degree the student is seeking. For athletes in general, but particularly for African Americans, academic standards are lowered to allow the student athlete admission so they could compete for the institution. Eitzen and Sage (1993) provide a clear example by describing that at Tulane, undergraduates in 1985 had an average SAT score of 1132, but that the average SAT score for revenue-producing athletes was 648. The report cited includes the fact that 80 percent of all black male athletes and 40 percent of white male athletes in 1977 and 1982 had SAT scores below 700 (p. 139). Consider the disadvantage with which the student athlete is faced when admitted under compromised standards. Now consider this disadvantage complicated by a demanding schedule that Edwards (1984) estimated: during the season, basketball players spend fifty hours and football players as much as sixty hours per week preparing for, traveling to, participating in, and recovering from competitions. Maintaining a minimum GPA to remain eligible to play "for the team" was addressed, as National Collegiate Athletic Association (NCAA) regulations demanded some documentation of progress toward a degree. Graduation rates are available to document the lack of academic success of African American athletes, however, as well as that of athletes in general. With some exceptions that must be recognized as a tribute to coaches such as Mike Krzyzewski at Duke University and Pat Summit at the University of Tennessee, many high-profile programs exploit ill-prepared African American student athletes to ensure success of the program, and not success of the athlete. As cited in Eitzen and Sage (1997), Edwards describes the situation as, "a case of the farmer caring for his turkeys—right up until

Thanksgiving Day. Then it's back to the ghetto, without an education, without a prayer" (p. 325).

Despite the acknowledgment of lowered admission standards and dismal graduation rates, particularly for revenue-producing sports, many would argue that athletic ability can provide students from low-income, underserved communities an opportunity to an education that can lead to financial opportunity and upward mobility. The media is quick to provide examples of African Americans from low socioeconomic backgrounds that have achieved fortune and fame as a direct result of their athletic ability. These athletes, particularly African Americans, are awarded the college scholarship, drafted into the professional arena, and paid incredible amounts of money. This scenario is reality only for a select few, but because of the attention the individuals receive, the media suggests that it is more common that it actually is. To further complicate this illusion for African American youth, Harry Edwards argues that African American families encourage children to aspire to careers in sport as opposed to other available opportunities. For those whose athletic abilities do not qualify them for entrance into the professional ranks, the college scholarship might be their most viable option for attending college. It has been established, particularly for men, that greater percentages of athletes as opposed to nonathletes expect to attend a four-year college. Ideally, even while anticipating a college athletic scholarship, many athletes may be inclined to strive for academic success in high school as they anticipate the demands of college and the opportunities that a degree may provide. As well, many athletes must maintain a minimum GPA even at the high school level to be allowed to compete.

This situation becomes problematic when high school athletes believe that their athletic abilities will propel them into the professional ranks without a college degree, or their specific high school environment allows them to earn academic grades without meeting the academic requirement attached to those grades. Research has documented that high school athletic participation does have positive affects on educational, occupational, and financial success, however. Additionally, research has established that college athletes from low socioeconomic families who compete for their four eligible years do attain a higher occupational status than their fathers did. The most valid indication of whether athletic participation can result in upward mobility is to compare athletes with nonathletes. Eitzen and Sage (1997) summarize the research and suggest that the college athlete can be considered upwardly mobile for three possible reasons: (1) they attain occupational sponsorship from alumni, (2) employers perceive that the athletic experience provides talents that

can be transferred into the business world, (3) the competitive experience of sport may provide competitive drive and interpersonal skills that
facilitate success in the marketplace (p. 313).

Whether athletic participation results in educational opportunity
or exploitation is a question that needs to receive more focused attention and research, and the answer is dependent on several factors, including the specific athlete, sport, and program. The possibility for exploitation of athletes is apparent and may continue to increase as the
"big business" aspect of college athletics intensifies. Yet for the countless numbers of African American athletes who have been awarded college scholarships for their athletic abilities, successfully completed their
academic requirements, and earned degrees, sports might have been
the way to advanced educational opportunity.

Stereotyping

Many currently believe that the sports world has been successful in
eliminating racial barriers for educational and financial opportunity.
Even if opportunity is available, however, we must recognize the problems that exist within sport regarding race. Many may believe that,
whether athletes or spectators, we are all enjoying the same game, so
why can't we all "get along" or "act the same"? Just as male and female
athletes or two male athletes from different family orientations might
play the game differently, however, individuals from different races may
also play the game differently. The attribution model may serve as an example of this. Many athletes are asked, "To what do you attribute your
success?" These athletes are asked to present their individual perceptions regarding what caused their success. Sport psychologists inform
us that the kinds of attributions that individuals make are based on a socialization process that may vary across cultures (Cox 2002). This socialization process teaches us what we learn to value. Cox (2002) notes that
for Iranian children, ability is important regardless of whether they are
successful. In contrast, he notes, American children value effort and intent regardless of ability. Other research supports these differences with
regard to race and suggests that American athletes of European descent
believe that success is something they caused, and because they are in
control of their level of effort, it will likely occur again. This internal perception of success is less evident in African American and Native American athletes.

Differences in orientations will help us understand why athletes,
particularly those not from the dominant culture, do not all play the
game the same way. Individuals from the culture of power in the United

States expect everyone to assimilate to their way of doing things, believing that it is the "right way." All Americans, however, must begin to understand and accept individual difference, especially as they may be attributed to race. As Cox (2002) discusses this issue in regard to sport psychologists' training, he refers to the U.S. census reports that minorities make up 29 percent of the population but that the percent of minority participants in NCAA sports is much higher—68 percent for men's basketball, 57 percent for men's football, and 43 percent for women's basketball.

One of the most visual examples of how individual differences are misunderstood or considered unacceptable is the "touchdown celebration" during professional football games. This issue surfaced during the 2002–2003 National Football League (NFL) season and seemed to fuel fires of racism and prejudice among fans as well as athletes. Some sports writers became critical of the premeditated end-zone dances of athletes like Terrell Owens. Suggesting that the behavior was inappropriate supports the notion that many in the mainstream culture have difficulty accepting behavior that is different from "the norm." This norm is a standard that the white mainstream culture of power has set. Shouldn't individual difference in behavior be accepted as long as it does not interfere with or violate the integrity of the game? Or could these explicit celebrations actually be statements against the imposition of "white" standards on professional athletes? Much more powerful statements have been made in the name of civil rights or in protest of the racism experience by high-profile athletes. To expect talented athletes to compete and then conform to the expectations of others is problematic and supports the notion that individual difference, particularly in terms of race, is not as accepted as much as society would like to believe.

"Stacking" refers to the disproportionate placement of African Americans and other minorities into positions of low centrality (Cox 2002). When stacking occurs, minorities are underrepresented in positions of high task dependence, observability, and visibility on the field of play. To the public, these high-task positions represent leadership and are often considered "thinking" positions in team sports. In football we think of the quarterback. In baseball we think of the pitcher and catcher. Some have suggested that, despite unparalleled speed or acrobatic catches, African American athletes did not possess the intelligence to play these positions. Only a decade ago, documentation of this phenomenon was expressed by the low percentages of African American athletes in these key positions. Eltzan and Sagel (1993) refer to the 1993 Racial Report Card compiled by Lapchick and Benedict, in reporting that in the NFL, where African Americans accounted for 68 percent of the players, only 6 percent of the quarterbacks were African American. Similarly, in Major League Baseball, where 16 percent of the players were African American, 5 percent were pitchers and 1 percent were catchers. To express stacking in terms of the positions in which minorities are over-represented, the report states that in the NFL, 92 percent of the running backs and 88 percent of the wide receivers were African American. Running backs and receivers, although often the most physically talented on the team, are considered the "work horse" positions that are not as mentally demanding as the quarterback! In MLB, 50 percent of the outfielders were African American. More current figures are suggesting that over the last ten years stacking is not as prevalent as it was; however, the reasons for the more appropriate distribution of minorities in leadership positions are questionable. The imbedded prejudice that caused stacking at the lower levels of participation from youth sports, into high school, and then through college may be diminishing, but some would suggest that changes in the game have resulted in less need for these stereotypical decisions. Cox (1994) speaks to the changes in coaching strategies, allowing responsibilities for decision making to shift from the athlete to the coach; quarterbacks are not allowed to call their own plays, coaches rather than the shortstop adjusts the outfielders in baseball, and point guards in basketball receive the plays from the coach.

Only two main concerns regarding racial issues have been discussed in this chapter. The low percentage of minority coaches and administrators is of major concern at all levels within the world of sports. The NCAA, colleges, professional owners, and players unions are all taking a look at hiring practices as well as considering issues of quotas and reverse discrimination. As long as racism and prejudice are embedded in our society, these issues will continue to be challenges faced in athletics.

THE INTEGRATION OF SPECIFIC SPORTS

Baseball

Baseball might be the sport that best epitomizes the racial discrimination and segregation that was part of our history and is still common in the United States today. Even though a few African Americans were members of white baseball clubs in the late 1800s, and some may have seen limited participation at the professional level in the minor leagues, they were basically prohibited from participating in professional Major League Baseball. No event had more significance on the integration of professional sport than the signing of Jackie Robinson in 1946, who on

April 15, 1947, became the first African American to play in a Major League Baseball game for the Brooklyn Dodgers. Even the NFL had formally banned African Americans from playing from 1934 until 1946 (Polidoro 2000). The signing of Jackie Robinson (additional information on Jackie Robinson can be found later in the chapter) by Branch Rickey was seen as the indication that the racial barrier to professional sport had been dismantled, but it also allowed the reality of racism in the United States at the time to be publicly documented in the world of professional sports.

What makes baseball an even more significant representation of racial discrimination in the United States was the formation of the Negro League in 1920, formally the National Association of Colored Professional Baseball Clubs. When the New York Knickerbocker Baseball Club was established, it excluded African American players from its roster; segregation became explicit in 1871 when the National Association of Baseball Players, as an organization, decided to ban "colored" players from their teams. In response, African Americans united to form their own teams and play among themselves. From 1871 to 1947, the League of Colored Baseball Clubs thrived. The founding teams were the Boston Resolutes, New York Gorham Philadelphia Pythians, Norfolk (Virginia) Red Stockings, Cincinnati Crowns, Lord Baltimores, Washington Capital Cities, Pittsburgh Keystones, and Louisville Fall Cities (http://www.cwpost.liunet.edu/cwis/cwp/library/aaitsa/htm).

By 1890, predominantly black colleges formed the Colored Intercollegiate Athletic Association to help develop future African American baseball players. Andrew "Rube" Foster, as a result of his efforts to keep the African American league prosperous, became known as the Father of Black Baseball. His success resulted in the establishment of the Negro National League, which sponsored the Negro World Series in 1926. With the success of Jackie Robinson and the subsequent inclusion of other talented African Americas in professional league teams, the Negro League ceased to exist, but its very establishment made a signficiant impact on the country's history. Great African American baseball players who first played in the Negro League were Leroy "Satchel" Paige, Josh Gibson, Walter "Buck" Leonard, James "Cool Papa" Bell, Ray Dandridge, and Bobby Robinson (http://www.cwpost.liunet.edu/cwis/cwp/library/aaitsa/htm).

Basketball

Dr. James Naismith is famous for the game he developed in 1891 that evolved into what we call basketball. It is considered the fastest growing game ever because it quickly spread across the nation and the world. Played by girls and women from its inception, Dr. Naismith actually married the first women to play the game at Springfield College, in Massachusetts. More than a century later, African Americans often dominate the sport in numbers and in their display of athletic excellence. Novak (1976) provides his interpretation of basketball, which speaks to this issue: "For basketball, although neither invented by blacks nor played only by blacks, came to allow the mythic world of the black experience to enter directly, with minimal change, into American life. The game is corporate like black life; improvisatory like black life, formal and yet casual; swift and defiant; held back, contained, and then exploding, full of leaps and breakaway fluid spirits" (p. 113). Novak (1976) continues to share his interpretation of the game as representing the black experience in the United States as he reviews the deceptive nature of the game. He refers to the fact that every motion of the game is disguised by the use of head feints, ball fakes, picks, backdoor plays, or steals. It is an interesting interpretation of the game, because it might be suggestive of the reality of life for African Americans, a life that in reality is much different from how it appears to outside observers.

With the success of African American players today, it may be difficult for some young people to believe that Jim Crow laws allowed almost complete segregation of teams, at both the college and the professional level. To combat this, the Colored Intercollegiate Athletic Conference was established to promote the game as well as the talents of the highly skilled African American players. Some northern colleges, including Boston University, Detroit University, and Long Island University, did allow African American players before 1950 (http://www.cwpost.liunet.edu/cwis/cwp/library/aaitsa/htm). The professional leagues that were established in 1925 excluded African Americans. Nonetheless, all-black teams evolved outside the leagues; the New York Rens and the Harlem Globetrotters were two well-known professional basketball teams formed for African Americans in the 1920s that toured the country and were responsible for making basketball a true "spectator sport" of unmatched popularity.

During the 1950s and 1960s, African Americans were finally welcomed to play professional basketball. Chuck Cooper became the first African American to play in the National Basketball Association (NBA), followed by Bill Russell, Wilt Chamberlain, Oscar Robertson, and Elgin Baylor.

One of the most significant moments in college basketball came in 1966 as the nation watched Texas Western become the first NCAA champion to start five black players, upsetting top-ranked Kentucky's all-white team in the NCAA final in College Park, Maryland. Texas took the lead midway in the first half and never relinquished it. The significant racial implications were not explicit but touched the hearts and minds of each participant and every observer. The number of African Americans playing at the elite level, whether professional or college, is still an issue that draws attention to the racial concerns of our society.

Boxing

The history of boxing reaches back to early America. Fighting was common on the American frontier, with many conflicts settled through hand-to-hand combat. Boxing as sport, however, was uncommon. The first famous American boxers were both African Americans who made their names in England. The first was William Richmond of Staten Island, New York, whom a British general named Lord Hugh Percy noticed during a fight on the docks with a sailor. Percy commanded the British forces occupying New York during the Revolution. In a number of matches against British soldiers, Richmond was unbeaten, and Percy took him to England in 1777. Known as the Black Terror, Richmond knocked out his first Englishmen in just twenty-five seconds. Not much is known of his career from that time through 1805, when British champion Tom Cribb knocked out the forty-one-year-old Richmond (http://www.bennett boxing.com/history.html). The Cribb verses Richmond fight was publicized for its racial implications, and with Richmond's loss, "the crowd was pleased that a black man had been put in his place" (http://www.cwpost.liunet.edu/cwis/cwp/library/aaitsa/htm). Tom Molineaux, a former slave who trained under Richmond, also fought Cribb. Molineaux knocked Cribb down in the twenty-eighth round, but Cribb was declared the winner because Molineaux was accused of rule violations. The first African American to win the world title was Joe Gans, who created opportunity for other African American boxers by attempting to win American boxing titles. Society mandated that the heavyweight champion of the world remain a white man, however. In the later half of the nineteenth century, boxing became very popular among the white working class in the United States. Jack L. Sullivan dominated the sport from 1882 to 1892, as the world's heavyweight champion from Boston. A black boxer from Australia named Peter Jackson came to American in 1888 with the hope of fighting Sullivan. Even though his talents and success were internationally recognized, Jackson was never given his chance to dethrone the champ. Sullivan, as well as his successor James Corbett, refused to "cross the color line" and fight him. The racism of the time demanded segregation in all walks of life, and sport was no exception.

African American boxers faced segregation until 1937, when Joe Louis won the world championship and became one of the most noted boxers in history. Henry Armstrong, "Sugar" Ray Robinson, Archie Moore, Ezzard Charles, "Jersey" Joe Wolcott, Floyd Patterson, Sonny Liston, Muhammad Ali, and Joe Frazier also won the world champion titles in various weight groups. In the last quarter of the twentieth century, black boxers dominated the sport. "Sugar" Ray Leonard, "Marvelous" Marvin Hagler, Thomas Hearns, Larry Holmes, Michael Spinks, and Mike Tyson are among them ("History of Boxing," n.d.).

Football

Just as baseball was "America's game," football was the "King of Intercollegiate Athletics." The first Rose Bowl was played in 1902. Intercollegiate football experienced integration in 1890 when two African American players became members of Amherst College's football team. The first recorded game between two black colleges was played in 1892 between Biddle University and Livingston College. Shortly after, the Tuskegee Institute in Alabama, Lincoln University in Pennsylvania, Atlanta University, and Howard University in Washington, D.C., were participating in intercollegiate football (Mechikoff and Estes 1998). Most of these schools were considered models for black education at the time.

In 1920, the owners of eleven football clubs organized professional football into the American Professional Football Association (APFA). The first president was Native American Jim Thorpe, who at the time was thought to be the country's greatest all-around athlete. In 1922, with the association in financial distress, it was reorganized and renamed the National Football League (NFL). In 1946, Kenny Washington and Woody Strode became the first African Americans to play professional football (Mechikoff and Estes 1998), often facing significant discrimination. Both men played for the Los Angeles Rams after attending the University of California at Los Angeles. Their names are not well known today because professional football was eclipsed by the enormous popularity of professional baseball at the time. The integration of football did not receive the attention that it did in other sports of the day.

Golf

From its inception in this country, the game of golf has been primarily a "white only" sport in which African American participation amounted to their serving as caddies for the white golfers. Blacks could not join clubs or compete in professional or amateur tournaments, but, as in other sports, this discrimination did not curtail the developing talent and desire African Americans had to compete professionally at golf. In 1926, Robert Hawkins organized African American golfers and staged a tournament; two years later, he founded the United Golf Association (UGA), an organization to further the game of golf among African Americans. A national tournament was conducted each year to determine the best male and female golfers in the country. Women were encouraged to participate in the UGA from its inception, but it was not until 1939 that an organization for women sought affiliation with the UGA. That organization was the Chicago Women's Golf Club (http://www.arga.org/ns_hist.htm).

In 1948, Bill Spiller became the first African American to play in a major Professional Golf Association (PGA) tournament. Charlie Sifford was the first African American golfer to play on the tour as a member; until 1960, he was denied playing privileges by a clause in the rules of the American PGA that permitted only Caucasians to be members (http://www.afrogolf.com/page18.html). In 1975, Lee Elder became the first African American to play in the Masters. Tiger Woods, was the first African American and Asian to win the Masters in 1997; many believe Woods may be the best golfer of all time.

Horse Racing

In colonial America, wealthy landowners in the south showcased their status by the owning, breeding, and racing thoroughbred horses. Care and training of these animals were generally delegated to slaves, and thus many young African Americans became skilled equestrians. Horse racing was among the most popular U.S. sporting event from 1823 until the start of the Civil War, and African American jockeys and trainers were its primary participants. After the war, horse racing surged in popularity, and during the later half of the nineteenth century riding was a physical skill that was seen as a means of upward social and economic mobility for marginalized groups. As a result, jockeys and trainers became the first identifiable African American sportsmen (http://www. cwpost.liunet.edu/cwis/cwp/library/aaitsa/htm). Fourteen of the fifteen jockeys in the first Kentucky Derby, held in 1875, were African American. Oliver Lewis was the winning jockey on Aristides. Isaac Murphy was the most famous African American jockey of the time, riding nearly every famous horse, winning almost every major race, and becoming the first African American jockey to win three Kentucky Derbies (Wiggins 1997). Other African American jockeys that followed in Murphy's footsteps were Monk Overton, Willie Simms, James "Soup" Perkins, Jimmy Lee, Jimmy Winfield, and Marlon St. Julien (http://www.liu. edu/cwis/cwp/library/aatisa). Because of his success on the track, Murphy earned a significant income. It was said that he fit into the white man's world well, but his acceptance was only superficial. Jim Crow laws and the social pressures of the 1890s created a climate of segregation within organized sports, and white athletes in several sports refused to participate in events and competitions in which African Americans were allowed to participate.

NASCAR

The birth of auto racing in the United States was significant in African American sports history. Little was know about the "Gold and Glory" auto races organized by and held for African American drivers who were banned from auto racing at the time. This racing circuit was actually brought to the attention of the nation through a February 16, 2003, ESPN special, "The Forgotten Race." The Gold and Glory Sweepstakes is the name given to the highly celebrated auto racing events for African Americans, held in Indiana and throughout the Midwest during the 1920s and 1930s. Because African Americans could not participate in the Indianapolis 500, William Rucker organized a group of the city's top black civic leaders and several noted white race promoters to create the Colored Speedway Association, the mission of which was "to perpetrate the principles and interest of sportsmanship in race driving and other sports" (Gould 2000). In 1924, the organization announced an event staged at the Indiana State Fairgrounds as part of Indianapolis's Emancipation Day celebration. Six years later, that event, known as the Gold and Glory Sweepstakes, was the largest sporting event for African Americans, often drawing crows in the tens of thousands. Famous drivers were highlighted in the races, most notably Charlie Wiggins, who was respected for his mechanical talents at Indy, but not allowed to race. After his amazing accomplishments at the Gold and Glory races, the *Indianapolis Recorder* dubbed Wiggins "the Negro Speed King." In 1991, Willy T. Ribbs became the first African American to qualify for the Indianapolis 500, which was a historic accomplishment, but it was only the pinnacle of a remarkably rich black racing legacy that preceded Ribbs by nearly seven decades (Gould 2000).

Tennis

In 1957, Althea Gibson became the first African American to win the U.S. women's tennis championship, and she went on to become the first

African American to win Wimbledon. Arthur Ashe was the first African American man to win the U.S. singles title. Because of his powerful influence on the game of tennis and in the sports world, he was considered an activist for social justice. (His story is presented within the prominent figures section of this chapter.) Most recently the domination of the women's game by African American sisters Venus and Serena Williams has proven that tennis is a game open to all races and socioeconomic classes. Nonetheless, many still perceive it as one predominantly for the wealthy.

PROMINENT AFRICAN AMERICAN ATHLETES AND DATES OF THE TWENTIETH CENTURY

1901   Jimmy Winfield wins the Kentucky Derby, becoming one of the best riders in the country.

1904   George Poage wins a bronze medal in the four-hundred-meter hurdles at the Olympics, held in St. Louis.

1908   Jack Johnson takes the heavyweight boxing title away from Tommy Burns.

1920   The National Negro Baseball League is organized.

1921   DeHart Hubbard, a track and field athlete, wins an Olympic gold medal in Paris.

1928   Bojangles Robinson performs in *Blackbirds,* the first of fourteen films, many with Shirley Temple.

1932   An African American team, the New York Rens, defeats the Boston Celtics to win the World Basketball Championship.

1933   Katherine Dunham makes her dance debut in Ruth page's La Guiblesse.

1934   Jesse Owens wins four gold medals at the Berlin Olympics.

1935   Joe Lewis knocks out Max Schmelling; he will hold the heavyweight title for eleven years.

1946   Kenny Washington and Woody Smith become the first African Americans to play professional football.

1947   Jackie Robinson plays first base for the Brooklyn Dodgers.

1948   American Alice Coachman became the first black woman to win an Olympic gold medal.
        Bill Spiller becomes the first African American to play in a major PGA tournament.

1950   Nat "Sweetwater" Clinton is the first African American to sign to play in the NBA.

Chuck Cooper is the first African American to be drafted into the NBA.

1955 Isaac Murphy is the first African American elected to the National Horse Racing Hall of Fame.

1957 Althea Gibson is the first African American woman to appear on the cover of *Sports Illustrated* as a result of her victories in professional tennis.

1958 Alvin Ailey forms his own American Dance Company.

1959 Muhammad Ali defeats Sonny Liston, gaining worldwide attention.

1960 National Baseball Congress names Satchel Paige an all-time outstanding player.

1961 Willie Mays retires from the New York Mets after playing in every All-Star game from 1954 to 1973.

1962 Willie Mays surpasses Babe Ruth's home-run record.

1984 Carl Lewis wins four gold medals at the Los Angeles Olympics; he will win nine gold medals throughout his Olympic career.

1985 Eddie Robinson of Grambling State University becomes the most successful football coach in history.

1990 Michael Jordan leads the Chicago Bulls to their first of six NBA Championships.

1997 Tiger Woods wins the Master's and is chosen Male Athlete of the Year by the Associated Press.

Source: Gates and West (2000). *The African American Century: How Black Americans Have Shaped Our Country.* New York: Touchstone.

GENDER

Sport competition and access to training have been denied to women throughout U.S. history, the result of firmly held beliefs that feminine virtues such as piety, purity, frailty, and submissiveness were not compatible with sport. Many people believed that girls and women should not be pushed physically to the point of extreme intensity that sport participation demanded.

In the 1970s, sport participation for female athletes received increased attention because of their success in the international arena. Now there was evidence that women could perform at intense, competitive levels, particularly in the sports of gymnastics, swimming, and running. As a result, opportunity and equity for female athletes needed to be addressed. The most significant event in relation to women and sport was the passage of Title IX to the *Educational Amendments of 1972*. The ramifications of this legislation on athletic opportunities for girls and women have been overwhelming. Nonetheless, the impact on athletics as a whole, and in particular the effect on boys' and men's sports, has resulted in significant controversy.

Title IX, an extension of the *Civil Rights Act of 1964*, mandated that no person in the United States, on the basis of sex, could be excluded from participation in, be denied the benefits of, or be subjected to discrimination under any educational program or activity receiving federal funding. This forced public schools to provide many more athletic teams for girls and women or allow them to participate on male teams. What many had believed would happen was soon realized. As soon as female athletes were given the opportunity to participate, they did so—and with great enthusiasm. According to the National Federation of State High School Associations, only 294,015 girls participated in high school sports in 1971, compared with 3,666,917 boys. The 1995 figures documented the response to Title IX: 3,536,359 boys and 2,240,461 girls were participating in high school sports (Polidoro 2000). By the late 1970s, public schools and colleges were including women's teams in their programs and hiring female athletic directors, full-time women's coaches, and female athletic trainers. Early on, however, the NCAA saw the implications of this legislation and immediately began an oppositional campaign. The NCAA's statement suggested that the mandates would create a crisis in intercollegiate athletics that would entirely alter the existing programs and would change the entire financial structure of athletics. What the NCAA did not realize was what they were pointing out as potential implications of the legislation was exactly what the legislation had intended. At the time, the existing programs served male athletes. It was not uncommon for programs to spend at little as 1 percent of their total operating budgets to meet the needs of their female athletes. By 1975, the NCAA realized that compliance with Title IX was inevitable, and as a result, it had consumed the governance of women's athletics by 1982, which forced the dismantling of the Association for Intercollegiate Athletics for Women (AIAW). Ten years later, gender equity was still not evident within interscholastic and intercollegiate programs. In 1993, the NCAA Gender-Equity Task Force recommended three significant changes to the existing conditions. Two of the recommendations called for (1) an increase in the number of female athletic scholarships with no increase for male athletes, and (2) equitable opportunities in all areas of athletics, specifically in regard to equipment, facilities, and travel expenses, for example. By themselves, these two recommen-

dations meant significant changes in budgets, but it was the third recommendation that had the most profound impact. It called for the opportunity to participate to be proportional to the percentage of undergraduate enrollment. At most universities, where enrollments were
typically equal or, in many instances, where females outnumbered male
enrollment, either the number of females athletes had to increase dramatically or the number of male athletes had to decrease. Compliance
with this recommendation, referred to as "proportion" was extremely
challenging, especially for schools with football teams that had rosters
of sixty or so men. To comply with Title IX, programs had no choice but
to drop some well-established men's sports. Typically, men's swimming,
gymnastics, and wrestling were the targets. Many argue that male athletes should not have been so profoundly affected; scholarships are no
longer available to many athletes and even the opportunity to compete
no longer exists as a result of Title IX. This scenario is unfortunate, but
establishing gender equity in athletics is a goal that must be realized.
Carpenter (in 2001) cites a 2000 *Wall Street Journal* and NBC poll regarding Title IX: "79% of those polled both knew of Title IX and approved
of it. When asked if they also approved the cutting of men's teams, if no
other way existed to give females a chance to play, 76% said, 'Yes' "(p.
151). In 2003, however, challenges to Title IX are meeting with more support than would be expected given the moral and ethical foundation of
the original legislation. Potential "adjustments" to the legislation have
jolted us back into a reality in which sexual stereotyping is still deeply
imbedded and men dominate the power structures. Siedentop (2001)
states, "Legislation such as Title IX is extremely important in the public,
legal arena, but the moral imperative to rid our culture of these preju-
dices is much more profound and considerably more difficult to
achieve" (p. 384).

Just as racial discrimination is evident in a society where equal
rights for all is a governing principle, so is gender discrimination,
post–Title IX, a reality for most female athletes. Following are a few issues related to gender discrimination.

The Female Physiology

Why does society continue to refer to women and men as opposite
sexes? Christensen (2001) believes that this "is a convenient but sexist
means of separation for a variety of purposes, none of which are supportive of women" (p. 180). This authority also points out that variations
within each sex are far greater than *between* the sexes. It is indisputably
obvious that elite females can physically out perform the vast majority

of the male population. When considering elite performance or ultimate gender capabilities, however, aspects of the male physiology are
optimal for performance. What is most important to provide are facts
that will help dispel myths and assist in the development of programs
for girls and women in educational settings. The following conclusions
are based on research and generally accepted by experts on women
physiology:

- Female athletes can train during menstruation and preg-
  nancy; they may choose to decrease training intensity.
- The menstrual cycle does not impair or enhance performance.
- In comparison with men, women have smaller hearts, less
  hemoglobin, and more body fat, which results in a lower
  VO2 max, which is the ability to consume oxygen.
- In general, men's longer legs, higher center of gravity, and
  faster approaches result in greater jumping performances
- In general, women's shorter limbs and lower muscle mass
  result in less speed
- Females have higher levels of body fat and lower aerobic
  capacities, resulting in a disadvantage in endurance events
  (Christensen, in Cohen 2001).

These considerations explain the differences at the elite level and
confirm the established distinctions documented by world records.
Outside this extremely narrow context, however, girls and women have
the capability to train and achieve levels of performance necessary to
compete with their male counterparts. Programs and policies should be
established based on this general premise.

Homophobia and Lesbians in Sport

Society's association of athleticism with a lack of femininity and les-
bianism is a culturally constructed myth that has subjected female athletes to stereotyping, prejudice, ridicule, embarrassment, and invasion
of privacy, to name a few. Griffin (2001) provides an explanation, "When
viewed through lenses of male superiority and traditional gender roles,
girls and women who excel in sports are threats to a gender system that
insists on separate and unequal social constructions of womanhood
and manhood" (p. 279). In other words, Griffin suggests that using labels
such as "faggot," "queer," "lezzy," or "dyke" have become accepted
means for addressing isolated situations in which individuals transgress

traditional gender boundaries. She continues to remind us that many girls and women, regardless of their athleticism, have difficulty adhering to the culturally constructed standards of beauty and femininity. Yet it is the girl or woman who infringes on the once exclusively male world of sports who is attacked with unjustified acquisitions. Consider lesbians outside of the context of sports. Does society respond with equal contempt?

Stereotypical beliefs about lesbians support prejudice against participation in sports. Prejudice is always based on ignorance, and therefore it is important to attempt to provide answers to questions that surface. Griffin (2001) provides answers to several common questions on this matter. Included is a list to summarize her answers.

- There is no evidence to suggest that association with individuals of different sexual orientations necessarily affects one's personal identity.
- Masculine characteristics are culturally defined, but women possess these characteristics as well. Women who transgress traditional gender-role expectations are often labeled lesbians.
- Statistics on rape, sexual harassment, sexual abuse of power, and other forms of violence against women indicate that male coaches and male athletes pose the greater risk than lesbian athletes.
- Most lesbians in sport do not "come out." They hide their sexual orientations because they fear discrimination and prejudice.
- Many high-profile athletes who are lesbians have played a major role in women's sports. Most are successful and respected for their dedication, leadership, high standards, and ethical performance; therefore, they are good role models.

Psychological and Social Challenges for Female Athletes

It is undisputed that participation in sport is physically beneficial, regardless of gender. It has also been well documented that most children and adolescents in the United States do not participate in regular physical activity. Therefore, any deterrents to sport participation should be confronted and strategies developed to address them. Murray and Matheson (2001) describe which psychological and social factors that female athletes confront may negatively affect their performance. Particularly useful to this text is their suggestions for what parents, teachers, and coaches can do to promote sports and physical activities among girls as well as to remedy challenges to their participation.

- ⇥ Encourage girls to participate in sports and physical activity at earlier ages.
- ⇥ Give girls equal attention.
- ⇥ Give girls equal access and ensure that girls get to play key positions.
- ⇥ See that girls receive appropriate feedback to improve skills and self-confidence.
- ⇥ Intervene in the face of discrimination.
- ⇥ Be aware of girls' motives for sport participation.
- ⇥ Recognize physiological and psychological patterns of disordered eating.

Incorporating these suggestions into sports programming will assist in promotion of safe, happy, and healthy life decisions for female athletes.

Basketball

No other sport tells the story of the challenges and triumphs of female athletics as well as the sport of basketball. Almost immediately after Naismith invented the game, Senda Berenson, a physical education teacher at nearby Smith College, introduced basketball to her female students. Women loved the game because it allowed competition and strategizing. Nonetheless, because of the beliefs about the female athletes' physical capabilities, modifications were made to the game. The court was divided into three equal portions with boundaries that the two players assigned to that area of the court could not cross. This prevented players from running the length of the court, a physical feat most believed women could not sustain. Basketball was very popular among women in the early 1900s, but the public felt the activity was inappropriate, and colleges began to dismantle their collegiate sports programs for women. States began to close women's sports programs in support of the belief that women were too dainty for vigorous physical activity.

The game had gained too much attention, however, and amateur and workplace teams replaced the college teams. Games within the private sector marketed the attractiveness of the payers, who were encouraged to act feminine, wear makeup, and "not sweat too much." One of the most popular teams was an all-black team called the Tribune Girls, with one of the first female basketball stars, Ora Washington (Smith 1998).

What was important about the Tribune Girls is that they played "boys rules" of three players from each team under each basket. Another team that traveled throughout the country to promote the game was the Arkansas Travelers, led by the amazing Hazel Walker. These female traveling teams typically played and defeated the best male teams in the towns. Other high-profile teams were the All-American Red Heads, Hanes Hosiery, and the Hutchinson Flying Queens (Smith 1998). Players from these teams played on the first U.S. team at the world championships held in Santiago, Chile, in 1953, which the United States won. The physical limitations placed on the women's game were slowly eliminated. One version in the 1960s allowed unlimited dribbling and ball stealing, and more than two players from each team were allowed to "rove" the court. (I remember playing with a "rover" at the high school level.)

Finally, in 1971, women gained entry to the game that Naismith invented; any of the five players per team could perform any of the game's skills and could run the entire court (Smith 1998). When Congress passed Title IX, things changed further, because it became illegal to prevent people from participating in any educational group or activity that received government money for support. Today, the participation rates at all levels in women's basketball document the popularity of the game. According to the NFHS 2001 participation survey, basketball remained the most popular sport for high school girls with 444,872 participants (http://www.hfhs.org/Participation/SportsPat01_files/sheet 001.htm). According to the NCAA Participation Statistics Report released in June 2000, the biggest gains were in women's sports, an increase of 6 percent from the previous year, and women's basketball was the most sponsored sport with teams at 1,001 institutions (http://www. ncaa.org/releases/makepage.cgi/research/2000060701re.htm). Women's basketball can be especially exciting at the professional level. With the success of the American Basketball League (ABL) and the Women's National Basketball Association (WNBA), crowds are increasing, player salaries are rising, and many feel that the women's game may soon attain a level to compete with the men's. Many fans admire women's basketball because it is still a team game, without excessive showmanship, that athletes play for the love of the game.

PROMINENT FEMALE ATHLETES AND DATES OF THE TWENTIETH CENTURY

1886   The first women's intercollegiate basketball game takes place between the University of California at Berkley and Stanford.

1900   Tennis player Charlotte Cooper becomes the first female Olympic champion.
1908   Forty-three female athletes compete in the Olympic Games.
1916   The U.S. Amateur Athletic Union (AAU) holds its first national swimming competition for women.
1917   The Committee on Women's Athletics (CWA) is established in the United States.
1921   Alice Milliat of France founds the Fédération Sportive Féminine International (FSFI).
1928   Sonja Henie of Norway wins her first Olympic Gold Medal for figure skating.
       Five track and field events are included for women in the Olympic Games,
1931   The first women's Alpine Skiing World Championships are held.
       The first women's Archery World Championship is held.
1932   The CWA is replaced by the National Section on Women's Athletics (NAGWS).
1936   The first women's Speed Skating World Championship is held.
1941   The first National Collegiate Golf Tournament for Women is held.
1943   The All-American Girls' Professional Baseball League is established.
1948   American Alice Coachman became the first black woman to win an Olympic Gold medal.
1949   The Ladies Professional Golf Association (LPGA) is established.
1951   Babe Didrikson Zaharias named "woman athlete of the half century."
1950   The first women's Gymnastics World Championships are held.
1952   The first women's Volleyball World Championships are held.
1953   The first women's Basketball World Championships are held.
1957   Althea Gibson becomes the first black woman to win the U.S. Open and Wimbledon tennis championships.
1956   Olympic diving gold mentalist Pat McCormick is named the Associated Press Athlete of the Year.
1958   The U.S. Olympic Committee approves its Women's Advisory Committee.
1964   The first women's softball world championships are held.
1965   The first women's cross-country world championships are held.
1971   Association of Intercollegiate Athletics for Women (AIAW) is formed.
       Billie Jean King is the first woman to earn more than $100,000 in professional sports.
1972   Title IX of the *Education Amendments* is passed.

Olga Korbut scores a perfect 10 in gymnastics at the Olympic Games.

1978 The Women's Professional Basketball League is established (WPBL).

1984 American Joan Benoit wins the gold medal in the Olympic debut of the marathon.

American Mary Lou Retton is the first American to win gold the all-around gymnastics competition.

1986 The Women's Professional Volleyball Association (WPVA) is formed.

1992 Bonnie Blair wins two Olympic gold medals in speed skating.

Jackie Joyner-Kersee wins an Olympic gold medal in the heptathlon.

1996 With more than 30 percent of participants being women, the Olympic Games are referred to as the "Games of the Women."

The Women's Professional Fast Pitch Softball League is formed.

1997 American Anita De Frantz is the first woman to be elected vice president of the International Olympic Committee.

The Women's National Basketball Association (WNBA) is formed.

Tennis star Martina Navratilova reaches the $20 million career earnings mark.

Source: Polidoro, J. (2000). *Sport and Physical Activity in the Modern World.* Boston: Allyn and Bacon.

SIGNIFICANT INDIVIDUALS

This is a short list of individuals who have had a significant influence in the world of sport. Their accomplishments, achievements, and attitudes have taught the world lessons, sometimes about sports, but just as often about society and life in general. The list is incomplete, but it represents a sampling of the impact that athletes can have on society.

Muhammad Ali

Athletic Accomplishments

Muhammad Ali is without controversy the greatest boxer of all time. In 1987, *The Ring* magazine officially named him the greatest heavyweight boxing champion of all time (Herzog 1995, 9). He successfully defended his heavyweight title nineteen times, becoming the first boxer to win back the championship twice after first attaining it. Born Cassius

Marcellus Clay Jr. in 1942, he won a gold medal at the 1960 Olympic Games in the 175-pound division. In 1964, he defeated Sonny Liston for the heavyweight title in one of the most stunning upsets in boxing history. On March 6 of that year, he took the name Muhammad Ali, after accepting the teachings of the Nation of Islam.

In 1967, Ali refused induction into the U.S. Armed Forces during the Vietnam draft. As a result, he was stripped of his title, banned from fighting for three and a half years, and sentenced to five years in prison; he remained free on bond until the Supreme Court overturned the decision. He began boxing again in 1970 and won his second heavyweight title after knocking out George Foreman during the "Rumble in the Jungle," held in Kinshasa, Zaire. His 1970, 1971, and 1973 heavyweight bouts against Joe Frazier were some of the most anticipated sporting events of the time.

In 1978, Ali lost his championship to Leon Spinks, but won it back seven months later. Muhammad Ali retired from boxing on June 27, 1979, returned for a few unsuccessful fights, and then was diagnosed with Parkinson's disease in 1984. Most recently, Ali is most remembered for carrying the Olympic torch to ignite the cauldron at the Summer Olympic Games in Atlanta in 1996 (Morrison 2003a).

Significant Influence

Muhammad Ali's influence probably began the day he threw the Olympic Gold medal he won in 1960 into the Ohio River. Most believe this action was a statement against the racial injustice to which he was subjected. Explicitly, his conversion to Islam provided him the context and his popularity provided him the platform to speak out against racism. His message of black pride and resistance to white power within society made him a significant force in the civil rights movement. Citing religious reasons, his refusal to fight in the Vietnam War was a testament to what he was willing to sacrifice for the statement he could make against treatment of minorities by the dominant culture. According to famed sports writer Brad Herzog, "Ali was probably the most photographed, interviewed, chronicled, and talked about athlete in history; the most loved and the most hated; one of the most triumphant and tragic; perhaps the most recognized person on earth, and as it turned out, a surprisingly important figure in American history" (Herzog 1995, 10). His flamboyant style, his thought-provoking lyrics, his stand against injustice, and his relationship with sports broadcaster Howard Cosell allowed the world to get to know the man Americans were proud of and eventually grew to love. When the fragile, shaking Ali lit the caldron at the 1996 Olympic Games in Atlanta, most Americans were moved to tears.

Arthur Ashe

Athletic Accomplishments

Arthur Ashe, one of the most prominent tennis players of his time, was defined by his competitive drive and professionalism. In 1963, Ashe was selected to represent the United States in the Davis Cup, becoming the first African American to be selected to play for this American team. In 1969, he won the U.S. Open. Because of the low prize money awarded to players despite the popularity of tennis as a spectator sport, Ashe and several colleagues formed the Association of Tennis Professionals (ATP). In 1975, at the age of thirty-one, Ashe won Wimbledon and attained the number-one ranking in the world. Following heart surgery in 1979, he retired from tennis in 1980. He was named to the Tennis Hall of Fame in 1985. His illustrious ten-year career included three Grand Slam singles titles and more than eight hundred career victories (Arthur Ashe 2003).

Activist

The life of Arthur Ashe taught several lessons. Despite discrimination, he lived as a trailblazer in a "white" sport. His dedication to issues of social justice was unwavering and extremely productive. Denied a visa to play tennis in South Africa, he took a bold stand against the apartheid government and raised the world's awareness of the oppression in that area of the world. Realizing the significance of his voice, he became involved in journalism, specifically as a commentator for ABC Sports and HBO Sports and as a columnist for the *Washington Post* and *Tennis Magazine*. Ashe published *A Hard Road to Glory* and founded numerous charitable organizations. In 1992, his announcement to the world that he was HIV-positive helped to change people's perceptions of the disease. Arthur Ashe "stood out when he chose to utilize his status to bring about change. That is what makes his legacy so unique and important" (Arthur Ashe 2003).

Larry Bird

Athletic Accomplishments

Larry Bird was drafted by the Boston Celtics in 1978 and played for them for thirteen seasons, from 1979 through 1991. Many believe he single-handedly helped rebuild the Boston franchise that had been suffering in the late 1970s. When David Stern was commissioner of the NBA, he explained Bird's influence in these terms: "Larry Bird helped define the way a generation of basketball fans has come to view and appreciate the NBA" (National Basketball Association 2003a). His accomplishments, cited on the NBA Website, can be summarized as follows:

- 1979 College Player of the Year at Indiana University
- 1980 NBA Rookie of the Year
- Nine-time All-NBA first team
- Three-time regular season Most Valuable Player (1984–1986)
- Led Boston to three NBA titles (1981, 1984, 1986)
- Two-time NBA Finals Most Valuable Player (1984, 1986)
- U.S. Olympic Dream Team member in 1992
- Inducted into the Hall of Fame in 1998
- Named coach of Indiana Pacers in 1997
- Won Coach of the Year honors in first season
- Coached Indiana Pacers to the NBA finals in 2000

Significant Influence

Larry Bird personified hustle, consistency, and dedication to team. He was the ultimate all-around player, who excelled at passing, scoring, rebounding, and defending. A perfectionist who thrived in high-pressure situations and inspired his teammates to excel, his influence may not have been as significant if it were not for the love-hate relationship he developed with Magic Johnson. From 1979 to 1991, Larry Bird and Magic Johnson faced each other on the basketball court thirty-eight times. They responded to each other's presence on the court by playing their hardest and challenging each other to reach their fullest potential. Bird's physical skills could not match the natural athleticism and grace of Magic, but he made up for it with determination and confidence. Together, these two outstanding basketball players first brought college basketball to a higher level and then did the same for the professional game. As *Sports Illustrated*'s Jack McCallum explained, "Individually they were great players; together they became an epic tale" (Herzog 1995, 153).

Howard Cosell

Journalistic Accomplishments

During his tenure, Howard Cosell was the best-known sports broadcaster in the United States. His journalist career began in the 1960s when ABC hired him as a reporter for *Wide World of Sports*. His unique style earned him a commentator position for *Monday Night Football*. His most notable accomplishment was the relationship he developed with Mohammed Ali. His impact on the journalistic world was that he allowed who he was as a person to become part of the way he told the story. His often abrasive and controversial approach made him a pioneer in the profession.

Significant Influence

In 1970, a *TV Guide* poll named Howard Cosell both the most liked and disliked American sportscaster. This distinction was something that Cosell took pride in, acknowledging that he believed he was "the most hated man on the face of the earth" (http://drake.marin.k12.ca.us/students/friedmad/announce/Cosell.htm). When pondering the words "honesty," "telling it like it is," or "in-your-face journalism," sports fans thought of Howard Cosell. His way with words and forthright delivery brought him the recognition of other sports journalists, athletes, and celebrities. His personality was best expressed through the memorable moments that he and Muhammad Ali spent together in the public eye. The way they teased and made fun of each other is legendary (Biography of Howard Cosell, n.d.). His confrontational style caught the world's attention, but it was his integrity, honesty, and dedication to sport that held it. He helped society recognize that one could view the world through a critical lens and still be admired.

Pierre de Coubertin

Olympic Administrative Accomplishments

Known as the father of the modern Olympic Games, Pierre de Coubertin was the International Olympic Committee (IOC) president from 1896 to 1925. Initially an educator in France, Coubertin was an active sportsman who participated in boxing, fencing, horseback riding, and rowing. He felt that sport was a vehicle by which men could develop moral character and as a result, society would be served. Coubertin was not in favor of women's participation in sport. It was this passion for sport and conviction to its worth that drove him to revive the Olympic Games. In June 1894, a conference at the Sorbonne University in Paris resulted in the creation of the IOC. Coubertin's influence was notable, because from its inception the IOC could have been significantly manipulated by the political powers of the time. Coubertin's wish that the games be played at a different location each time was upheld. He was also determined to maintain an amateur level of competition, with athletes participating for the love of the game rather than money (Polidoro 2000). In 1896, the first Olympic Games of the modern era were held in Athens.

Significant Influence

Coubertin believed the Olympics should uphold four principles: the games should be something like a religion, that is, they should "adhere to an ideal of a higher life, to strive for perfection"; they should represent an elite "whose origins are completely egalitarian" and at the same time "chivalry" with its moral qualities; they should create a truce, "a four-yearly festival of the springtime of mankind"; and they should glorify beauty by the "involvement of the philosophic arts in the Games" (http://www.olympic.org/uk/passion/museum/permanent). Coubertin's concept of the Olympic Games was far from a simple sports competition. He was a contemplative man who reflected on the ideas and ideals of sport, education, art, culture, and peace. Even though he was opposed to the inclusion of female athletic competition, his efforts to maintain the integrity of the games is the legacy from which the Olympic Games benefit today.

Babe Didrikson Zaharias

Athletic Accomplishments

From the 1930s through the 1950s, Babe Didrikson Zaharias's athletic accomplishments are second to those of no athlete, man or woman. Bobby Jones called her one of the ten best golfers of all time. She established world records and won the Olympic Gold medal in track and field. She was an All-American Semi-professional Basketball player, and excelled at baseball and softball. She had a 170 bowling average and won several tennis and diving championships. Didrikson Zaharias was often called the Jim Thorpe of women's athletics. Her record for athletic versatility stands at the top for both men and women. Details of all her athletic accomplishments are cited at http://www.babedidricksonzaharias.org, but a short summary follows.

- •• Voted the world's greatest woman athlete of the first half of the twentieth century by the Associated Press
- •• Six-time Woman Athlete of the Year by the Associated Press (1931, 1945, 1946, 1947, 1950, and 1954)

- Member of the Ladies Golf Hall of Fame and Helms Athletic Foundations Golf Hall of Fame
- Three-time All-American basketball player (1930, 1931, 1932)
- Held U.S. AAU record in four events
- Won two gold and one silver medals for the United States in the 1932 Olympics, where she qualified for five events but was allowed to enter only three
- Won eighty-two golf tournaments
- Pioneer of the Ladies Professional Golf Association tour
- Won the 1954 U.S. Women's Open within three strokes per round of the best ever shot by the men in either the U.S. Open or the British Open
- Qualified for the Los Angeles (men's) Open twice
- Was the leading money winner on the LPGA tour four years in a row (1948 to 1951)
- In baseball, pitched, played shortstop, and third base for the House of David team, managed by Grover Alexander
- In softball, played on two teams that won city championships in Dallas, Texas
- In 1976, was inducted into the National Women's Hall of Fame

Significant Influence

The athletic accomplishments described here occurred at a time when society had not yet accepted the idea of female athletes. As Herzog (1995) declares, "At a time when female athletes were considered freakish at best, downright unacceptable at worst, Didrikson became one of the most popular athletic figures in the nation" (p. 110). Her presence and success provided the world with an increased awareness of the female athletic potential. It was her desire to become the greatest athlete of all time, and in the 1960s she finished seventeenth in international voting to determine history's greatest athlete (Herzog 1995). Her accomplishments were not without controversy, however. She did not conform to the socially constructed view of acceptable female appearance, and she was a feminist before the concept was widely accepted. Most in the sporting world criticized her ambitions, and many made challenging accusations in regard to her gender. The founder of the LPGA, she is considered George Halas and Red Grange rolled into one (Herzog 1995). The tangible accomplishments are stunning, but it is the intangible, tacit influence that has been most significant on the future of female athletics, the world of sports, and society as a whole.

Harry Edwards

Accomplishments

Harry Edwards's accomplishments are within the world of sports, but he is not known for his athletic abilities. Instead, he is known as the most important sports activist of all time. Edwards won an athletic scholarship to Fresno City College and then to San Jose State for basketball and track, but his master's and doctorate degrees were earned at Cornell University. His organized protest and subsequent publications are his major accomplishments, some of which follow.

- Organized a protest in 1967 at San Jose State that led to cancellation of the football game and resulted in the college administration meeting the black students' demands
- Assisted in the formation of the Olympic Committee for Human Rights (OCHR) and the Olympic Project for Human Rights (OPHR)
- Organized a potential boycott of the 1968 Olympic Games by African American athletes
- Motivated the famous protest of Tommie Smith and John Carlos on the medal stand during the national anthem at the 1968 Olympic Games
- Wrote *The Revolt of the Black Athlete* (1969)
- Wrote *Sociology of Sport* (1973)
- Acted as consultant to the San Francisco 49ers and Golden State Warriors
- Hired by Major League Baseball in 1987 to address the lack of minorities in administrative positions

Social Activist

Edwards was probably the most significant figure in the fight to acknowledge the discrimination and exploitation of the African American athlete. In 1967, Edwards organized a movement in protest of the circumstances surrounding African Americans in sports. This movement is best realized for its call to African American athletes to boycott the1968 Olympic Games. His book *Sociology of Sport,* which was published in 1973, became the most widely used text in schools of physical education across the country. This allowed the perspectives of an African American sociologist to be taught to future sport and physical education professionals. The 1960s were a time of protests, riots, and activism. Sports were believed to be that aspect of society immune from the turmoil and a haven for racial equality. Harry Edwards was responsible for organizing the efforts of many that would dispel these myths and "help America grow up" (Herzog 1995).

Mia Hamm

Athletic Accomplishments

Mia Hamm is generally considered the best all-around female soccer player in the world. Her accomplishments are provided in detail at http://www.womensoccer.com/biogs/hamm.html, but a summary appears here.

- Played on the U.S. World Cup champion team in 1991 and 1999
- First-ever three-time U.S. Soccer athlete of the year, male or female (1994, 1995, 1996)
- Member of the Gold Medal–winning U.S. Women's National Team at the 1996 Olympic Games
- Named U.S. Soccer's Female Athlete of the Year for three consecutive years (1994, 1995, 1996), the first player honored three times
- Most Valuable Player of the Women's World Cup in Sweden in 1995
- Youngest member of the 1991 FIFA Women's World Cup championship team
- In 1987, at age fifteen, became the youngest woman ever to play with the U.S. National Team
- Most Valuable Player of the 1984 Chiquita Cup and 1995 U.S. Cup
- Played in three Olympic Festivals, winning gold medals in 1989 and 1990, and silver in 1987
- Played in 136 International games, scoring eighty-one goals
- U.S. National Team has a record of 62–2–2 in matches in which Hamm has scored
- Featured on the July/August 1997 cover of *Women's Soccer World Magazine*
- Appeared on the second *Sports Illustrated—Women' Sport* cover in 1997
- Named the Women's Sports Foundation Athlete of the Year for 1997
- Four-time member of the NCAA champion team from the University of North Carolina, 1989–1993

- ⚬ All-time leading scorer in NCAA women's soccer with 103 goals and seventy-two assists
- ⚬ Three-time All-American

Significant Influence

Following the 1991 Women's World Cup, the 1996 Olympic Games, and the 1999 Women's World Cup, Mia Hamm quickly became one of the most identifiable female athletes in the world. She was immediately showered with endorsement opportunities, most notably from Nike and Gatorade. In the sports marketing world, she became the female counterpart to Michael Jordan. This level of endorsement from the sports world seemed to validate the female athlete. The most explicit expression of this came from the Gatorade commercial in which she challenged Michael Jordan to, "Anything you can do, I can do better"! Mia Hamm was the perfect female athlete for the role of challenging Jordan. On the field, her aggressive style of play and tenaciously competitive personality allowed the world to fall in love with a female athlete who challenged a stereotype. Her athletic ability on the soccer field was unmatched, she was smart, and she was attractive. Her dedication, skill, and love of the sport of soccer were apparent every time she stepped onto the field. In recognition of her physical abilities and in memory of her brother Garrett, who died in 1996 from aplastic anemia, Hamm pledged to make a difference by helping others who suffer from the illness. The Mia Hamm Foundation was founded to raise funds and awareness for bone marrow diseases and the encouragement and empowerment of young female athletes. This creation of the foundation was a dream for the five-time recipient of the U.S. Soccer Female Athlete of the Year award. The Mia Hamm Foundation can be located on the Internet at http://www.miafoundation.org.

Magic Johnson

Athletic Accomplishments

No other athlete could have lived up to his nickname of "Magic" as Earvin Johnson did. When the name was declared, his mother was afraid that it might be too much to live up to: it was, but he did (Herzog, 1995; 148). His accomplishments are found at the NBA Website (NBA 2003c) but are summarized here:

- ⚬ Led Michigan State to NCAA title in 1979
- ⚬ All-NBA first team nine times

- Three-time Most Valuable Player (1987, 1989, 1990)
- Led Los Angles Lakers to five NBA titles (1980, 1982, 1985, 1987, 1988)
- Three-time finals Most Valuable Player (1980, 1982, 1987)
- Second in all-time in NBA assists (10,141)
- Twelve-time All-Star
- Retired on November 7, 1991; returned to score twenty-five points in 1992 NBA All-Star Game
- U.S. Olympic Dream Team member (1992)
- J. Walter Kennedy Citizenship Award (1992)
- Announced NBA comeback then retired again before start of 1992–1993 season
- Named head coach of Lakers on March 23, 1994
- As a minority owner of the Lakers, came back to play thirty-two games during 1995–1996 season
- Elected to Naismith Memorial Basketball Hall of Fame in 2002
- Named one of fifty greatest players in NBA history (1996)

Significant Influence

Magic Johnson's athleticism was undeniably fitting of his nickname. His overall significance to the game of basketball came from his competitions with Larry Bird, however. They faced each other on the court thirty-eight times from 1979 to 1991. Beginning on March 26, 1979, Magic and Michigan State met Larry Bird and Indiana State in the finals of the NCAA tournament, resulting in one of the largest television audiences ever to watch a basketball game. That single game transformed the annual tournament into what we now know as March Madness. The competition continued for the ten years of professional basketball that followed between the Los Angeles Lakers and the Boston Celtics. Additionally, Magic brought the widest smile and the most radiant personality to the world of professional sports. It was this captivating personality that made his November 7, 1991, announcement of having tested positive for the HIV virus that much more painful for NBA fans to bear. He was transformed from sports figure to cultural symbol, as the nation was forced to question issues of promiscuity and their attitudes toward AIDS. AIDS activists like Randy Shilts and health educators saw the silver lining in this situation, believing that "No human being in the history of the AIDS epidemic is better positioned to get the battle against AIDS moving than Johnson" (Herzog 1995, 151). Magic continued his NBA career and has declared that he knows one day he will not be a sports role model, but a human being facing life dealing with AIDS.

Michael Jordan

Athletic Accomplishments

Michael Jordan's athletic accomplishments were so remarkable that it propelled him to "Celebrity of the World" status. Larry Schwartz, a writer for ESPN writes, "As the 20th century drew to a close, Jordan was recognized as an icon. Tall, dark, and bald, he was the first man of the planet. The Chicago Bulls guard had the rarest of gifts, the ability to transcend his sport. His fame and skill were intertwined, much as they were in earlier generations from a select few, such as the Babe and Ali" (http://msn.espn.go.com/sportscentury/features/00016048.html). Without controversy, Michael Jordan is the best player ever to play professional basketball. He played college basketball at North Carolina, where as a freshman he hit the game-winning shot of the 1982 NCAA championship game. *The Sporting News* named him College Player of the Year in 1983 and 1984, he won the Naismith and John Wooden Awards in 1984, and, after his junior year, was the third overall pick in the 1984 NBA draft to play for the Chicago Bulls. In his first season, he was named Rookie of the Year, held the majority of NBA records, and won two Olympic Gold medals. In 1991, he led the Chicago Bulls to the first of six NBA championships, where he was named NBA Finals Most Valuable Player. Jordan retired in 1993, played Major League Baseball in 1994, and returned to the NBA to play for the Chicago Bulls in 1995. In 1996, 1997, and 1998 he led the Chicago Bulls to their fourth, fifth, and sixth NBA Championships. As cited at the NBA Website (NBA 2003c), his career accomplishments are unprecedented. Following are some of the highlights.

- Five-time NBA Most Valuable Player (1987–1988; 1990–1991; 1991–1992; 1995–1996; 1997–1998)
- Ten-time All NBA First Team Selection
- Selected as one of the Fifty Greatest Players in NBA History (1996)
- Led the Chicago Bulls to Six NBA championships
- Six-time NBA Finals Most Valuable Player
- 1987–1988 NBA Defensive Player of the Year
- Nine-time NBA All-Defensive First Team
- As of 2002–2003 season, first in NBA history in scoring average (thirty-one points per game), second in steals (2,391), fourth in total points (30,652)
- Ten years led the league in scoring (NBA record)
- Most consecutive games scoring in double digits (842; NBA record)

➠ Led the NBA in steals in 1987–1988, 1989–1990, 1992–1993
➠ NBA finals highest single scoring average (41) in 1993 (NBA record)
➠ NBA playoffs record for highest career scoring average (33.4 points per game)
➠ Established NBA playoffs record with sixty-three points against Boston Celtics (1986)
➠ Recorded two playoff career triple-doubles in 1984 and 1993
➠ Participated in Thirteen NBA All-Star Games (1985, 1987–1993, 1996–1998, 2002, 2003)
➠ Named Most Valuable Player of NBA All-Star Game in 1988, 1996, and 1998
➠ All time NBA All-Star Game leader in steals, second in field goals attempted, third in points scored, fourth in scoring average, and eighth in assists
➠ First triple-double in All-Star Game history (1997)
➠ Won slam-dunk in 1987, 1988

Michael Jordan retired for the second time on January 13, 1999, and began a new career on January 19, 2000, as president of basketball operations and part owner of the Washington Wizards. On September 25, 2001, he came out of retirement to play for the Wizards and was an impressive force during the 2002–2003 season. Jordan announced his third retirement after the Wizards failed to make the 2003 playoffs. His career as a player may be over, but his influence on the game will remain as he continues to be a part of NBA management.

Significant Influence

What made Michael Jordan such a significant influence in the world of sports was that along with his physical accomplishments and world-renowned status, his personality was captivating. This resulted in the unparalleled level of endorsements. The Jordan name became almost synonymous with Nike, the apparel and sporting goods giant. At all times, Jordan displayed an "aura of class," always remaining dignified and professional. At the same time, Jordan's drive to win was a life lesson in and of itself. This drive to succeed produced a level of confidence in key, high-pressure game situations that most often resulted in his hitting the winning shot. Fans often shared in Jordan's frequent personal amazement of his accomplishments. It seemed at times there was nothing he could not do. As adults admired him, youth worldwide looked to him as a superstar and role model. The number twenty-three holds significance in a far broader context than the world of sports.

Jackie Joyner-Kersee

Athletic Accomplishments

Known as the First Lady of Track and Field, Jackie Joyner-Kersee was considered the best all-around female athlete in the world. Highlights of her career are cited at the TopBlacks Website (Jackie Joyner-Kersee 2001). Among these are the following:

- First woman to earn more than seven thousand points in the heptathlon
- Has held the world record in the heptathlon since 1986
- Holds the American record in the long jump
- 1984 Olympic silver medal
- 1988 Olympic gold medal
- 1992 Olympic gold medal
- Most decorated woman in U.S. Olympic track and field history with six medals

Significant Influence

What makes Jackie Joyner-Kersee so special among elite athletes is her courage and determination to rise above the challenges that life presented to her. She grew up in a rough area in East St. Louis and overcame poverty, tragedy, and discrimination. She stayed away from the drugs and alcohol that were so readily available, growing up across the street from a liquor store and pool hall. She graduated in the top 10 percent of her high school class and was awarded a scholarship to the University of California, Los Angles.

Mike Krzyzewski

Coaching Accomplishments

In his twenty-third season as the Head Basketball Coach for Duke University, "Coach K" has established a basketball dynasty that has won him the respect of everyone associated with the world of sports. As cited on the Duke University Website (Mike Krzyzewski 2003) his accomplishments are unprecedented:

- Inducted into the Naismith Basketball Hall of Fame, class of 2001

➡ Named America's Best Coach in 2001 by *Time* magazine and CNN
➡ Named Sportsman of the Year in 1992 by *The Sporting News*
➡ Eleven-time Coach of the Year
➡ Five-time ACC Coach of the Year
➡ NCAA National Championships in 1991,1992, and 2001
➡ Six National Players of the Year
➡ Five National Defensive Players of the Year
➡ Eighteen NCAA Tournament Bids
➡ Sixteen All-American selections
➡ Nine Final Four Appearances
➡ Seven Atlantic Coast Conference (ACC) Championships
➡ Nine ACC Regular Season Championships
➡ 564 total victories (215 ACC wins)
➡ Seventy-two weeks ranked as number one in the country
➡ Fifty-eight NCAA Tournament victories (second all-time)
➡ Thirty-two NBA draft selections, including sixteen first round picks

Significant Influence

Coach Mike Krzyzewski is not included in this text for these coaching accomplishments. He is profiled because of the manner in which he achieved these accolades and for the testimony he is to moral character. At a time when the "winning at all costs" coaching philosophy is widely accepted in big-time collegiate athletics, Coach K is considered proof that winning and success can be achieved while maintaining high academic standards and moral character. Among the statistics of which he may be most proud is the fact that from 1986–2002, fifty of the fifty-four players who completed their four years of eligibility played in a final-four game and in at least one championship NCAA game. Tyrangiel of *Time* writes the following: "Krzyzewski has accomplished all this with a program that turns out real-deal scholar athletes—kids who go to class, graduate and don't mind telling everyone about it." *The Sporting News* named him Sportsman of the Year, noting, "On the court and off, Krzyzewski is a family man first, a teacher second, a basketball coach third, and a winner at all three. He is what's right about sports" (http://goduke.ocsn.com/sports/m-basketbl/mtt/krzyzewski_mike00.html). Mike Krzyzewski has made a statement to the world of sports that high standards can be maintained, integrity must be a priority, that winning isn't everything, and that life lessons are sports' most valuable lessons to be taught to athletes.

Mark McGwire

Athletic Accomplishments

The list of Mark McGwire's accomplishments may not be as long as other significant figures, but the impact of his presence in Major League Baseball during the 1990s and into the new millennium is why he is included here. Here are a few of his accomplishments:

- *The Sporting News* college player of the year (1984)
- Member of 1984 U.S. Olympic Baseball Team
- Won American League Rookie of the Year and hit a rookie record forty-nine home runs (1987)
- Became the first player to hit seventy home runs in a regular season (1998)

Significant Influence

At a time in U.S. history when many things were going wrong (a presidential sex scandal, Major League Baseball strikes), the home run battle between Mark McGwire and Sammy Sosa seemed to be just what the country needed. It is said that Mark McGwire saved baseball and gave the nation's boost in pride it needed. Because Americans knew baseball was going to be OK again, they believed the country would be, too. Living through those times was a testimony to the affect that sports, specifically baseball, had on U.S. society. What might have been significant about the events could be more than the athletic accomplishments. Both of the athletes involved were genuine "good guys." Both were relatively unassuming athletes, family men who participated in charitable organizations and seemed to convey a sense that they had their priorities in line. Mark McGwire was a quiet hero at a point in time when the country needed him.

Cal Ripken Jr.

Athletic Accomplishments

In 1995, Cal Ripken Jr., shortstop for the Baltimore Orioles, broke Lou Gehrig's fifty-six-year record of 2,130 consecutive games played and became professional baseball's "Iron Man." If you lived in Baltimore, you might be able to recite the following short list of his accomplishments, but for the rest of us, a summary follows.

- 1982 American League Rookie of the Year

- 1983 and 1991 American League Most Valuable Player
- 1991 and 1992 American League Gold Glove Short Stop
- 1991: All-Star Game Most Valuable Player
- 1995 Played in 2,131 consecutive games to establish a new record
- 1996 ESPY Male Athlete of the Year and ESPY Showstopper of the Year
- 2001 All-Star Game Most Valuable Player

Significant Influence

At a time when it was acceptable for multimillion dollar athletes to choose to sit out of competitions with minor injuries or for personal reasons, Cal Ripken Jr. was one shining star that proved there were professional athletes who played because they loved their game. Sitting out was not an option. He declares that his father, the late Cal Ripken Sr., taught him that his teammates depended on him and that commitment was important. But Cal Ripken Jr. was not just committed to his teammates; his commitment to the city of Baltimore was quite obvious to those hardworking blue-collar types that, like him, put in their long days every day. Cal Ripken Jr. was also devoted to his wife and two children and to the charitable organization he and his wife established for the benefit of those underserved in the city of Baltimore. Changing teams probably would have made Cal Ripken Jr. more money, but it is refreshing to realize that his commitments were more important.

Jackie Robinson

Athletic Accomplishments

Jackie Robinson was the first African American to play Major League Baseball. Rickey Branch, then president of the Brooklyn Dodgers, signed Robinson to a contract in 1946 and sent him to the team's minor league affiliate, the Montreal Royals. On April 15, 1947, Robinson made his major league debut for the Brooklyn Dodgers at Ebbets Field against the Boston Braves. After a slow start, Robinson's performance helped the Dodgers win the National League Pennant. He finished the season with the most stolen bases and tied for team's home runs, being named National League Rookie of the Year. The Dodgers played the New York Yankees in the 1947 World Series, as Robinson experienced the joy of playing against Rizzuto, Berra, and DiMaggio. Robinson was named National League Most Valuable Player in 1949, retired from baseball in 1957, and was inducted into the Baseball Hall of Fame on January 23, 1962.

Significant Influence

Jackie Robinson's influence on the game of baseball was important, but not as significant as his influence on society as a whole. Upon his entrance into the major leagues, Robinson became the role model for other African Americans determined to realize their right to participate in all aspects of society. However, Robinson was the target of significant discrimination and racism. Despite the racial insults, he persevered and eventually his fellow teammates, appreciating his talents and accepting him for the person he was, began to support him on and off the field in the face of controversy. Robinson was also known to speak out against racism, as demonstrated by his appearance before the House Un-American Activities Committee in Washington, D.C. (http://www. cwpost.livnet.edu/cwis/cwp/library/aaitsa.htm). Herzog includes a detailed description of Robinson's first games and memorable moments. Within the account, Herzog includes quotes from a few new stories of the day, which speak volumes: "Alone, Robinson represents a weapon far more potent than the combined forces of all our liberal legislation," "Jim Crow Dies at Second," and "Triumph of Whole Race Seen in Jackie's Debut in Major League Ball" (Herzog 1995, 2–4).

Dean Smith

Coaching Accomplishments

Dean Smith coached basketball for thirty-six years, having finished his career at the University of North Carolina as the all-time winningest coach in basketball history with a record of 879–254. These figures and his accomplishments are cited on the University of North Carolina's athletic Website (www.tarheelbue.oscn.com).

- Two NCAA Championships
- Thirteen Atlantic Coast Conference (ACC) Championships
- Carolina was ranked in the final top 10 from 1981 to 1989
- Eleven Final Four appearances (second only to John Wooden)
- Twenty-three consecutive appearances in the NCAA tournament
- Twenty-seven appearances in the NCAA Tournament in thirty-one years
- Eight-time ACC Coach of the Year
- Named 1997 Sportsmen of the Year by *Sports Illustrated*

•→ Inducted into the Naismith Basketball Hall of Fame in 1983
•→ Inducted into the North Carolina Hall of Fame in 1981

Significant Influence

His coaching accomplishments have earned him the respect of everyone in the world of basketball. His significance beyond the court is also
remarkable. He was successful while demanding academic excellence of
his players, having 96 percent of his players graduate since his first year
at Carolina in 1961. Additionally, in his thirty-six years of coaching, he
never had an NCAA violation. He received the Arthur Ashe Award for
Courage at the ESPY Awards and is well known as a social activist in the
state of Carolina. Rick Reilly writes of this "Man of Substance" in the
March 17, 2003, issue of *Sports Illustrated*. Reilly's article describes some
of the situations and actions that resulted in his description of Smith as
"Abe Lincoln in a world of Stepford Jocks, where speaking out on social
issues is likened to a class A felony" (Reilly 2002, 78). The article continues to describe how Dean Smith

> •→ Supported the action of Toni Smith of Manhattanville
> College, when she turned her back on the flag in protest
> (He declared, "I'm sure it took a lot of courage," and contin-
> ued to explain his position that basketball players don't give
> up their individual rights when they put on a basketball
> uniform.)
> •→ Helped desegregate Chapel Hill restaurants in the early '60s
> by taking one of his black students into a restaurant to eat
> •→ Allowed one of his players to miss practice to protest against
> the low wages paid to the University of North Carolina's cafe-
> teria workers
> •→ Discussed the words of Martin Luther King Jr. with his team
> •→ Passionately spoke out against the 2003 war in Iraq
> •→ Continuously speaks out against the death penalty in North
> Carolina
> •→ Took his basketball players to a prison to meet death-row
> inmates in their cells
> •→ Wants to ban gambling on college sports
> •→ Wants newspapers to stop printing point spreads
> •→ Feels college athletes should get paid by the NCAA

Dean Smith is certainly a voice to be heard, and as Reilly suggests,
in the world of sport speaking up for what you believe is not always the

safest thing to do. In Smith's case, it has earned him the respect he deserves. He is an example to follow for those in high-profile positions.

Pat Summit

Coaching Accomplishments

During the University of Tennessee's 2002–2003 basketball season, the team volunteers should witness their head coach, Pat Summit, earn her 800th win, an accomplishment only four other coaches have achieved. Pat Summit will have done it faster than any of them; in her twenty-eighth season, her record stands at 788–158 (http://utladyvols.ocsn.com/sports/w-baskbl/mtt/summitt_pat). A detailed account of her career can be found at the University of Tennessee Lady Volunteer's Website, but a brief summary is included here.

- Six NCAA titles
- Three consecutive titles (1996, 1997, 1998)
- Twenty-one Southeastern Conference (SEC) tournament and regular season championships
- Coached eleven Olympians
- Sixteen Kodak All-Americans named to twenty-eight teams
- Fifty-five All-SEC players
- Named to the Basketball Hall of Fame in 2000
- Named Naismith Coach of the Century in 2000
- Thirteen NCAA Final Four appearances
- Named Naismith Women's Basketball Coach of the Decade in 1999
- First female coach to be pictured on the cover of *Sports Illustrated* in 1997
- Three-time SEC Coach of the Year (1993, 1995, 1998)
- *The Sporting News* Coach of the Year; Naismith Coach of the Year; Associated Press Coach of the Year, and the U.S. Basketball Writers Association Coach of the Year in 1998
- Most NCAA tournament victories, winning seventy-six of eighty-six NCAA contests
- Coached the 1984 USA women's basketball team to an Olympic Gold medal

Significant Influence

Just as her career coaching accomplishments are underserved in this brief section, so, too, are her accomplishments off the court. She is involved in all of the following:

- Verizon Wireless's HopeLine program
- The United Way
- The Race for the Cure
- Juvenile Diabetes
- Big Brothers/Big Sisters
- Tennessee Easter Seal Society (honorary chair in 1985, 1987, 1988, 1989)
- In 1994, Tennessee chair of the American Heart Association
- In 1996, named Distinguished Citizen of the Year by the Great Smoky Mountain Council of the Boy Scouts of America
- In 1997, Tennessee Lung Association presented her the Tennessee Woman of Distinction Award

Perhaps the one accomplishment that places Summit in this section is that the graduation rate of her players who complete four years of eligibility at the University of Tennessee is 100 percent (Beckett Publications 1999). This accomplishment speaks to her perspective on the kind of players she recruits and what she demands of them. She explained in an interview in *USA Weekend,* "I don't want average people. Average people cut corners. Winners know there are no shortcuts" (Beckett Publications, 1999).

Tiger Woods

Athletic Accomplishments

The world was introduced to Tiger Woods in 1978 when at the age of two he putted against comedian Bob Hope on the *Mike Douglas Show* (Morrison 2003b). His career accomplishments are presented at http://www.infoplease.com/spot/tigertime1.html, but a summary is provided here.

- Won the Optimist International Junior Championships at age 8, 9, 12, 13, 14, and 15
- At age 15, became the youngest U.S. Junior Amateur Champion in golf history
- Voted 1991 *Golf Digest* Amateur Player of the Year
- Won the U.S. Junior National Championships for the third time in 1993

- Won the U.S. Amateur Championship in 1994, to become the youngest amateur champion
- Voted Pac-10 Player of the Year, for Stanford University
- Played in 1995 Masters, tying for forty-first as the only amateur to make the cut
- At age twenty, became the first golfer to win three consecutive U.S. Amateur titles
- Turned professional in 1996 and signed a $40 million Nike endorsement and a $20 million Titleist endorsements
- Voted *Sports Illustrated* Sportsman of the Year in 1996
- Won the Masters in 1997 by twelve strokes, the widest margin of victory ever, becoming the youngest as well as the first African American or Asian to win
- Ranked number one in the world rankings in forty-second week as a pro
- Voted PGA Player of the Year and Associated Press Male Athlete of the Year in 1997 and 1999
- Selected as ESPY Male Athlete of the Year in 1997
- Earned the most money on the PGA tour in 1999: $6,616,585 for the year
- Won PGA Championship in 1999 and 2000
- Became the fifth player in history (youngest) to complete the career Grand slam in 2000 and one of only two players to win three majors in one season
- In 2001, won the Masters and became the first golfer to be champion of all four majors at the same time; named PGA Player of the Year for the third consecutive year
- In 2002, won second consecutive Masters, third overall, and became the youngest golfer in history to win seven PGA majors

Significant Influence

Tiger Woods is recognized as a remarkable athlete as well as the epitome of dedication, hard work, integrity, and professionalism. As the most decorated golfer in history and one of the most recognized African American athletes of the twentieth century, Woods became a role model for many young African Americans who aspire to accomplish what stereotypes and racism seem to suggest is unattainable. He is said to be the hardest working athlete of his time and is seen as having mastered the mental aspect of what many believe is the most challenging sport. Woods was placed in the political limelight, just before the 2003 Masters, which is played at Augusta National, an all-male-membership country club. When a *New York Times* editorial called on Tiger Woods to boycott this most prestigious tournament to make a statement against the discrimination, Woods declined but declared that he felt there should be female members. He added that it was not his position to make the statement against the club. Woods's position not to enter into political or controversial social issues of the times does not diminish the influence he has had on the world of golf and as a role model for many of today's youth.

REFERENCES

African-American in the Sports Arena. (n.d.). Retrieved March 17, 2003, from http://www.cwpost.livnet.edu/cwis/cwp/library/aaitsa.htm.

Arthur Ashe: CMG Worldwide represents many famous legends of the 20th century. (2003). Retrieved on March 9, 2002, from http://www.cmgww.com/sports/ashe/index.html.

Beckett Publications Staff. (1999). *Good Sports: Athletes Your Kids Can Look Up To.* Beckett: Dallas.

Biography of Howard Cosell. (n.d.). Retrieved from the Internet Movie Database: http://www.imdb.com/Bio?Cosell,%20Howard.

Carpenter, L. J. (2001). Letters Home: My Life with Title IX. In *Women in Sport: Issues and Controversies,* G. L. Cohen, editor. Oxon Hill, MD: AAHPERD Publications.

Christensen, C. L. (2001). Women's Physiology and Exercise: Influences and Effects. In *Women in Sport: Issues and Controversies,* G. L. Cohen, editor. Oxon Hill, MD: AAHPERD Publications.

Cox, R. (2002). *Sport Psychology: Concepts and Applications.* McGraw Hill, Boston.

Dean Smith. (2003). Retrieved on April 3, 2003, from http://tarheelblue.ocsn.com/sports/m~baskbl/mtt/unc-m-baskbl-dean-smith.html.

Delaney, J. (1996). Pay for Play in College Sports? Retrieved June 25, 2003, from http://www/umich.edu/~mrev/archives/1996/9-18-96/13/htm.

Edwards, H. (1984). *The Black "Dumb Jock": An American Sports Tragedy. The College Board Review,* No. 131, spring 1984.

Eitzen, D. S., and G. Sage. (1993). *Sociology of North American Sport.* Madison, WI: Brown & Benchmark.

Football Violence in Europe. (n.d.). Retrieved June 24, 2003, from http://www.sirc.org/publik/fvhist.html.

Gates, H. L., Jr., and West, C. (2000). *The African American Century: How Black Americans Have Shaped Our Country.* New York: Touchstone.

Gould, T. (2000). *For Gold and Glory.* Retrieved April 28, 2002, from http://www.indianahistory.org/pub/traces/gould.html.

Griffin, P. (2001). Heterosexism, homophobia, and lesbians in sport. In *Women in Sports: Issues and Controversies,* G. L. Cohen, editor. Reston, VA: National Association for Girls and Women in Sports, a division of AAPERD Publications.

Herzog, B. (1995). *The Sports 100: The 100 Most Important People in American Sports History.* New York: Macmillan.

History of Boxing. (n.d.). Retrieved from the Official Site of the Klitschko Brothers. http://www.klitschko.com/eng/ist2_e.

Jackie Joyner-Kersee: The First Lady of Track and Field. (2001). Retrieved April 3, 2003, from http://www.topblacks.com/sports/jackie-joyner-kersee.asp.

Madden, M. (2001). Madden: Alcohol is root of fan violence. Post-Gazette.com (*Pittsburgh Post Gazette*), December 22, 2001. Retrieved October 2, 2002, from http://www.post-gazette.com/sports/columnists/20011222 madden1222p.6.asp.

Mazur, A. F. (2001). Nutritional supplement use puts student-athletes eligibility at risk. Retrieved June 27, 2003, from http://www.ncaa.org/news/2001/20011008/actve/3821n22.html.

Mechikoff, R., and Estes, S. (1998). *A History and Philosophy of Sport and Physical Education: From Ancient Civilizations to the Modern World.* Boston: McGraw-Hill.

Mike Krzyzewski. (2003). Retrieved on April 4, 2003, from http://goduke.ocsn.com/sports/m~baskbl/mtt/krzyzewski_mike00.html.

Monitoring the Future. (1996). Retrieved June 27, 2003, from http://vax.vmi.edu/MARION/ACA8918.

Morrison, M. (2003). Muhammad Ali timeline: The ups and downs of the champ's career. Retrieved on April 22, 2003, from http://www.infoplease.com/spot/malitimeline1.html.

Morrison, M. (2003). Tiger Woods timeline: A glance at the golf sensation's life and career. Retrieved on April 22, 2003, from http://www.infoplease.com/spot/tigertime1.html.

Murray, M., and H. Matheson. (2001). Psychological and Social Challenges for Females in Sport. In *Women in Sport: Issues and Controversies,* G. L. Cohen, editor. Oxon Hill, MD: AAHPERD Publications.

National Association of College Athletic Directors. (n.d.). Retrieved June 26, 2003, from http://nacda.ocsn.com/nacda/nacda-admin.html.

National Basketball Association. (2003a). NBA history: Larry Bird biography. Retrieved June 20, 2003, from http://www.nba.com/history/players/bird_summary.html.

National Basketball Association. (2003b). NBA history: Magic Johnson biography. Retrieved June 20, 2003, from http://www.nba.com/history/players/johnsonm_summary.html.

National Basketball Association. (2003c). Michael Jordan biography. Retrieved June 20, 2003, from http://www.nba.com/playerfile/michael_jordan/bio.

National Interscholastic Athletic Administrators Association. (n.d.). Retrieved June 26, 2003, from http://www.niaaa.org.

NCAA Basketball "Reforms" Come Up Short. (May 1, 2000). Retrieved June 26, 2003, from http://pqasb.pqarchiver.com/USAToday/53326837.html.

NCAA Graduation Reports. (n.d.). Retrieved June 30, 2003, from http://www.ncaa.org/eligibility/cbsa/index1.html.

Novak, M. (1994). *The Joy of Sport: Endzones, Bases, Baskets, Balls, and the Consecration of the American Spirit.* NY: Basic Books.

Polidoro, J. R. (2000). *Sport and Physical Activity in the Modern World.* Boston: Allyn and Bacon.

Povich, S. (1995, May 2). Telling it like it was about Howard Cosell. Retrieved on April 18, 2002, from http://www.washingtonpost.com/wp-srv/sports/longterm/memories/1995/95pass11.htm.

Preventing Drug Abuse Among Children and Adolescents: Some Research-Based Drug Abuse Prevention Programs. (n.d.). Retrieved June 25, 2003, from http://www.drugabuse.gov/Prevention/PROGRAM.html.

Reilly, R. (2003, March 17). A man of substance. *Sports Illustrated,* p. 78.

Schwartz, L. (2002–2003). Sportscentury biography: Michael Jordan transcends hoops. Retrieved on April 22, 2003, from http://msn.espn.go.com/sportscentury/features/00016048.html.

Siedentop, D. (2001). *Introduction to Physical Education, Fitness, and Sport.* Mountain View, CA: Mayfield.

Smith, L. (1998). *Nike Is a Goddess: The History of Women in Sport.* New York: Atlantic Monthly Press.

Sports Announcers Past to Present. (1999, January 15). Howard Cosell. Retrieved on April 3, 2003, from http://drake.marin.k12.ca.us/students/friedmad/announce/Cosell.htm.

They Altered the Course of Golf History (n.d.). Retrieved May 6, 2003, from http://www.arga.org/ns_hist.htm.

Tyrangiel, J. (1992). Not-so-dumb jocks. *Time,* April 20.

Wiggins, D. K. (1997). *Glory Bound: Black Athletes in a White America.* Syracuse, NY: Syracuse University Press.

Chapter Five

•‹ **Organizations**

The following organizations, associations, and agencies provide support for individuals associated with sports, physical education, or sports within the context of education.

GLOBAL

International Olympic Committee (IOC)
www.olympic.org

The IOC is an international nongovernmental non-profit organization and creator of the Olympic movement. It serves as an umbrella organization of the Olympic movement, and owns all rights to the Olympic icons: symbols, the flag, motto, anthem, and Olympic Games. Its primary responsibility is to supervise the organization of the summer and winter Olympic Games.

World Alliance of Young Men's Christian Association (YMCA)
www.ymca.net

Based in Chicago, Illinois, the mission of the YMCA is to put Christian principles into practice through programs that build healthy spirit, mind, and body. The YMCA is not a particular facility, and it does not provide direct programs and services to the public. Each YMCA is separate and autonomous from the umbrella of the YMCA of the USA, and each makes its own decisions based on local community needs.

World Young Women's Christian Association (YWCA)
www.ywca.org

The YWCA works to empower women and girls by offering a wide range of services and programs that enrich and transform their lives. It seeks to nurture young girls' minds with the YWCA TechGYRLS™ Clubs, and encourages women to exercise their political clout at the Institute for Public Leadership. Also, the YWCA embraces and promotes social justice by annually presenting the YWCA Week Without Violence and the YWCA National Day of Commitment to Eliminate Racism.

International School Sport Federation

The primary aims of the ISF are: to foster better mutual understanding between countries; to solicit close collaboration with the school authorities of member countries; to promote better interaction between international sporting federations; to cooperate with international organizations that have similar goals; and to be completely free from political, religious, and racial considerations.

International Council for Health, Physical Education, Recreation Sport, and Dance (ICHPERSD)
www.ichpersd.org

The mission of the council is to publicize and disseminate information about the studies and results dealing with the field of sport science. The council also makes recommendations on how to apply this information in cultural and educational contexts.

The International University Sports Federation (FISU)
www.fisu.net

The FISU (International University Sports Federation) was formed within university institutions to promote sporting values and encourage sporting practice in harmony with, and complementary to, the university spirit. Its mission to promote sporting values means encouraging friendship, fraternity, fair play, perseverance, integrity, cooperation, and application among students who will one day hold responsible, even key positions in politics, the economy, culture, and industry.

The International Amateur Athletic Federation (IAAF)
www.iaaf.org

The IAAF is a national governing body for athletics (track and field). Each country sends a member to review and modify the rules and regulations of international athletic competition.

NATIONAL

The Center for the Study of Sport in Society
www.sportinsociety.org

The goal of Northeastern University's Center for the Study of Sport in Society is to promote an awareness of sport and its relation to society, and to implement programs that pinpoint problems, provide solutions, and identify the benefits of sport.

American Alliance for Health, Physical Education, Recreation and Dance (AAHPERD)
www.aahperd.org

This is the largest organization of professionals that supports and assists those involved in physical education, fitness, dance, leisure, health promotion and education, and all disciplines related to achieving a quality lifestyle. Through a combination of programs, resources, and other support, practitioners are encouraged to improve their professional skills.

National Association of Sport and Physical Education (NASPE)
www.aahperd.org/naspe

The NASPE grows the body of knowledge of, and increases the level of professional practice in, sport and physical activity through the dissemination of the results of scientific study and experiential knowledge.

American Association for Health Education
www.aahperd.org/aahe

The AAHE assists health professionals concerned with health promotion through education and other programs.

National Association for Girl's and Women's Sports (NAGWS)
www.aahperd.org/nagws

The NAGWS advocates equality of all kinds for girls' and women's sports: funding, quality, and respect. It is the leading organization that works with these issues.

The National Dance Association (NDA)
www.aahperd.org/nda

The NDA increases knowledge, improves skills, and encourages sound professional practices in dance education through the use of high-quality dance programs.

National Association of Physical Education in Higher Education (NAPEHE)
www.napehe.org

This is an organization designed for professionals in higher education. Its provides a forum for interdisciplinary ideas, concepts, and issues that are related to the role of physical education in higher education with respect for social, cultural, and personal perspectives.

North American Society for Sport History (NASSH)
www.nassh.org

The NASSH promotes, stimulates, and encourages study, research, and writing of the history of sport, and supports and cooperates with local, national, and international organizations having the same goals.

Women's Sports Foundation
www.lifetimetv.com

This foundation supports the participation of women in sports activities and seeks to educate the public about athletic opportunities for women. It publishes a quarterly newsletter, *The Women's Sports Experience.*

The Association of the Advancement of Applied Sport Psychology (AAASP)
www.aaasponline.org

This association promotes the development of psychological theory, research, and intervention strategies in sport psychology. It also provides a forum for individuals interested in research and theory development, as well as in the application of psychological principles in sport and exercise.

United States Olympic Committee
www.usoc.org

The USOC preserves and promotes the Olympic ideal as an effective, positive role model that inspires all Americans. It challenges U.S. athletes to sustain the highest levels of competitive excellence, and, through their successes, become a source of inspiration for the U.S. Olympic ideal.

ESPN
www.espn.com

This Website provides current information and comprehensive coverage of all sports. Sport-related issues in the news are discussed, as are statistics, standings, and competitions.

YOUTH SPORTS

Little League Baseball
www.littleleague.org

Little League Baseball is a non-profit organization whose mission is "to promote, develop, supervise, and voluntarily assist in all lawful ways, the interest of those who will participate in Little League Baseball." The program aids youth in developing the qualities of citizenship, discipline, teamwork, and physical well-being. In doing so, Little League believes its efforts will result in developing superior citizens rather than superior athletes.

The National Congress of State Games (NCSG)
www.stategames.org

The NCSG is the membership organization of all states conducting state game competitions. It is a community-based member of the United States Olympic Committee. It develops grassroots sports through statewide Olympic-style sport festivals.

Pop Warner Little Scholars (PWLS)
www.popwarner.com

This is a non-profit organization that requires some scholastic aptitude in order to participate. It works at developing America's youth, on the field and off, by encouraging team sports as well as involvement in community outreach programs.

American Youth Soccer Association (AYSO)
www.soccer.org

The AYSO is a nationwide non-profit organization that develops and delivers quality youth soccer programs in a fun, family environment based on its "Five Philosophies": everyone plays, balanced teams, open registration, positive coaching, and good sportsmanship.

Institute for the Study of Youth Sports (YSI),
Michigan State University
http://ed-web3.educ.msu.edu/ysi

The Michigan Legislature founded the YSI in 1978 in order to research the benefits as well as unfavorable conditions of participation in youth sports; to produce educational materials for parents, coaches, officials, and administrators; and to offer educational programs to these same groups of people.

The Mendelson Center for the Study of Sport, Character, and Culture
www.nd.edu/~cscc

This organization at the University of Notre Dame wishes to "create a sense of human solidarity and concern for the common good that will bear fruit as learning becomes service to justice." The center challenges sport participants, sport organizations, and educational institutions to promote social justice, such as valuing diversity, creating equal opportunity, and advocating for the disadvantaged.

The American Sport Education Program (ASEP)
www.asep.org

The ASEP develops and delivers both online and instructor-led courses and resources for coaches, officials, sports administration, athletes, and athletes' parents. It helps improve the sport experience for young people by proving quality instructional resources, workshops, and courses for coaches, administrators, officials, and parents.

HIGH SCHOOL SPORTS

National Federation of State High School Athletic Associations
(NFHS)
www.nfhs.org

The NFHS provides leadership and national coordination for the administration of interscholastic activities, which will enhance the educational experiences of high school students and reduce the risks of their participation in sports. It develops good citizens through interscholastic activities that provide equitable opportunities, and positive recognition and learning experiences to students while at the same time achieving their educational goals.

National Interscholastic Athletic Administrators Association (NIAAA)
www.niaaa.org

This association provides opportunities for athletic administrative growth, leadership potential, professional publications, continuing education, conference opportunities, and more. The site allows administrators to research these concepts that provide direction and guidance benefiting athletic administrators, corporate people, and decision makers who embrace knowledge and change.

COLLEGIATE

National Collegiate Athletic Association (NCAA)
www.ncaa.org

This is a voluntary association of about 1,200 colleges and universities, athletic conferences, and sports organizations devoted to the sound administration of intercollegiate athletics. Through the NCAA, member schools and conferences consider any athletic problem or issue that is national in character. Volunteer school representatives establish rules that govern the association and programs designed to further its purposes and goals.

National Association of Intercollegiate Athletics (NAIA)
www.naia.org

Since 1937, the NAIA has administered programs and championships that balance out the overall educational experience. In 2000, it reaffirmed its purpose to enhance the character-building aspects of sport. Through "Champions of Character," the NAIA seeks to create an environment in which every student-athlete, coach, official, and spectator is committed to the true spirit of competition through "five tenets": respect, integrity, responsibility, servant leadership, and sportsmanship. With this program, the NAIA hopes to educate and create awareness of the positive character-building traits that sports offer, and maintain the integrity of competition at the collegiate and youth levels.

National Association of Collegiate Directors of Athletics (NACDA)
www.nacda.ocsn.com

NACDA serves as the professional association for those in the field of intercollegiate athletics administration. It provides educational opportunities and serves as a vehicle for networking, the exchange of information, and advocacy on behalf of the profession.

PROFESSIONAL

Association for Professional Basketball Research (APBP)
www.abpr.org

Robert Bradley founded the APBR with the following objectives in mind: to promote interest in the history of professional basketball; to correct historical inaccuracies of basketball and uncover missing information; to provide a central library and database of books, historical facts, and statistics for researchers, authors, and fans; and to promote awareness of extinct basketball leagues and their teams, players, coaches, and executives.

Professional Golf Association (PGA)
www.pga.com

The PGA of America is the largest working sports organization in the world, comprising more than 27,000 dedicated men and women who promote the game of golf to everyone, everywhere. It was founded in 1916 and has enjoyed a rich history. A comprehensive list of highlights from each year of the PGA's history is available on its Website.

Major League Baseball (MLB)
www.mlb.com

This is the official Website of Major League Baseball.

National Football League (NFL)
www.nfl.com

This is the official Website of the National Football League.

EDUCATION

Educational Testing Service (ETS)
www.ets.org

The ETS advances quality and equity in education by providing fair and valid assessments, research, and related services. Its products and services measure knowledge and skills, promote learning and performance, and support education and professional development.

OTHER

Athletes for a Better World (ABW)
www.aforbw.org

ABW's "Code for Living" provides guideposts for personal and leadership development. The code reflects the desire to live a responsible life as an individual, as a member of a team, and as a member of society. ABW believes that people who have grown up with its Code for Living will have been formed by a set of values that will provide a foundation for life.

Outward Bound
www.outwardbound.com

Outward Bound is one of the nation's leading, non-profit adventure-education organizations. It serves and supports four wilderness schools and two urban centers—all of which are in the United States. Its programs emphasize personal growth through experience and challenge in the wilderness, and in classroom settings around the world. Students are challenged to learn self-reliance, responsibility, teamwork, confidence, compassion, and environmental and community stewardship through experiential education.

Sporting Goods Manufacturers Association (SGMA)
www.sgma.com

SGMA is the global business trade association of manufacturers and marketers of sports apparel, athletic footwear, licensed outdoor products, fitness, sporting goods equipment, and related business/professional organizations. It advances members' interests through a major trade show, market research, communications, public policy, sports promotion, and international business development programs.

SPORTS MEDICINE

American College of Sports Medicine (ACSM)
www.acsm.org

The ACSM uses sports medicine and exercise sciences in order to improve fitness, health, and sport performance.

National Athletic Trainers' Association (NATA)
www.nata.org

NATA enhances the quality of health care for athletes and others who are engaged in physical activity, and advances athletic training through education and research in prevention, management, and rehabilitation of injuries.

American Sports Medicine Institute (ASMI)
www.asmi.org

ASMI improves the understanding, prevention, and treatment of sports-related injuries through research and education.

NATIONAL AMATEUR SPORTS

United States Olympic Committee (USOC)
www.usoc.org

The USOC preserves and promotes the Olympic ideal as an effective, positive role model that inspires all U.S. citizens. Its goal is to empower U.S. athletes to sustain the highest levels of competitive excellence, and through their achievements be a source of inspiration for the Olympic ideal.

Amateur Athletic Union (AAU)
www.aausports.org

The AAU is one of the largest, non-profit, volunteer, sports organizations in the United States, and is dedicated to the promotion and development of amateur sports and physical fitness programs.

Chapter Six

⊷ Selected Print and Nonprint Resources

Contained in this chapter is a collection of resources that should provide the reader with the opportunity to continue to investigate the issues raised throughout this text. Those interested should review many sources on each issue to provide a clear understanding of the scope of the perspectives involved. The works listed here are divided into two categories. The first section lists both popular and scholarly books that deal with the variety of aspects of sport reviewed by this text. The second section contains nonprint resources such as Websites and Internet research sites.

PRINTED SOURCES

Arnold, Peter, J. (1997). *Sport, Ethics, and Education.* Herndon, VA: Cassell. ISBN: 0-304-70000-2.

This unique text philosophically examines the relation between sport and education and the moral implications of each. The author believes that sport is a valued human experience as well as a necessary part of a quality education. Topics covered include universalism, competition, fairness, character development, and sportspersonship.

Bailey, W. S., and Littleton, T. D. (1991). *Athletics and Academe: An Anatomy of Abuses and a Prescription for Reform.* New York: Macmillan.

This text presents an overview of collegiate athletics and addresses the perceptions of the state of abuses within intercollegiate athletics as a whole. Medical terminology is used throughout the text to provide an ideal approach for the analysis of and causes of the abuses. The authors hope to provide an understanding of the nature and interrelationship of the fundamental and contributing causes of abuse, from which an accurate and effective diagnosis can be made.

Beckett Publishing Staff. (1999). *Good Sports: Athletes Your Kids Can Look Up To*. Dallas, TX: Beckeett. ISBN: 1-887432-62-0.

The short introduction addresses the issue of athletes as role models, followed by the stories of thirty amazing individual who just happen to be some of the most well-known athletes of our time, as well as some who are less well known. The list is interesting, as is the information the authors include that is little known among the general public.

Bissinger, H. G. (2000). *Friday Night Lights: A Town, a Team, and a Dream*. New York: DaCapo Press. ISBN: 0-306-80936-2.

This national best-seller tells the thought-provoking story of a town in Texas and the impact the high school football team has on life there. Sociological elements of the society are weaved through the sport story that results in a "can't put down book."

Coakley, J. J. (1994). *Sport in Society: Issues and Controversies*. St. Louis, MO: Mosby. ISBN: 0-8016-7557-X.

This textbook provides an initial look at sport from a sociological perspective. The author intends to push students in physical education or sociology to think more critically about sports and how they are related to their social lives.

Cohen, G. L. (2001). *Women in Sports: Issues and Controversies*. Reston, VA: National Association for Girls and Women in Sports, a division of AAPERD Publications ISBN: 0-88314-813-7.

This edited text provides a broad-based examination of topics related to female participation in sports. The contributing authors are well-known authorities, and the forward is by Jackie Joyner-Kersee. This text includes an overwhelming amount of detailed historical and current data regarding girls and women in sports.

Cox, R. (2002). *Sport Psychology: Concepts and Applications*. Boston: McGraw-Hill. ISBN: 0-07-232914-9.

This offers a comprehensive review of the psychological principles that relate to athletic performance and provides practical application of these concepts, which results in a better understanding of behavior within sport and by exercise participants. The content is organized within the following sections: introduction; motivation in sport and exercise; arousal, attention, and personality of the athlete; and situational factors related to anxiety and mood.

Edwards, H. (1973). *Sociology of Sport.* Homewood, IL: Dorsey Press. ISBN: 0256014159.

Edwards may be the most well-known sport sociologist of our time. This was the landmark text used by most physical education programs. It presents a comprehensive analytical profile of the institution of sport in the United States, its development, the complexities of its functions for the individual and society, and its potential as a significant and influential factor in the future of "the American way of life."

Egendorf, L. (1999). *Sports and Athletes: Opposing Viewpoints.* San Diego, CA: Greenhaven Press. ISBN: 0-7377-0056-4.

This is one volume in the *Opposing Viewpoints* series. The editor selected experts in the field to present both sides of the most controversial issues related to sports. The following chapters organize the essays: Do Sports Build Character? Should College Sports Be Reformed? Is Racial Discrimination a Problem in Sports? Is There Sexual Equality in Sports? and Is Drug Use a Problem in Sports? A book review states, "Those who do not know their opponents' arguments do not completely understand their own." Highly recommended.

Eitzen, D. S., and Sage, G. (1993). *Sociology of North American Sport.* Madison, WI: Brown and Benchmark. ISBN: 0-697-12625-0.

This sociology of sport text provides an enjoyable read with interesting facts as the authors cover the major issues facing sport in society. The issues are organized into the following sections: analysis of sport in society, social and cultural sources of the rise of sport in North America, sport and social values, children and sport, interscholastic sport, intercollegiate sport, sport and religion, sport and politics, sport and economy, sport and mass media, sport and social stratification, social mobility, race and sport, women in North American sport, and contemporary trends and the future of sport in North America. A pleasurable read of a very thorough review of the related issues.

Gates, H. J., Jr., and West, C. (2000). *The African American Century: How Black Americans Have Shaped Our Country.* New York: Touchstone. ISBN: 0-684-86415-0.

This book is written by two leading African American scholars. It presents how significant African Americans have been in shaping the twentieth century by presenting biographies of those who Gates and West believe have been most influential. Thoughtful inclusion of photos provides additional information.

Gerdy, J. (2000). *Sport in Schools: The Future of an Institution*. New York: Teachers College Press. ISBN: 0-8077-3970-7.

This edited text is an outstanding collection of essays intended to challenge the notion that sports necessarily promotes positive educational and social values, physical fitness, and character development. The editor has selected leading authorities to contribute in such a way that the readers are pushed to assess carefully the nature, value, and purpose of sport in our society. Essays are organized to question the educational benefits of sport, the preparation of coaches, race and gender issues in sport, and the value of athletics in the educational setting. I highly recommend this text.

Herzog, B. (1995). *The Sports 100: The One Hundred Most Important People in American Sports History*. New York: Macmillan. ISBN: 0-02-860402-4.

This author is a sportswriter in the great sports town of Chicago and has written several books. This text is not simply a list of best athletes, but includes biographies of individuals based on their impact in the world of sports. Well researched, it contains information not included in typical textbook versions. As one reviewer notes, "You will be surprised who is on the list and who is not, and how "the greatest" often is not the most important." I agree.

Kohn, A. (1992). *No Contest: The Case against Competition*. Boston: Houghton Mifflin. ISBN: 0395631254.

Competition has been looked upon as the basis for most of the problems that plague sports today. This text stirs up controversy as it critiques competition as the sabotage of self-esteem. The author argues that competition is an unavoidable part of our world and that competing against each other in sports, at work, in schools, and at play results in defeat for all.

Mechikoff, R. A., and Estes, S. G. (1998). *A History and Philosophy of Sport and Physical Education: From Ancient Civilizations to the Modern World*. Boston: McGraw-Hill. ISBN: 0-697-25883-1.

Over the years, there have been hundreds of books written for under-graduate physical education students in an attempt to provide them with the historical and philosophical orientations they need to precede through their professional development. The authors of this particular text use their experiences as coaches, athletes, and teachers to produce a text that incorporates the experiential aspects of learning into the content they present. Facts are incorporated into thought-provoking content.

National Collegiate Athletic Association. (2002). *2002–2003 NCAA Division I Manual: Constitution, Operating Bylaws, and Administrative Bylaws.* Indianapolis, IN: National Collegiate Athletic Association. ISBN: 1093-3174.

This publication incorporates the final legislative actions taken by the Division I Board of Directors from 1 August 2001 through 25 April 2002. Included are interpretations of the Division I Academics/Eligibility/ Compliance Cabinet Subcommittee on Legislative Review Interpre-tations.

NCAA News: The Official Publication of the National Collegiate Athletic Association. Published biweekly by the NCAA (700 W. Washington, Indianapolis, IN 46206-6222). ISBN: 0027-6170.

This newspaper provides up-to-date coverage of all NCAA-related is-sues. Sections include Comments, Division I News, Division II News, Division III News, Membership Information, NCAA Record, and the Market.

Novak, M. (1976). *The Joy of Sports: Endzones, Bases, Baskets, Balls, and the Consecration of the American Spirit.* NY: Basic Books. ISBN: 0465036791.

This well-known author of more than twenty influential books on a va-riety of subjects such as philosophy, religion, politics, and culture, who also writes a column for *Forbes* magazine, is an expert on public policy. This particular book provides the sports fan with insight into the "taken for granted-ness" by which sport has been victimized. It is excellently re-searched, historical, and provides enough perspective to get the reader thinking.

Polidoro, J. R. (2000). *Sport and Physical Activity in the Modern World.* Boston: Allyn & Bacon. ISBN: 0-205-27158-8.

This textbook provides a concise and comprehensive review of the major developments in sport and physical activity from the end of the eighteenth century to the beginning of the twenty-first. The book focuses on an international perspective in the identification and analysis of major issues confronting sport in the global context. The text begins with a historical section and contains an abundance of interesting facts. There are many contributing authors.

Shea, E. J. (1996). *Ethical Decisions in Sport: Interscholastic, Intercollegiate, Olympic and Professional.* Springfield, IL: Charles C. Thomas.

This text presents a model for assisting those involved in sports to judge whether decisions made involve ethical or unethical behavior. Because making tough decisions are a regular occurrence at every level of sport, the author believes that imposing a model on the decision-making process will provide well-formulated statements of principles for guiding this important process. Parallels are presented between decisions made in sport contexts to all of universal life.

Siedentop, D. (2001). *Introduction to Physical Education, Fitness, and Sport.* Toronto: Mayfield. ISBN: 0-7674-1662-7.

This author is one of the leading educators in the field. This comprehensive introduction includes the history, subfields, professional issues, and trends in physical education and human movement. The content is current, resulting in an exceptional resource for those interested in the professional activity in the broad area of sport.

Sinnette, C. (1988). *Forbidden Fairways: African Americans and the Game of Golf.* Chelsea, MI: Sleeping Bear Press. ISBN: 1886947422.

This excellent coverage of the game of golf is a testimony to the early African American golfers and caddies who would not be deprived of the game they loved. The racism of the nation and the hardships it produced are better understood from this text.

Smith, L. (1998). *Nike Is a Goddess: The History of Women in Sports.* New York: Atlantic Monthly Press. ISBN: 0-87113-726-7.

This edited text covers the history of female participation in sports, organized by sport. After a thought-provoking introduction, the sports that are presented are track and field; baseball and softball; tennis; golf, canoeing, kayaking, rowing, and sailing; skiing; figure skating; swimming; equestrian sports; gymnastics; soccer; ice hockey; and basketball. The author presents foundational information that allows the reader to understand how female athletes have gotten this far, as well as information to address the following questions: How do women grow in sport? How can we win? and Where does courage come from?

Sperber, M. (2000). *Beer and Circus: How Big-time College Sports Is Crippling Undergraduate Education.* New York: Henry Holt. ISBN: 0-8050-3864-7.

This author has received significant attention for his controversial stand that there is a strong inverse relationship between excellence in undergraduate education and performance in athletics among U.S. universities. This high-profile book attributes athletics, the party scene, and the excessive emphasis on graduate training and research at most NCAA Division I schools to the lack of attention to the quality of academic programming provided to undergraduate students. Additionally, the author discusses the effect of high-profile athletics on faculty issues as well as the student-athletes themselves. This book provides a provocative perspective on the concept of sport as big business.

Thomas, B., and Lewis, G. (1994). *Good Sports: Making Sports a Positive Experience for Everyone.* Grand Rapids, MI: Zondervan. ISBN: 0310482615.

This easy read for the layperson provides insights into how those involved in sports can help ensure that the positive lessons we believe sports can provide are actually realized. The author draws on personal experience at various levels of sports to address the pitfalls and distortions and then to provide advice, resources, and the basic tools for those who want to make good sports better.

Thomas, I. (2001). *The Fundamentals: 8 Plays for Winning the Games of Business and Life.* New York: HarperCollins. ISBN: 0-06-662074-0.

This autobiography presents Isaiah Thomas's journey from a westside Chicago ghetto to professional basketball, from his high school and Indiana University days forward; readers follow his career with the National Basketball Association (NBA), as an NBA owner, and as a successful businessman. The challenges he faced and the lessons he learned are inspiring.

Wiggins, D. K. (1995). *Sport in America: From Wicked Amusement to National Obsession.* Champaign, IL: Human Kinetics. ISBN: 0-87322-520-1.

This text is edited by one of the leading authorities on U.S. sports. It brings together nineteen essays that delve deeper into sport history than do typical textbooks on the subject. The book is organized around five chapters addressing distinct eras in U.S. sports: the pattern of sport in early America; health, exercise, and sport in a rapidly changing society (1820–1870); sport in the era of industrialization and reform (1879–1915); sport consumer culture and two world wars (1915–1945); transformation of sport in the age of television, discord, and personal fulfillment (1945–present).

Wiggins, D. K. (1997). *Glory Bound: Black Athletes in a White America.* Syracuse, NY: Syracuse University Press. ISBN: 0-8156-2734-3.

This author is well known for his work in the field of American sport. This book examines the relationship between the African American athletic experience and mainstream white America. Seminal moments and individuals are discussed as the black athlete's role in white America has changed the face of American athletics and society forever.

Wuest, D. A., and Bucher, C. A. (1995). *Foundations of Physical Education and Sport.* New York: Mosby. ISBN: 0-8151-9612-1.

This text is written for use in introductory courses within the broad field of sport and physical education. It is comprehensive and current and encourages future professionals to become engaged in the profession to develop their potential fully in this exciting and dynamic field.

NONPRINT RESOURCES

There is an abundance of information related to sports at all levels on the Internet. Many sport organizations have their own Websites, which are presented in chapter 5. The following section includes sites that provide information on sports-related issues.

American Alliance for Health, Physical Education, Recreation, and Dance (AAHPERD)
1900 Association Dr.,
Reston, VA 20191-1598

www.aahperd.org

This is the largest organization of professionals supporting and assisting those involved in physical education, leisure, fitness, dance, health promotion, and education and all specialties related to achieving a healthy lifestyle.

AAHPERD is an alliance of six national associations and six district associations and is designed to provide members with a comprehensive and coordinated array of resources, support, and programs to help practitioners improve their skills and so further the health and well-being of the American public. The five associations are listed here as well as the research consortium.

- ➥ The American Association for Health Education (AAHE) serves health educators and other professionals who promote the health of all people. AAHE encourages, supports, and assists health professionals concerned with health promotion through education and other systematic strategies. http://www.aahperd.org/aahe.
- ➥ The National Dance Association (NDA) seeks to increase knowledge, improve skills, and encourage sound professional practices in dance education through high-quality dance programs. http://www.aahperd.org/nda.
- ➥ The American Association for Active Lifestyles and Fitness (AAALF) serves professionals conducting programs of physical activity and fitness and the professors who train them. AAALF advocates for underrepresented populations and interests. http://www.aahperd.org/aaalf.
- ➥ The American Association for Leisure and Recreation (AALR) serves recreation professionals—practitioners, educators, and students—who advance the profession and enhance the quality of life of all Americans through creative and meaningful leisure and recreation experiences. http://www.aahperd.org.aalr.
- ➥ The National Association for Girls and Women in Sport (NAGWS)—the leading organization for equity issues in sports—champions equal funding, quality, and respect for girls' and women's sports programs. http://www.aahperd.org/nagws.
- ➥ The National Association for Sport and Physical Education (NASPE) seeks to enhance knowledge and professional practice in sport and physical activity through scientific study and

dissemination of research-based and experiential knowledge to members and the public. http://www.aahperd.org/naspe.

➡ The Research Consortium provides services and publications that assist the HPERD researcher and promote the exchange of ideas and scientific knowledge within the HPERD disciplines. http://www.aahperd.org/research.

American Youth Soccer Organization

AYSO National Support and Training Center, 12501 S. Isis Avenue, Hawthorne, CA 90250
(800) USA-AYSO
www.soccer.org

AYSO is a nationwide nonprofit organization that develops and delivers quality youth soccer programs in a fun, family environment based on AYSO's Five Philosophies: everyone plays, balanced teams, open registration, positive coaching, and good sportsmanship.

Healthy People 2010

www.healthypeople.gov

This government publication, *Healthy People 2010,* displays the goals and agendas of the national health promotion and disease prevention strategy for improving the health of Americans.

Institute for the Study of Youth Sports

Michigan State University, 213 IM Sports Circle Building, Department of Kinesiology, East Lansing, MI 48824-1049;
Tel: (517) 353-6689; Fax: (517) 353-5363;
e-mail: ythsprts@msu.edu

The Institute for the Study of Youth Sports was founded by the Michigan Legislature in 1978 to research the benefits and detriments of participation in youth sports; to produce educational materials for parents, coaches, officials, and administrators; and to provide educational programs for coaches, officials, administrators, and parents.

African Americans in the Sports Arena

www.liu.edu/cwis/cwp/library/aaitsa

This is a Web-based exhibit that presents a glimpse into the history of sports and the role of African Americans. Seven major sports are covered. Special tributes are included to Jackie Robinson and Michael Jordan.

International Olympic Committee (IOC)
Château de Vidy 1007, Lausanne, Switzerland;
Tel: (+41) 21 621 61 11; Fax: (+41) 21 621 62 16
www.olympic.org

The IOC is an international nongovernmental nonprofit organization and the creator of the Olympic movement. The IOC exists to serve as an umbrella organization of the Olympic movement. It owns all rights to the Olympic symbols, flag, motto, anthem, and Olympic Games. Its primary responsibility is to supervise the organization of the summer and winter Olympic Games.

The National Collegiate Athletic Association (NCAA)
700 W. Washington Street,
P.O. Box 6222,
Indianapolis, IN 46206-6222

This is a voluntary association of about 1,200 colleges and universities, athletic conferences, and sports organizations devoted to the sound administration of intercollegiate athletics. Through the NCAA, member schools and conferences consider any athletics problem that has become national in character. Volunteer school representatives establish rules that govern the Association and programs designed to further its purposes and goals.

National Federation of State High School Associations (NFHS)
P.O. Box 690,
Indianapolis, IN 46206;
Tel: (317) 972-6900
www.nfhs.org

The mission of the NFHS is to serve its members and its related professional groups by providing leadership and national coordination for the administration of interscholastic activities that will enhance the educational experiences of high school students and reduce risks of their participation. The NFHS promotes participation and sportsmanship to develop good citizens through interscholastic activities that provide equitable opportunities, positive recognition, and learning experiences to students while maximizing the achievement of educational goals.

School Sports.com
www.schoolsports.com

This Website is the leading site for national news on current high school sports and athletes.

The Mendelson Center for the Study of Sport, Character, and Culture
University of Notre Dame, 10 IEI Building, Notre Dame, IN 46556;
Tel: (574) 631-4445; e-mail: cscc@nd.edu
www.nd.edu/~cscc

The Mendelson Center brings social scientists and sports practitioners together to build character and promote civic responsibility through sports. Through its research, educational programs, and consulting, the center strives to put the tools of character development into the hands of athletic leaders and educators. The center encourages sport participants, sport organizations, and educational institutions to embody those values and behaviors that promote social justice, such as valuing diversity, creating equal opportunity, and advocating for the disadvantaged.

Sports Illustrated.com: A CNN Website
www.cnnsi.com

On July 17, 1997, CNN/*Sports Illustrated* launched a twenty-four-hour sports news Website, CNNSI.com. This Website brought together the combined sports assets of Time Warner and Turner Broadcasting Systems and offered a combination of CNN, the world's largest and most trusted news organization, and *Sports Illustrated,* the publishing world's premier sports magazine. It also uses the valuable resources of *Sports Illustrated* reporters, editors, and analysts who cover sports around the world. The Website continues to provide the complete story—with scores, stats, highlights, interviews, analysis, and commentary by some of the best journalists in sports today.

The Center for the Study of Sport in Society
Northeastern University, 360 Huntington Avenue, Suite 161 CP,
Boston, MA 02115-5000;
Tel: (617) 373-4025; Fax: (617) 373-4566/2092;
e-mail: sportinsociety@neu.edu
www.sportinsociety.org

The mission of Northeastern University's Center for the Study of Sport in Society is to increase awareness of sport and its relation to society and to develop programs that identify problems, offer solutions, and promote the benefits of sport. The center also supports quality projects with more narrow focuses: Project TEAMWORK provides critical training that teaches the value of diversity and conflict resolution; the Mentors in Violence Prevention (MVP) Program works to reduce men's violence against women; the Urban Youth Sports Program enables a growing number of young people in Boston to participate in organized athletic programs while gaining important life skills; Athletes in Service to America helps support students promote racial harmony, reduce violence, and achieve academic success.

●◆ Index

❧ About the Author

Anna Marie Frank, Ed.D., is assistant professor of physical education and fitness management in the School of Education and serves on the athletic board and Athletic Academic Eligibility Committee at DePaul University, Chicago. She received her doctoral degree in instructional leadership, master's degree in human performance, and her bachelor's degree in physical education and health.